DATE DUE			
Nov 15 '84			
DEC 0 7 2009			

VERSAILLES TWENTY YEARS AFTER

VERSAILLES TWENTY YEARS AFTER

BY PAUL BIRDSALL

ARCHON BOOKS
HAMDEN, CONNECTICUT
1962

FOR HELEN

CONTENTS

PREFACE, xi

CHAPTER I: *THE PEACE CALLED
CARTHAGINIAN,* 1
1. German Alternatives
2. Mirrors of Versailles
3. American Prophet
4. What Price a League of Nations?
5. Design for Diplomacy

CHAPTER II: *WILSONIAN PRINCIPLES AND
NATIONALIST AMBITIONS,* 22
1. The Contract—Pre-Armistice Agreement
2. Before the London Conference—French Traditions
3. London Conference, December 1-3, 1918—Rhineland
   and Reparation
4. December Elections—Squeeze the Orange
5. Aboard the *George Washington*—Wilson and The Colonial Problem
6. Buckingham Palace—German Colonies
7. Eve of the Peace Conference—The League of Nations

CHAPTER III: *THE GERMAN COLONIES AND THE
MANDATES PRINCIPLE,* 58
1. Annexationist Demands—January 23-28
2. Veiled Annexation—January 29
3. Hughes—January 30
4. The French and "Nigger Armies"—January 30

CHAPTER IV: *JAPANESE STRATEGY,* 83
1. Two Pounds of Flesh and One Ounce of Prestige
2. Hughes Opposes Racial Equality—February 4-April 28
3. Pound of Flesh—Shantung—April 15-30

CHAPTER V: *LEAGUE OF NATIONS—FRENCH STYLE,* 116
1. The Higher Strategy
2. Anglo-Saxon Moralism
3. "They Can Christen It The Society of Nations"
4. French Amendments—Act One
5. American Amendments
6. "Lest Old Acquaintance Be Forgot"

CHAPTER VI: *DISARMAMENT OF GERMANY,* 148
1. The Policy of Pin-Pricks
2. Preliminary or Final Treaty?
3. Conscription Again
4. Inspection Again
5. General Disarmament Once More

CHAPTER VII: *DISMEMBERMENT OF GERMANY— I. THE EAST,* 172
1. "Poland Must Be Very Big and Strong"
2. The Battle of Danzig
3. The Battle of Memoranda
4. Upper Silesia

CHAPTER VIII: *DISMEMBERMENT OF GERMANY— II. THE WEST,* 195
1. "Today We Have The Rhine"
2. Colonel House and Self-Determination
3. New Guarantees for Old

4. Occupation, and Inspection Again
5. Deadlock and Compromise
6. The Conscience of Marshal Foch
7. Federalism for Germany and Separatism in the Rhineland

CHAPTER IX: *DISMEMBERMENT OF GERMANY—
III. THE SAAR VALLEY, 224*
1. "Clear Violation of the President's Principles"
2. Battle of the Saar—Self-Determination
3. Battle of the Saar—Special Political Régime
4. The League Commission

CHAPTER X: *GERMAN INDEMNITIES, 238*
1. Justice and Common Sense
2. The Battle of Words—"War Costs" and "Reparation"
3. German Capacity—The Fixed Sum
4. German Capacity—The Time Limit and Reparation
Commission
5. "I Don't Give a Damn for Logic"
6. "War Guilt"
7. "This Is a Complete Departure from the Principles
upon Which We Have Been Working for Three
Months"
8. "That Makes Me Very Tired"

CHAPTER XI: *PRESIDENT WILSON AND COLONEL
HOUSE, 264*
1. The Jackal Tradition of Italian Politics
2. Fiume
3. The American Delegation—A Split Personality
4. "Who Are the Experts?"
5. House and Wilson

6. House and the Experts
7. Fiume for the Last Time
8. The Aftermath

CHAPTER XII: *RETROSPECT AND PROSPECT,* 289
1. Who Were the Realists?
2. Versailles to Hitler
3. National Traditions
4. "Union Now"—or Never?

NOTES, 313

BIBLIOGRAPHY, 333

INDEX, 339

PREFACE

THE PRESENT BOOK is an analysis and interpretation of the diplomatic factors which shaped the general character of the Treaty of Versailles. It is in no sense a formal history of all the negotiations at the Paris Peace Conference, or even of all the negotiations which resulted in the Versailles Treaty. It is an appraisal of the forces, personal and political, which determined the outcome of the struggle between Wilsonian principles of a new world order and the principles of reactionary nationalism. It is a purely empirical study which began and continued for six years as a seminar course for advanced students of history. The author admits his predisposition, as an American and a professional historian, to take seriously American efforts at Paris to achieve the Wilsonian program. Yet the conclusions offered in this book have been arrived at with full consciousness of that predisposition, and only after years of debate and discussion with students, with colleagues, and with Americans who participated in the negotiations at Paris. This interpretation is offered now in the belief that it is relevant to the immediate issues of war and peace, as they affect the United States and the world in general. The introductory and final chapters attempt to put the problem of Versailles in its historical setting and to indicate the present relevance of its lessons.

The book owes a very particular debt of gratitude to Professor Emeritus Theodore Clarke Smith, who inaugurated seminar methods of instruction in Williams College and trained the author in its mysteries. Special acknowledgment is also due the custodians who have made private papers available to the author. President Charles Seymour of Yale University permitted extensive use of the Edward M. House Collection in the Sterling Memorial Library. While maintaining his invariable rule that no one may see Colonel House's unpublished diary, he extended every courtesy consistent with that restriction. He looked up many specific matters in the diary and made the relevant extracts available to the author, and his Assistant Curator, Mr. Russell G. Pruden, gave invaluable help and advice in the use of the House Collection. Both officials and staff of the Division of Manuscripts in the Library of Congress at Washington, D. C., afforded every assistance in the utilization of the papers of former Secretary of State Robert Lansing, but particular thanks are due Mr. John de Porry. The Woodrow Wilson papers in the Division of Manuscripts were not available during the preparation of the book. Dr. James T. Shotwell of Columbia University and the Carnegie Endowment for International Peace provided the unpublished diary of George Louis Beer, and thanks are due both Mrs. Beer and Dr. Shotwell for permission to quote from the diary. Mr. Norman Davis kindly loaned his typescript memorandum on the reparation negotiations and permitted quotation from it.

The author is indebted to many members of the American Peace Delegation for the expression of their personal views in conversation. President Seymour, Dr. Shotwell, Mr. Davis, gave generously of their time and of their opinions; as did also President Isaiah Bowman of the Johns Hopkins University, Professor Douglas Johnson and Professor William Westermann of Columbia University, and Sir William Wiseman, formerly of the British Delegation. The author himself

xii

bears exclusive responsibility for the conclusions presented in the book.

Grateful acknowledgment is made for special permission granted by publishers to quote from books copyrighted by them:

> Edith Bolling Wilson, *My Memoir*. The Bobbs-Merrill Company, Indianapolis, 1939.
> Ray Stannard Baker, *Woodrow Wilson and World Settlement*. Doubleday, Doran, New York, 1922.
> Philip Mason Burnett, *Reparation at the Paris Peace Conference*. Columbia University Press, New York, 1940.
> Allan Nevins, *Henry White: Thirty Years of American Diplomacy*. Harper and Brothers, New York, 1930.
> Charles Seymour, *The Intimate Papers of Colonel House*. Houghton Mifflin Company, Boston, 1928.
> David Lloyd George, *Memoirs of the Peace Conference*. Yale University Press, New Haven, 1939.

The Honorable Hunter Miller has kindly permitted extensive quotations from two books copyrighted by him, *My Diary at the Conference of Paris*, privately printed, New York, 1928, and *Drafting of the Covenant*, G. P. Putnam's Sons, New York, 1928.

Finally, the author wishes to express his appreciation to the authorities of Williams College, and especially to his colleagues of the History Department, for the semester leave of absence during which the book was completed. Mrs. Mary L. Hurt has performed the laborious and skilful task of indexing the book.

P. B.

Williamstown, Mass.,
January, 1941.

★ 1 ★

THE PEACE CALLED CARTHAGINIAN

1 : *German Alternatives*

FOR TWENTY YEARS all the ills of Europe have been blamed ▓▓▓▓▓▓▓▓▓▓ nd its satellites of St. Germain, ▓▓▓▓▓▓▓▓▓▓ . Hitler's view that the present ▓▓▓▓▓▓▓▓▓▓ quities of Versailles may not be so widely accepted, yet American isolationists are convinced that Woodrow Wilson made a mess of Versailles and that the United States must never again intervene in European affairs.

Perhaps the United States can remain non-belligerent, though Woodrow Wilson tried to keep out of the first World War and the forces which destroyed his efforts are stronger today than ever. Yet the present war in Europe raises fundamental questions with which the United States is very seriously concerned. What will be the character of a purely European peace without American intervention? Will it be better, or will it be worse? Will it be any more durable than the last one? What are the conditions for a stable peace, and is there a better chance for the achievement of such conditions with or without American participation?

There cannot be even a tentative answer to any of these questions without a study of the Treaty of Versailles and its

1

alternatives. What would that Treaty have been without the prominent rôle of President Wilson in shaping it? What terms would Germany have imposed if she had defeated the Allies?

The Treaty of Brest-Litovsk is a good guide to official German doctrine about a satisfactory peace.[1] Imposed on a defeated Russia in 1918, it clearly foreshadowed Hitler's policy of German domination in central and eastern Europe. Combined with the Treaty of Bucharest, later imposed on Rumania, it established a chain of puppet states bound in political and economic vassalage to the Reich, from the Baltic to the Black Sea. Hitler has had to treat Russia as partner rather than as victim in the new Brest-Litovsk Treaty, but that is a matter of political exigency, not a change of political doctrine.

Imperial Germany never had a chance to show its hand in western Europe, because a decisive military victory never occurred. Yet her generals had devised a set of peace terms at least as early as 1916. These terms, which assumed a complete military victory, ironically became the cause of military disaster. The generals, more particularly Ludendorff who achieved a virtual dictatorship of Imperial Germany, refused to modify the terms in any detail to meet the deteriorating military situation. When the great offensives of 1918 had spent their force without a break-through, Ludendorff admitted that he could not win the war. Yet he fondly supposed that by keeping German troops on French soil he could in the end enforce Germany's maximum terms. It was a case of all or nothing. On September 1, 1918, Ludendorff succumbed to panic and ordered the new Imperial Chancellor, Prince Max of Baden, to get him an armistice immediately.

What were the terms which Ludendorff thought so essential that to gain them he gambled with Germany's very existence in 1918? Germany was to obtain the Longwy-Briey ore

2

basin, a portion of the valuable Lorraine deposits which had been overlooked in 1871, and most of the French colonies. Political and economic control of Belgium would assure an adequate strategic base to offset English maritime ascendancy. Added to the provisions of the Brest-Litovsk and Bucharest treaties, these western arrangements would create a German mastery of Europe and a German world power of menacing proportions. Germany would also exact suitable indemnities from the victims to compensate her for the tremendous financial cost of these achievements.[2]

The post-war political association of Hitler and Ludendorff was no mere coincidence. These dictators were the future and the past, both with identical views of Germany's mission. There is very little in Hitler's version of that mission in *Mein Kampf* that is not present in Brest-Litovsk, or in those western terms which never materialized. The ideological trappings of Hitler's book clothe a traditional German military logic which can be traced far back in the nineteenth century to the great Prussian philosopher of war, von Clausewitz. It stamped with unmistakable imprint much of Imperial German diplomacy in the post-Bismarck period. It is a logic so rigid that it has no room for what Bismarck called the "imponderables." Its victims lose all flexibility of mind, all imagination about the attitudes of other people, of "public opinion" in general. Hitler has already displayed the same inflexibility which destroyed Ludendorff and the political system he served, and it is even possible that he is preparing for himself and the Nazi system the same fate which overtook Imperial Germany. While 1941 is too early to predict that fate, it is none too soon to recognize what kind of peace Hitler will give Europe if he has his way.

There is always the possibility of a negotiated peace resulting from a military stalemate. Ludendorff could probably have had such a peace any time up to August of 1918 if he had been willing to forgo Germany's extreme demands. Hitler may have the same opportunity. A restoration of the *status quo ante* must always have an irresistible appeal to the peoples of democratic states who have taken up arms to resist aggression. It is only when those peoples are finally convinced that the aggressors refuse to stop short of complete conquest and domination, that they dig in for a finish fight. Assuming that the logic of Hitler's position commits him to the same all-or-nothing attitude of Ludendorff, there is no more possibility of a negotiated peace with him than there was with Ludendorff. We know what Ludendorff would have done with his victory, and we know equally well what Hitler would do with his, but until we have some reasonably fair appraisal of the Treaty of Versailles and of the negotiations which produced it, we have no reliable way of forecasting what a victorious Britain would do to a defeated Germany. We shall also run the risk of accepting the Hitler thesis that the present war is directly attributable to the iniquities of Versailles and of the coalition which attempted to perpetuate them.

2 : *Mirrors of Versailles*

If the first World War taught us anything, it taught us that after four years of bloodshed democracies become thoroughly vindictive toward the enemy who has caused them to suffer. The peoples of England and France were in a mood to "hang the Kaiser" and to "squeeze the orange until the pips squeak." It is by now a commonplace that a hysterical populace in Allied countries called for punishment and destruction of Germany, and Allied leaders, true to the principles of democracy, bowed to the storm. Belief in the unique guilt of the Kaiser for the horrors of the World War was unanimous.

4

Can the peoples of Great Britain and France entertain many doubts about the guilt of Hitler? If they could regard the people of Imperial Germany as "Huns" and barbarians, how will they think of their Nazi enemies?

How can such passions be controlled? They must be controlled if democracy is to solve the problem of a stable peace and of a durable world order. Only in a stable world can democracy survive. Those who decry idealism and justice as sentimental and unrealistic terms in world politics miss the point. For idealism and justice are the very rudiments of common sense. They amount to a practical realization of what the traffic will reasonably bear. They require the sacrifice of immediate vengeance for the sake of long-term enlightened self-interest.

Woodrow Wilson symbolized the forces of reason in the fight for a peace of justice. He spoke too much the language of idealism and self-sacrifice and too little the plain language of a genuine community of interest, and to that extent he brought upon himself the misrepresentation which obscured his real rôle in the Paris Peace Conference and contributed to the defeat of his program in the United States. A hard-boiled and disillusioned age is quick to gibe about cant and hypocrisy, and Keynes' characterization of the Presbyterian theocrat who was "bamboozled" by Clemenceau and Lloyd George and could not be "debamboozled"[3] has found recent echoes in Harold Nicolson's references to the "arid revivalism" of the "American Prophet," in whose pronouncements Nicolson observed "a slight tinge of revivalism, a touch of Methodist arrogance, more than a touch of Presbyterian vanity."[4]

The simple thesis of such writers is that the doctrinaire and unrealistic program of Wilson collapsed under the impact of the power politics of Europe. Nationalist aims triumphed over his principles. There was division of the spoils

5

of war, "bartering about of peoples and provinces from sovereignty to sovereignty as if they were chattels or pawns in a game," in defiance of his principle of self-determination. Worst of all, there had to be pretense. The Allied governments had accepted Wilson's program. While violating it, still they must pay it lip-service and hence, according to Keynes, they joined with Wilson in weaving "that web of sophistry and Jesuitical exegesis that was finally to clothe with insincerity the language and substance of the whole Treaty." Keynes in his disillusionment has fixed the legend of a Carthaginian Peace in Wilsonian disguise.

This is caricature, not history, but like most successful caricature it has enough verisimilitude to be plausible. Scarcely as much can be said for Lloyd George's recent *Apologia*, which presents the exactly opposite thesis that Versailles was a purely Wilsonian peace.[5] Only he does not call it Wilsonian, because it was he, Lloyd George himself, who achieved the peace of justice practically single-handed. Always adept at sleight of hand, in his latest masterpiece he demonstrates that he achieved Wilson's program in spite of Wilson. Like most commentators, he deplores the choice of war-worn Paris as the seat of the Peace Conference, but hastily adds, "I cannot point out that in the sequel the purely Parisian influence made any serious impression on the actual stipulations of the document finally agreed to, since *I cannot discover a single particular in which it has departed from the terms of peace laid down by the Allies before the War came to an end.*"[6] That statement acquires a peculiarly fine flavor of irony from the fact that Lloyd George himself bears major responsibility for the most egregious breach of faith contained in the entire treaty. The "Reparation" chapter of the Treaty of Versailles, besides being a clear violation of the Pre-Armistice Agreement with Germany, proved in the outcome to be the most

6

disastrous section of the treaty. Keynes spoke with authority and even with clairvoyance on that subject.

The prosaic truth is that elements of good and bad were combined in the treaties. There were Carthaginian features like the Reparation settlement and Wilsonian features like the League of Nations. There was actually a distribution of colonial spoils of war, but only after the valuable principle had been established that colonial powers administered their new estates under specified conditions and subject to review and correction by an international tribunal, the League of Nations. The territorial settlement in Europe was by no means the wholesale, iniquitous, and cynical perversion of Wilson's principle of self-determination which has been pictured.

Harold Nicolson has explained many of the worst boundary decisions as resulting from sheer lack of coördination between the various expert commissions charged with a supremely difficult task. Yet most critics of the settlement forget the difficulties of that task. One of the commonest criticisms is directed against the shattering of the former Dual Monarchy of Austria-Hungary into those fragments called the Succession States. In this view the negotiators at Paris should have foreseen the economic and political need of a Danubian Confederation to combine the fragments. Yet Austria-Hungary had fallen apart before the Peace Conference convened and *de facto* national governments ruled the pieces. British and American delegates in Paris actually proposed a customs union for the area, only to encounter Italian objection, based on the principle of "divide and rule." [7]

The populations of central Europe are hopelessly mixed, and therefore Simon-pure self-determination is impossible. Any boundary will leave national minorities on one side or the other. Moreover, the history of the past few years has certainly justified the commissioners in taking account of

7

strategic factors in the award of boundaries to the new states of Europe. The aftermath of the Munich settlement proved that Czechoslovakia could not exist without possession of its historic and strategic boundaries in the Bohemian mountains, even if that area is inhabited by 3,000,000 Germans. It is equally clear that a special status for the purely German city of Danzig, involving segregation from the political structure of the German Reich, is essential to the security of the Polish Corridor, which on the basis of pre-war German statistics is "indisputably" Polish territory. Hitler's demand for the reincorporation of Danzig in the German Reich was accompanied by a demand for territory across the Corridor itself. To have granted the demand for Danzig would have left the way open for the "fourth and final partition of Poland," even without the formality of war. If the Allies should ever conquer Germany again, the negotiators of the new Versailles will face precisely the same dilemma. They can simply accept the traditional German thesis that Slavic peoples as an inferior racial breed have no right to independent national existence and permit Germany to rule Poland, Bohemia, Moravia, and Slovakia, or, if they acknowledge any right of self-determination to these peoples, they must inevitably violate in some degree the rights of German minorities. Hard as it is to visualize in 1941, it would not be surprising if the negotiators of the new Versailles were to recreate Poland and Czechoslovakia within something like the original Versailles boundaries.

In any case, it is well to be reminded by Professor Seton-Watson that it was not directly the Great Powers which profited from the partition of former German and Austro-Hungarian territory, but those new Slavic states which had themselves been partitioned and dominated for centuries.[8] If their sense of injury was deep and their territorial appetite greedy in 1919, those sentiments are not likely to be

8

extinguished by their present plight. If they received an unduly large measure of sympathy from the victorious Great Powers at that time, they would again secure at least their due share.

Finally, the territorial settlement contained in the various treaties negotiated at Paris is still, with all its faults, the closest approximation to an ethnographic map of Europe that has ever been achieved. If the next Peace Conference does better, it will be because of the achievements as well as the mistakes of Versailles. It can scarcely hope to do better unless some leading figure is prepared to undertake the rôle of Woodrow Wilson in restraining the forces of extravagant nationalism. It will take a brave man to assume that rôle.

3 : *American Prophet*

President Wilson's own claims were modest. When the rough and tumble of negotiation was over in early June, 1919, he said to the entire American Delegation, "though we did not keep them [the British and French] from putting irrational things in the treaty, we got very serious modifications out of them. If we had written the treaty the way they wanted it, the Germans would have gone home the minute they read it. Well, the Lord be with us." [9]

Unfortunately, purely negative accomplishments, the prevention of positive harm, rarely attract public attention. Yet the record of what Wilson prevented is just as important as his one great positive achievement, the League of Nations, which, however dead at this moment, is certain to be revived in some form in the event of another Allied victory over Germany. The story of Wilson's struggle to restrain nationalist demands is equally important for an understanding of the problems of the next Peace Conference. Unless his successor is even better equipped to cope with the forces of reaction,

9

the second chapter of the League of Nations can hardly have any happier ending than the first. An understanding of Wilson's difficulties will be the beginning of wisdom for anyone bold enough to reënact his part.

The difficulties began before Wilson sailed for Paris, reactionary nationalism being equally at home on both sides of the Atlantic. To Wilson it seemed particularly strong in the ranks of the Republican Party. Naturally, though unwisely, he invited the American electorate to return only faithful Democrats to Congress, on the assumption that they alone could be counted upon to support his program. This purge, like a more recent one in American history, failed to come off. Republicans captured control of both branches of the legislature in the elections of November, 1918, and the most conspicuous and bitter opponent of Wilson's program—Henry Cabot Lodge—became chairman of the Senate Committee on Foreign Relations. Lodge's lifelong friend, Theodore Roosevelt, interpreted the election for the benefit of the nationalists of Europe:

Our allies and our enemies and Mr. Wilson himself should all understand that Mr. Wilson has no authority whatever to speak for the American people at this time. His leadership has just been emphatically repudiated by them. The newly elected Congress comes far nearer than Mr. Wilson to having a right to speak the purposes of the American people at this moment. Mr. Wilson and his Fourteen Points and his Four Supplementary Points and his Five Complementary Points and all his utterances every which way, have ceased to have any shadow of right to be accepted as expressive of the will of the American people. . . .[10]

Acceptance of the Wilsonian principles referred to had become a contract between the Allied and Associated Powers on the one hand and Germany on the other, as a condition for the granting of an armistice and the convening of a Peace Conference. In effect, Roosevelt was inviting the Allied governments to repudiate their pledges to both President Wilson and the German Government. Though noisy, Theodore Roosevelt was only a private citizen. It was one thing for him to announce that the American people had themselves rejected the whole contractual basis for peace. It was quite another for his friend Henry Cabot Lodge, as Chairman of the Senate Committee on Foreign Affairs, to indulge in similar pronouncements. On December 21, 1918, less than a week after Wilson's arrival in Paris, the *Congressional Record* published the substance of Lodge's speech to the Senate, in which he advised Europe that what it did to Germany was no concern of the United States.[11] Let the Allies administer a severe peace to leave Germany disabled and helpless, and exact heavy indemnities. No attention need be paid to Wilson's principles with regard to new boundaries in Europe, for that was none of his business. Above all, postpone all plans for the construction of a League of Nations until Germany had been summarily disposed of.

The alliance of reactionary nationalisms in Europe and America undermined Wilson's position from the start. The alliance was tacit but real. Colonel House records that "the elections of last November have been a deterrent to free action by our delegates,"[12] and Lloyd George is smugness itself in describing the contrast between his own and Wilson's position. Lloyd George enjoyed an overwhelming popular mandate, and knowing the weakness of Wilson's position, could be nonchalant about Wilson's threats to appeal to public opinion. "His occasional threats to appeal to American opinion, when he did not get his way at the Conference, conveyed no real menace. There was no assurance that his country would support him in a break with the Allies on any issue."[13]

Many writers have commented on this initial handicap, but few have bothered to analyze the more subtle and complicated difficulties created by the behavior of the American Delegation at the Peace Conference. It is notorious that Secretary of State Lansing was hostile to the whole idea of a League of Nations as contrary to American traditions of isolation, and that he logically joined forces, at a later date, with the Republican "Irreconcilables" to wreck the peace settlement. Wilson, at least, knew where Lansing stood and therefore excluded him from any appreciable part in the peace negotiations. The rôle of Colonel House, the President's closest friend and most intimate adviser, is so difficult to estimate that it is still clouded by controversy. This much, at least, is clear. He was so devoted to one part of the President's program—the establishment of a League of Nations— that he was willing to sacrifice almost any amount of the rest of that program to reach his goal. He was so afraid that Italy, or Japan, or France, or even Great Britain, would refuse to join the League of Nations, that he was ready to satisfy their nationalist ambitions for territory or indemnities in order to be assured of their support. He would "satisfy the greedy ones by giving them what they want." House was, moreover, a genial man with a flair for human relations, and much too adroit for either his own or Wilson's good. He got on with Europe's leaders far better than the President, and they formed the habit of using him as their intermediary when Wilson proved stiff and difficult. They constantly explained to him that, unlike the President, he was a diplomat to his finger-tips, and the Colonel's diary for this period shows that he was not wholly immune to this form of flattery. Indeed, one of his colleagues among the American Commissioners, the professional diplomat Henry White, goes so far as to suggest that House became the unwitting ally of European nationalism. White's letter to Lansing of November 8, 1919, deserves fairly full quotation:

12

I was not aware until recently of the extent to which intrigue went on "upstairs" during the earlier months of the Conference, with a view to preventing any of the views of our experts, which happened to be contrary to those held there, from reaching the President. Still less had I any idea of the attempts made to get some of the experts to change their views and adopt those advocated in the small upper chamber previously mentioned.

Since your departure I have realized more and more how grievously misled the Italians and others were by the tendency to compromise and by the assurances of friendship and sympathy, of a general nature at least, if not actually with their particular views, expressed during their interviews upstairs: and there is no doubt in my mind that Fiume and other questions would have been settled while the President was still here, if they had been left in your hands or kept in the President's, and had not been hampered by a feeling upstairs that no decision should be attempted, much less reached, which would in any way be likely to cause jeopardy to the adoption of the League of Nations Covenant. . . .

Under these circumstances and in view of the undue influence which I cannot but think our British friends exercise over our late colleague, I cannot help feeling anxious . . . about participation in the League of Nations if we are to be represented there by a man . . . given to compromise and not strong enough and willing to make a fight in which our interests (which besides being commercial are those of world peace as against special national interests such as land-grabbing and sphere-of-influence capturing, now rife in Europe) are likely to be overridden unless carefully guarded and defended. . . .[14]

It is only fair to add that, in part, the Colonel's behavior is to be explained by a deep and entirely natural sympathy with the sufferings of France and the other victims of German arms. It was a sympathy widely shared by the American experts of the Peace Delegation, and however chivalrous its basis, it greatly complicated Wilson's task by making him seem ungenerous. Clemenceau openly accused the President of being pro-German on one issue where even Wilson's own experts were against him. One of the most usual complaints

13

against Wilson made by European writers is this same lack of sympathetic understanding, in contrast to the greater warmth of other members of the American Delegation. In case after case he held out against concessions urged upon him by the experts and Colonel House.

What, then, is the true picture of the man who tried against such odds to maintain his principles? Undermined at home, imperfectly supported by his own colleagues in Paris, his frequent refusals to compromise may well have seemed the inflexible rigidity of an arid revivalist or the arrogance of a prophet. The harsh lines of the caricature fade out in the kindlier and more realistic portraiture of Henry White, and White's portrayal is all the more convincing because of the absence of any natural bonds of affinity between himself and Wilson. A professional diplomat with thirty years' experience of old-world diplomacy, he was scarcely an eager disciple of any prophet of a new world order. Republican Party affiliations and a lifelong friendship with Senator Lodge ought to have kept him immune from too much sympathy for Wilson. Yet this is what he wrote his friend, Representative Rogers, from Paris on April 7, 1919:

I have discovered since knowing him that he is really shy, and in an atmosphere which he does not feel to be entirely sympathetic, much more in one which is antagonistic, his reserve increases in proportion to the absence of sympathy. That he has a very human side there is no doubt, and I have also found him at various times attractive. . . . I have also noticed that he is much more "get-at-able" in conversation with one other person: whether on account of his natural shyness or what, I do not know . . . certainly when we talk to him as a Delegation, he is apt to do most of the talking, whereas when I see him alone, I have found him a very good listener and apparently appreciative of what is said to him. I suppose it is for that reason that he deals so much with and through Colonel House, rather than taking advantage of the collective information of all those by whom he is imme-

14

diately surrounded; whether it be the Peace Conference or his own Cabinet at home.[15]

When one considers the deplorable lack of understanding available in Paris, the President's reputation for stiffness is more readily understood. It was not the stiffness of prophet or revivalist, but the protective covering for the sensitiveness of an academic temperament. Lloyd George is, therefore, much nearer the mark when he abandons talk of the missionary and the theocrat, and contrasts the toughness of his own hide with Wilson's sensitiveness, because the President's nerves had not been "hardened for the stinging and scorching arrows that burn and fester in the ruthless conflicts of a political career." It is clear why Lloyd George did not regard Wilson as "comparable to his great rival, Theodore Roosevelt." [16]

For all the weaknesses of the academic temperament, Wilson remained a man of courage in the face of almost insuperable obstacles. White admitted that he became more and more impressed with the greatness of that quality, and he repeatedly sought to impress upon Senator Lodge that "dignity and distinction" characterized everything which Wilson did in Europe. He tried in vain to convince Lodge of the soundness of the President's program and begged him not to wreck it. He maintained that Wilson's activity in Europe had vastly increased American prestige.[17]

4 : *What Price a League of Nations?*

The cardinal point of Wilson's program was its most vulnerable spot. The Allied premiers well knew Wilson's determination to establish a League of Nations in the treaties themselves as the corner stone of a new world system, and they were not scrupulous in exploiting that determination to extract concessions from him. Henry White suggests that

15

Colonel House was responsible personally for fatal concessions to nationalist greed in order to purchase support for the League, but he has said more generally of Wilson:

The fact is that the League of Nations in which he has been more deeply interested than anything else from the beginning . . . has been played to the limit by the French and Japanese in extracting concessions from him; to a certain extent by the British too, and the Treaty as it stands is the result. The Italians overshot the mark.[18]

That remark is the most valuable clue to the labyrinthine maze of Peace Conference negotiations that has yet been offered. It may be true, as Harold Nicolson has said, that there was no recognizable pattern of negotiation, that in the confusion and fog of Paris there was "amazing inconsequence, the complete absence of any consecutive method of negotiation or even of imposition."[19] Yet it is extraordinary what a clear scheme of diplomatic strategy emerges from the fog, once the major territorial and other problems are studied in relation to the contemporaneous negotiations in the League of Nations Commission.

It was one thing to secure acceptance of the principle that there should be a League of Nations in the treaty. It was quite another to expect the states of Europe to adopt any particular constitution of a League that Wilson might formulate. Indeed, he was wise enough to avoid the presentation of any cut-and-dried proposition of his own. The actual construction of a League was bound to raise fundamental questions affecting the sovereign rights of all nations, and the Great Powers, at least, had the right to decide as to what provisions should or should not be embodied in the charter to which they were invited to subscribe. The negotiations which dealt with the actual text of the Covenant in the League of Nations Commission were a magnificent opportunity for obstruction. French, Japanese, or even British representatives

ality; it also forms
individual aspects
deal with French
y; for the endow-
at the expense of
a buffer state out
west; for the an-
ion of the entire

n the British con-
anese concerning
ery particular of
s active and con-
pened by his ex-
ssion, his anxiety
orld, his intimacy
ceau, led him to
very major issue
t the expense of
ery case beyond
t he assisted the
ch in extracting
ery instance ex-
lson successfully
se to which the
nce and method
lian Delegation
They revealed a
deep to roots of
break with the
d the Colonel's
with President
mbolic of the
order to emerge

ch
ly art
/ilson
anent
compri
er, form
ems gai
Clemen
of the Fre
ce of that
e of Natio
nd to oppo
nd to pres
ually to crea
with the poli
f Nations Cor
g of the deep

in the Commission could press their own proposals, or with-hold assent to Wilson's, not necessarily on the merits of the proposals themselves, but for the sake of "nuisance value" or bargaining advantage.

Wilson's dilemma was serious enough without such complications. He must devise a Covenant which would genuinely assure America's support to a system of collective security, without at the same time too patently violating American traditions of isolation. A small group of Senate "Irreconcilables" led by Senator Lodge was determined to reject any League of Nations which Wilson could devise, and he must at all costs avoid giving them the ammunition with which to compass that destruction. He must, therefore, resist French and Japanese proposals which would seem to endow the League with the authority of a superstate to restrain the exercise of sovereign rights by member states. He must equally secure the adoption of American provisions explicitly safeguarding certain distinctively American rights, like the Monroe Doctrine, as sacred and inviolable.

On both fronts the President was in a peculiarly vulnerable position. Too much restraint on the authority of the League, either from resistance to French and Japanese proposals or from insistence on American reservations, would justify the foreigner in saying that such a League afforded him no security and that he must, therefore, look to more tangible guarantees. Since these tangible guarantees usually involved an annexationist scheme totally at variance with the rest of Wilson's program, the horns of his dilemma were particularly sharp. This dilemma is the clue to the maze of Peace Conference diplomacy, and it determines the structure of the present book.

17

Nationalist aims of territor|
and Africa and Asia took sha|
his Fourteen Points, and Chapt|
of the conflict between the real|
ernments and their professions|
ciples.

The main body of the book is|
lomatic strategy of the British, J|
tions in the attainment of their|
arranged to indicate the relation l|
of the nationalist program of eac|
ticularly designed to reveal how ea|
ducted its negotiations in the Leagt|
with a view to the achievement of |

First, chronologically and logica|
certain of the British Dominions—s|
Delegation—to annex former Germa|
in the Pacific. Such claims were a dire|
proposal that all the former Germa|
property of the League of Nations, |
mandatory powers chosen by the Lea|
supervision. There was as yet no Leag|
tainly no code for Wilson's mandatory|
be regarded as binding the Dominions|
the mandatory principle was necessar|
some concession to their demand for|
tional control of former German territo|
ing to sell their support to a League o|
including the mandates principle—at a p|

Next, logically, appeared the Japane|
cluded annexationist aims in the Pacific,|
accorded the same consideration which the|

between Anglo-American and French ment|
a necessary introduction to the study of |
of the French program. Succeeding chapter|
proposals for the disarmament of German|
ment of Poland with maximum territories|
Germany in the east; for the creation of |
of Germany's Rhineland provinces in the |
nexation of the Saar Valley; for the exact|
cost of the war from Germany.

In every phase of these negotiations—wit|
cerning colonies and mandates, with the Ja|
Shantung, above all with the French in e|
their national demands—Colonel House wa|
ciliatory. His concern for the League, shar|
perience in the League of Nations Commi|
about protracted negotiation in a chaotic w|
with the Allied premiers, especially Clemer|
adopt an "appeasement" philosophy. On e|
he advocated compromise and concession a|
the accepted principles of peace, and in e|
definite limits set by Wilson. To this exter|
strategy of the British, Japanese, and Fren|
concessions from Wilson, although in ev|
cept that of the Reparation Settlement Wi|
stopped short of the extremes of compromi|
Colonel was urging him. Yet in both substa|
Colonel House's negotiations with the Ita|
proved a climax of appeasement philosophy.|
rift within the American delegation, cutting|
philosophy and method; they led to an open|
Italian Delegation; and they apparently end|
own relations of mutual trust and confidence|
Wilson. Fiume and its consequences are s|
deeper reasons for the failure of a new world|

from Versailles. The Fiume episode, though distinct from the Versailles negotiations, forms an appropriate conclusion for any analysis of the diplomatic factors which shaped the general character of the treaties at the end of the first World War.

★ 2 ★

WILSONIAN PRINCIPLES AND
NATIONALIST AMBITIONS

---

1 : *The Contract—Pre-Armistice Agreement*

The armistice was signed this morning. Everything for which America fought has been accomplished. It will now be our fortunate duty to assist by example, by sober, friendly counsel and by material aid in the establishment of just democracy throughout the world.[1]

SUCH WAS THE triumphant announcement President Woodrow Wilson made to the American people on Monday, November 11, 1918. He had every apparent justification for the confidence and hope it proclaimed.

The Imperial German Government had appealed directly to Wilson, as the acknowledged spokesman for the Allied and Associated Powers, for an armistice, and had unreservedly accepted the President's principles as the precedent condition for the armistice. On October 23, 1918, he had communicated his correspondence with Germany to the chiefs of the Allied governments in Paris and commissioned Colonel House as his special agent to secure their assent to the same principles. The Colonel cabled President Wilson from Paris on November 5, 1918:

I consider that we have won a great diplomatic victory in getting the Allies to accept the principles laid down in your January 8 speech and in your subsequent addresses. This has been done in the face of a hostile and influential junta in the United States and the thoroughly unsympathetic personnel constituting the Entente Governments.[2]

Wilson knew as much as the Colonel about the "hostile and influential junta" at home. The recent Congressional elections had increased its strength, and Wilson frankly feared the Republican victory would encourage domestic opposition to his foreign policy.[3] Yet for the moment his mind was absorbed by world problems, and here the chief difficulty was the "thoroughly unsympathetic personnel" of the Allied Governments.

The most significant thing about Allied acceptance of the President's program was the reluctance with which it was accorded. The Allies were in no position to refuse, since from the time of America's entrance into the war they had tacitly acquiesced in the President's leadership. The propaganda value to the Allied cause of his ringing appeals for a new and democratic world order was immense. If they now openly repudiated these principles just when Imperial Germany had accepted them, the President would certainly notify Congress that the Allied Powers were evidently fighting a war for conquest, and America would withdraw, leaving them to face Germany alone. Colonel House had to make precisely that threat before the Allied premiers finally agreed to the President's proposals.

Lloyd George opened the floodgates on October 29 when he put the question:

Do we or do we not accept the whole of President Wilson's Fourteen Points? I am going to put quite clearly the points which I do not accept. Should we not make it clear to the German Government that we are not going in on the Fourteen Points of peace?

23

Clemenceau agreed that he would not commit himself and France blindly to any such program. He had never been asked by Wilson if he accepted it, and Lloyd George said that he also was not committed. They asked the Colonel if agreement to an armistice with Germany would commit them to the Fourteen Points, and he replied, "That is my view." [4] He warned them that if they refused the conditions, President Wilson would have no choice but to notify the German Government of that fact and wipe the previous negotiations off the slate. "That would amount to a separate peace between the United States and the Central Powers," said Clemenceau. "It might," Colonel House replied. And he reported to the President that his remarks "had a very exciting effect on those present." [5]

Lloyd George persisted in his objection to one of the provisions of Wilson's program, Point Two, which embodied the principle of "Freedom of the Seas." Under no conditions would Lloyd George accept a principle which seemed to destroy the power of blockade. It was in vain that House told him that Freedom of the Seas involved no such drastic proposal, that it simply meant a codification of maritime law dealing with neutral rights of trade "during a war between a limited number of nations when that war involves no issue upon which the League of Nations cares to take sides." [6] The effect of Lloyd George's obduracy was to encourage Clemenceau and also the Italian Foreign Minister Sonnino to prepare their own memoranda of objection to the Fourteen Points.[7] Colonel House had already threatened a separate peace between the United States and Germany in the event of a complete rejection of Wilson's program by the Allied premiers. He now amplified that threat:

. . . If the Allied Governments felt constrained to submit an elaborate answer to the President containing many objections to his programme, it would doubtless be necessary for the President to go to Congress and to place before that body exactly what Italy, France, and Great Britain were fighting for, and to place the responsibility on Congress for the further continuation of the war by the United States in behalf of the aims of the Allies . . .[8]

Colonel House was disposed to permit two reservations, as reasonable in themselves and as a guarantee against more extensive demands. Clemenceau abandoned his more elaborate plans and Sonnino had to abandon his.[9] They all agreed to the British draft, which became the official reply of the Allied premiers to President Wilson. The note read:

The Allied Governments have given careful consideration to the correspondence which has passed between the President of the United States and the German Government. Subject to the qualifications which follow they declare their willingness to make peace with the Government of Germany on the terms of peace laid down in the President's address to Congress of January 8, 1918, and the principles of settlement enunciated in his subsequent addresses. They must point out, however, that clause two, relating to what is usually described as Freedom of the Seas, is open to various interpretations, some of which they could not accept. They must, therefore, reserve to themselves complete freedom on this subject when they enter the Peace Conference.

Further, in the conditions of peace laid down in his address to Congress of January 8, 1918, the President declared that invaded territory must be restored as well as evacuated and freed. The Allied Governments feel that no doubt ought to be allowed to exist as to what this provision implies. By it they understand that compensation will be made by Germany for all damage done to the civilian population of the Allies, and their property, by the aggression of Germany by land, by sea, and from the air.[10]

The German Government at once accepted the principles of this note and the reservations it embodied, and the note thus became a binding contract generally known as the "Pre-Armistice Agreement." House was jubilant. "I am glad the exceptions were made," he wrote, "for it emphasizes the acceptance of the Fourteen Points. If they had not dissented in any way, but had let the Armistice be made without protest, they would have been in a better position at the Peace Conference to object to them." [11]

He underestimated the resourcefulness of Lloyd George and Clemenceau.

2 : *Before the London Conference—French Traditions*

French foreign policy for centuries has shown a remarkable consistency of aim which has varied little with the extraordinary number of changes of internal régime which have occurred during the whole period of French national history. From Cateau Cambresis (1559) to Versailles (1919), Valois Kings, French Cardinals, Revolutionary leaders, Napoleonic adventurers, and statesmen of the Third Republic, all have labored to prevent the creation of a strong and centralized Germanic state east of the Rhine, or have sought to weaken or destroy such a state once it had been created. What, otherwise, is the meaning of Thiers' remark that France was beaten at Sadowa in 1866 but that the Second Empire had permitted the defeat of a decadent German state by one charged with a vigorous militarism, that Prussia would succeed where Austria had failed in the construction of a united and powerful Germany? In the outcome, Bismarck had to crush France before he could complete his unification of Germany. Clemenceau remembered that event, and Marshal Foch was trained in its lessons at St. Cyr.

Like French aims, French methods also show remarkable consistency. Whenever opportunity offers, France has intervened directly in the internal affairs of the German state to disrupt the very fabric of the state itself. From Francis I to Richelieu, His Catholic Majesty made leagues with the Protestant Princes of the Holy Roman Empire against their Catholic Emperor for fear that religious unity in the Germanic

26

states meant political unity as well. During the Thirty Years' War at the precise moment when the Protestant powers could no longer hold their own against the Catholic Imperial power, Cardinal Richelieu sent French armies to their aid. A comparison of the constitutional provisions of the Treaty of Prague (1635) with those of the Treaty of Westphalia (1648) reveals the reason for French intervention. The provisions of the former treaty forbade princes of the Holy Roman Empire to maintain private armies or to make leagues or treaties without imperial assent—a premature establishment of centralized authority in the Germanic states. After French victory the Treaty of Westphalia registered the virtually complete independence of the petty states of Germany and today it is treated as a textbook of sovereign rights. Napoleon, with the much wider opportunity afforded by complete military conquest, simply dissolved the Holy Roman Empire by decree in 1806. Clemenceau and Foch remembered in 1919 that the new German Reich of Bismarck which had nearly destroyed them was still constitutionally not a completely centralized and unitary state but a federation.

Equally desirable, if not always obtainable, is direct French control of strategic German territory. The historic French slogan of "natural frontiers" has usually had that application, and both Louis XIV and Napoleon well knew its meaning. No one in 1919 disputed French claims to Alsace-Lorraine, but few were disposed outright to concede the Saar Valley, much less the Rhineland. Moreover, the French Government had accepted the general principle of "self-determination" which seemingly precluded any claim to German territory other than Alsace-Lorraine. Yet if historical tradition were any clue it seemed that age-old French instincts would reassert themselves in a demand for some sort of control of distinctively German territory. Actually, they had laid their plans in 1916.

Finally, to supplement direct political intervention and direct territorial annexation, French rulers had for centuries maintained the strongest possible alliances to the east of Germany. Poland vanished from the map of Europe at the end of the eighteenth century, but eventually Russia came—in more ways than one—to occupy her place in the nineteenth century. Russia in 1919 was host to Bolshevism, only less obnoxious to the French than Germanism because further removed and thereby more susceptible to immunization by *"cordon sanitaire."* Fortunately, Wilson's thirteenth point provided for the resurrection of the Polish state "which should include territories inhabited by indisputably Polish populations, which should be assured a free and secure access to the sea." Clemenceau and Foch could be counted upon for their loyalty to French tradition in demanding that the widest areas possible be assigned to the new Polish state. Nor would they be too scrupulous about ethnographic principle where the strategic strength of the new state was concerned. Foch would have assigned the whole of East Prussia to Poland, and Pichon said simply that Poland should be *forte, forte, et très forte.*[12]

It cannot be charged against the French that they worked in the dark. They were indeed amazingly frank, to the point of indiscretion. Within a week of the armistice, only two weeks after their acceptance of the Fourteen Points, the Quai d'Orsay drafted a program for the Peace Conference which not only attacked the fundamentals of Wilson's program but also revealed characteristic French intentions toward Germany.[13] The essence of the French scheme was to postpone the establishment of a League of Nations until after all other matters had been settled by treaty—a direct challenge to President Wilson's insistence that the League form an integral part of the treaty settlement—and to sweep away the whole of the Fourteen Points as insufficiently defined to "furnish a concrete basis for the labors of the Conference." One suspects that from the French point of view many of the Fourteen Points were too precise. Indeed, Harold Nicolson, taking issue with the current view, considers them "precise to the point of recklessness." [14]

The real objection of the French to Wilson's program appears in their own concrete proposals, which assigned primary importance to the "federalization" of Germany. The significance of that proposal becomes clear from a remark of Clemenceau (March 7, 1919), "that the more separate and independent republics were established in Germany, the better he would be pleased." [15] The French memorandum was given to President Wilson in Washington by Ambassador Jusserand on November 29, 1918. A reply was never vouchsafed.

Other French schemes lurked in secret files, only to be produced at a favorable moment. They embodied familiar principles—French control of strategic German territories. In September 1916 the French Cabinet with the privity of President Poincaré had decided to annex not merely Alsace-Lorraine, but the Saar Valley as well, to take from Germany the entire left bank of the Rhine and to constitute it an autonomous republic under military occupation by French armies. Chary of discussing the project with the British Government, they sent Doumergue to Russia to purchase the support of their Imperial Ally by offer of French support to any designs which Russia might have for territorial acquisitions at Germany's expense in the east. The pact was sealed by an exchange of notes in February 1917, shortly before the collapse of the Czarist régime.

One brief flash of publicity illumined the transaction at the end of that year, when the Bolshevist Government published to the world the pertinent contents of the imperial archives— a complete set of the Secret Treaties to which the Imperial Russian Government was party—including the Franco-Russian exchange of notes. It is surprising that the revelations made but little stir. They undoubtedly prompted the moderate exposition of war aims by both Lloyd George and Wilson in January 1918, but aside from embarrassing questions addressed in Parliament to the British Foreign Secretary, Lord Balfour, there seems to have been little disquiet as to the nature of French purposes.[16] The British Government did not take seriously this clear warning.

It is now possible to see the real significance of the debate (October 30 and November 1, 1918) between Marshals Haig and Foch and Premiers Lloyd George and Clemenceau about the armistice terms. Foch and Clemenceau were insistent that Allied armies should at once occupy all of the left bank of the Rhine and four bridgeheads of the right bank, including a radius of 30 kilometers. Both Lloyd George and Haig thought occupation of the right bank unwise. Haig would have confined occupation to those areas which the Allies had decided to take back from Germany at the Peace Conference—Belgium, Luxembourg, and Alsace-Lorraine. Haig said, "If you had these, you have in hand everything you desired in the west at the Peace Conference." Neither Foch nor Clemenceau dared at this time say that if the French were to insist on the Rhine River as their permanent military frontier they must at once get it in hand by means of the armistice terms. Clemenceau did state that "he could not maintain himself in the Chamber of Deputies unless this remains in the Armistice," but he gave "his word of honor that France would withdraw *after peace conditions had been fulfilled.*" He was still hopeful that one of those conditions of peace would permit French troops to remain there permanently. The Supreme War Council gave unanimous assent to the occupation provisions drafted by Foch.[17]

The next step was obvious. Marshal Foch prepared a memorandum on November 27, 1918. It began where the armistice terms left off, providing the transition from a provisional to a permanent arrangement for French control in the whole Rhineland area. It implements fully the general principles of the Franco-Russian exchange of notes in February 1917, and in some particulars goes far beyond even those principles. It found its justification in the undoubted fact of two German invasions of France within fifty years and in the permanent inferiority of French man-power *vis-à-vis* Germany. East of the Rhine, Germany still had between 64,000,000 and 75,-000,000 subjects as against a total of 49,560,000 for France, Belgium, Luxembourg, and Alsace-Lorraine, all lumped together. Even if Germany were deprived of all her territory of the left bank, west of the Rhine, and its population were added to the French bloc, the French total would be only 54,960,000 as against the German total east of the Rhine of 64,000,000 to 75,000,000. There was no longer a Russian ally to immobilize considerable German forces in the east, to provide that essential breathing space before British forces could appear on French soil in sufficient numbers to offset German superiority.

Foch proposed, therefore, to group at once all the populations of the left bank of the Rhine in the same military organization to be capable of defending the line of the Rhine. The details of that program add up to the most thinly disguised military imperialism.

1. Extinguish German sovereignty in the purely German territory west of the Rhine.
2. Organize one or more autonomous republics in this former German territory.
3. Conscript the male population of this area into military units to fight Germany in case of war.
4. "Equally treaties or arrangements should assure the conduct of these new states, with a view to specifying their political attitude, and to determining their military burden. . . . That is to say that the different States on the left bank . . . should have a common policy, controlled by some of

31

them in proportion to the risks to be encountered in war [France, Belgium, Great Britain]. . . ."

5. "Equally treaties should assure, by maintenance of allied contingents at strongholds of the left bank, the defense of the new frontier for at least a certain period of time."

6. Finally, in order to secure guarantees for German execution in full of all treaty terms, especially reparation payments, it is "indispensable to maintain intact the occupation of the bridge-heads of the right bank. . . ." [18]

Frenchmen might sincerely describe such a program as "not a policy of annexation, but of protection," but they could scarcely object if Lloyd George and Wilson failed to appreciate the distinction. The former would certainly object to the creation of new Alsace-Lorraines in Europe; the latter would as certainly resist such a patent violation of his cardinal principle of self-determination, and would most particularly resent the affront to the League of Nations, which in his view was to provide adequately and permanently for French security within the framework of a new world order. All of which Clemenceau realized perfectly well. He must simply do the best he could while walking very warily. After the armistice he maintained a rigid press censorship to suppress all editorial demands for the left bank of the Rhine. Among his daily instructions to the press there is a specific order forbidding publication of the Foch memorandum.[19] One of the French journalists of this period testifies that the apparent absence of popular demand for the Rhineland "was rather because official and semi-official circles abstained from arousing popular feeling on such a delicate subject." [20]

Besides, there would shortly be an opportunity to sound out the British in London, where a meeting of the Allied and Associated Powers' representatives was scheduled for December 1, 1918. On November 25, Colonel House received the following invitation from Lloyd George:

32

Monsieur Clemenceau is coming to London on 1st December and I earnestly hope that you will be able to come also, as a number of urgent questions require discussion. As I shall not be able to attend any conferences in Paris before the election of the 14th of December, this is especially important. I am inviting Signor Orlando also.[21]

House was ill with influenza and could not attend, but Lloyd George has given an account of what occurred.

3 : *London Conference, December 1-3, 1918—Rhineland and Reparation*

Clemenceau and Foch arrived November 30 and that evening Foch held a preliminary discussion with Lloyd George, Balfour, and General Sir Henry Wilson at Downing Street. Clemenceau pleaded a social engagement to excuse his absence. "When I discovered the real topic which was to be raised," says Lloyd George, "I realized why he was absent. The wily old politician, knowing our partiality for Foch and the debt of gratitude we owed him, deemed it advisable that the first introduction to French ideas as to the future of the Rhineland should be left to him." Foch had brought his memorandum of November 27 and summarized its contents with complete fidelity. ". . . it was essential that there should be a permanent mutual assistance between all the countries of the west. France, Belgium, Luxembourg, the Rhineland left of the river, and Great Britain—all organized for the defense of the Western front. We ought to prepare an Alliance, *including the Rhenish Provinces,* whether they were in an autonomous organization or not (a question which he did not wish to discuss) which would provide forces fully organized to safeguard the position. The control of the organization should be under Great Britain, France, and Belgium." Lloyd George asked how the Marshal reconciled his plan with President

33

Wilson's Fourteen Points. Foch thought it conceivable that the German population of the area could be reconciled by "the attraction of our economic organization," and in any case "it was better to be on the side of the victors than of the conquered." Lloyd George wanted to know if Foch did not fear the danger of creating a "new Alsace-Lorraine" which must result eventually in a new war of revenge. The Marshal promised again that he would do his best "to conciliate the feelings and interests of these people." Lloyd George agreed to study the memorandum very carefully, but he made it clear that he would never be party to arrangements which created new problems in Europe.[22] President Wilson was, therefore, assured of Lloyd George's support in resisting French schemes of military imperialism in the Rhineland. Fundamental British interest in continental stability was certain to assist the realization of the President's territorial program—based on the principle of self-determination—*in Europe*.

While the French Rhineland project was thus shelved, the full conference of December 1-3 considered two other matters of fundamental importance: Reparation, and the Trial of the Kaiser. Concerning the latter, Lloyd George's account is complete and revealing, for he is able to prove from the record that far from originating any such project himself he merely followed the French proposals and secured unanimous agreement from all representatives of the Allied and Associated Governments, including the United States.[23] While the decision to try the Kaiser as "the criminal mainly responsible for the War" has ever since been cited as proof of Allied vindictiveness, it is chiefly interesting as testimony to the universality of belief that the Kaiser personally plotted and planned the war, and it is well to remember that the legend of the "Potsdam Crown Council" which supported that belief came from German sources.[24]

Far more significant was the Reparation question, which

was given first place on the agenda of the London Conference. Public opinion in all Allied countries wanted from Germany all the money that could be got. The question was, how much could be obtained; and since the general public was prone to illusions on the extravagant side, Lloyd George proposed the creation of an Inter-Allied Commission of Experts to find out just how much the defeated enemy could pay. It was so resolved, with the additional stipulation that each of the Allied Governments was to make out its own bill of claims to present to the Commission.[25] If there were anything disquieting about the discussion, it was the absence of any reference to the Pre-Armistice Agreement which limited Allied claims to "compensation . . . for all damage done to the civilian population of the Allies and their property." There might have been additional cause for worry in the actual wording of the resolution which recommended an Inter-Allied Commission "to examine and report on amount enemy countries are able to pay for reparation *and indemnity*." Colonel House thought so, for when he forwarded the resolutions of the conference to President Wilson for his approval, he suggested that the word "indemnity" be struck out.[26] The historical connotations of the word were certainly much wider than the limited construction to be put upon "reparation," or "compensation for damage." They might cover "costs of the War." When read in the context of the vocal demands of the British and French public for War Costs, "indemnity" seemed to convey that meaning. It was clearly precluded by the very intent of the Pre-Armistice Agreement, positively by the promise only to exact compensation for civilian damage, negatively by Wilson's more general prohibition of "punitive damages."

Despite Lloyd George's apparent nonchalance about principle and contract, his practical desire to confine Allied demands to an expert assessment of what the traffic would bear gave some hope of a reasonable solution, provided always

35

that he could practically achieve such an expert determination of financial capacity. Otherwise his abandonment of the ground of principle was bound to be disastrous. He started on a slippery path at the London Conference which led rapidly downhill into the morasses of the December British elections.

4 : *December Elections—Squeeze the Orange*

Lloyd George was so little bothered by his commitment to the Pre-Armistice Agreement that he was quite ready to make pledges to the British electorate which defied one of its cardinal principles. His concern for a practical determination of enemy capacity had nothing whatsoever to do with a scrupulous regard for principle or for his pledged word; it was dictated solely by his conception of British economic interest as an exporting nation. Throughout his own account of the Reparation question the constant theme is not his superior virtue, but his superior wisdom. He assumed the complete justification of the British demand for full war costs, provided the enemy practically could pay that much, and provided also that the payment would not injure British trade. Thus at a meeting of the Imperial War Cabinet November 26, 1918, when the Australian premier, Mr. Hughes, "strongly urged the exaction of a full war indemnity," Lloyd George reported:

. . . I asked if it was Mr. Hughes' intention that Australia should be paid in gold, or by Germany selling goods, and to this question Mr. Hughes replied "by credit." I then pointed out that, in order to pay the debt in this manner, it would be necessary for Germany to sell goods, and asked who was going to buy them. The total liability of Germany would probably amount to some £20,000,000,000, and it would be very easy for the Allied Powers to say to Germany that she had got to pay this amount, but I suggested that it would mean that for two generations we would

36

make German workmen our slaves. I further pointed out that someone must buy the goods manufactured in Germany, and for the moment, I did not see which nation would provide the dumping ground for such goods. Further, we would have to allow Germany to import raw material for the manufacture of the goods. I thought the only way in which Germany could pay a large indemnity would be by manufacturing cheaper than other nations and by selling to them.[27]

Lloyd George was particularly anxious "that members of the Government should not be responsible during the election for arousing or encouraging any false hopes in the minds of the electorate." Unfortunately on the very eve of the elections Lloyd George's hand-picked committee proposed fantastic figures. He had counted on practical city bankers, officials of the Bank of England, economists, to cure Hughes of his optimism, but Gibbs, Cunliffe, Hewins, Foster, and Long caught the contagion. Both Bonar Law and Lloyd George regarded their report "as a wild and fantastic chimera." It began —reasonably enough in the latter's opinion—with the principle that "the total cost of the War to the Allies is the measure of the indemnity which the Enemy Powers should in justice pay." But it concluded that there was no reason why the Enemy Powers should not pay annually £1,200,000,000 as interest on a capital debt of £24,000,000,000, which was their estimate of the total cost of the war. They saw no reason to fear "economic ill-effects to Allied countries from the repayment of the cost of the War." Worst of all, this report represented the opinions of the Associated Chambers of Commerce and the Federation of British Industries.[28]

"So much," lamented Lloyd George, "for the infallibility of business men in business matters which go beyond their day-to-day transactions." One can grant so much without necessarily endorsing his corollary concerning the superior wisdom of the politician. Once admit the principle of full war indemnity and fantastic figures are sure to follow. It was Lloyd George himself who had opened the floodgates. He was in a hopeless dilemma and he refused to take the one possible and the only honorable way out by retreating to the firm ground of the Pre-Armistice Agreement. That way was political suicide.

When the Imperial War Cabinet met to consider the committee's report, one rather reluctant member justified his own acquiescence on purely political grounds, that ". . . the fact that men of such standing in the business world as Lord Cunliffe and Mr. Gibbs were emphatic in their belief that a large indemnity could be imposed, *and that similar conclusions had also been arrived at in the Reports of the Federation of British Industries and the Associated Chambers of Commerce,* would create a very awkward situation if the Government did not press its full demands in accordance with the cost of the war to ourselves." [29] Only one member of the government suggested an honorable retreat. Bonar Law warned the Cabinet that President Wilson might justly complain of their violation of his Fourteen Points. The Inter-Allied Conference had already decided on a preliminary examination by an expert commission of what Germany could actually pay. If the commission were to report that Germany was barely able to pay *reparation,* why quarrel about *indemnities* at all? Why raise the thorny question of principle without knowing the facts? Lloyd George replied:

. . . unless President Wilson was prepared to pool the whole cost of the war, and for the United States to take its share of the whole, he was not in a position to reject our claims for *indemnity.*
As regards the figure claimed for Reparations, he did not believe that sum could be obtained.[30]

In other words, Lloyd George, knowing that German financial capacity was inadequate to meet even strict claims for *reparation,* still insisted on raising the issue of *war costs.* He committed himself to the impossible task of satisfying the electorate by promise of full war costs; of satisfying common sense by reservations about German capacity to pay and about British capacity to receive. He was ready to satisfy every necessity except that of keeping his word, but to a seasoned politician like Lloyd George loyalty to pledges is never a necessity.

On December 11, 1918, Lloyd George gaily rode both horns of his dilemma into the electoral arena at Bristol to the tune of "Who is to foot the bill?" (A voice—"Germany!" and "The loser pays.") Lloyd George made an ambiguous speech, and, in conclusion, said:

Let me summarize. First, as far as justice is concerned, *we have an absolute right to demand the whole cost of the war from Germany*. The second point is that *we propose to demand the whole cost of the war*. (Cheers). The third point is that when you come to the exacting of it you must exact it in such a way that it does not do more harm to the country that receives it than to the country which is paying it. The fourth point is that *the Committee appointed by the British Cabinet believe it can be done*. . . . You may depend upon it that the first consideration in the minds of the Allies will be the interests of the people upon whom Germany has made war, and not in the interests of the German people who have been guilty of this crime against humanity.[81]

An enthusiastic electorate may be excused for remembering the positive promise of war costs and for forgetting the reservations, particularly since many of Lloyd George's colleagues were less scrupulous than he in admitting that any practical difficulties of collection existed. The most famous phrase that has ever since echoed out of that hurly-burly is Eric Geddes' triumphant shout in the Cambridge Guildhall, "We shall squeeze the orange until the pips squeak." [82] There was certainly a popular impression that the British Government had promised to collect from Germany every penny that the war had cost them. It may well be, as Harold Nicolson has said, that it was merely unfortunate that "a British Liberal should

39

have placed himself at the mercy of a jingo Commons and a jingo Press," but Lloyd George himself bears the initial responsibility for a cynical departure from President Wilson's principles and from his own pledged word to abide by them.[33] His own betrayal placed the British Liberal on the same level with jingo Press and jingo Commons.

French plans in the Rhineland, though opposed by Lloyd George, and British commitments to collect the costs of the war, certain to receive French support, were a serious challenge to the Wilsonian program and a clear repudiation of the Pre-Armistice Agreement. They were not likely to remain the only obstacles in Wilson's path. Even before he arrived in Europe there were plain evidences of annexationist ambitions on the part of British Dominions which had conquered German colonies and were determined to keep them.

5 : *Aboard the* George Washington—*Wilson and the Colonial Problem*

President Wilson was already well on his way to Paris aboard the *George Washington* when, on December 8, he received Colonel House's wireless report of the London Conference resolution for an Inter-Allied Commission to determine the capacity of enemy powers to pay "Reparation and indemnity," with the latter's recommendation to approve it only after the word "indemnity" had been struck out. Even so Wilson was disturbed. He hastily summoned Henry White and Secretary Lansing into a confidential meeting to express his alarm. He rightly interpreted the purpose of the resolution as an investigation of enemy capacity to pay "indemnity" before any formulation of the Allied bill of damages, "the plan being to assess the latter in proportion to the former." Wilson condemned this procedure as "getting the cart before

40

the horse"; as a "repetition of the selfish Allied procedure after the Boxer Rebellion."[34]

Two days later, as the *George Washington* passed close by the Azores,—just one day before Lloyd George's equivocal speech to the electors of Bristol—Wilson convened a solemn council of the entire American Delegation including the plenipotentiaries and the experts of the Inquiry, shortly to be rechristened "The American Intelligence." President Isaiah Bowman of Johns Hopkins University has preserved a summary of Wilson's remarks.[35]

Suspicions as to the good faith of Allied professions appeared at the outset in Wilson's phrase that ". . . *we would be the only disinterested people* at the Peace Conference," though he certainly miscalculated when he added *"that the men whom we were about to deal with did not represent their own people. . . ."* Again, "The European *leaders* reminded one of the *episode in Philippopolis*—for the *space of two hours they cried, 'Great is Diana of the Ephesians'*—to which the President appended in an aside, *'in the interest of the silversmiths.'* "[36]

The President insisted that the reparation problem be settled on the basis of "just claims" and not by a preliminary study of how much Germany could afford to pay. Above all, the question must be taken out of the hands of politicians and put in charge of an expert commission. To this extent he was in agreement with the procedure outlined by Lloyd George.[37]

He was also insistent on the incorporation of a League of Nations bodily in the structure of the peace treaties. He ". . . could not see how a treaty of peace could be drawn up or how both *elasticity and security could be obtained save under a League of Nations. . . ."* But his concern for the League led him on into highly optimistic forecasts of a colonial settlement which would utilize League machinery.

His proposal was ". . . that the *German Colonies* should

41

be *declared* the *common property of the League of Nations and administered by small nations.*" The League would act as "residuary trustee" for the inheritance of the German colonial empire, and the possession of property would tend to stabilize the institution of the League, while safeguarding the rights of natives and assuring the equality of economic opportunity for all nations.

Such was, in essence, the "Mandates" principle. In Wilson's formulation it excluded German claims for restoration of colonies and equally the claims of her enemies based upon conquest and possession. If the small nations were to receive mandates from the League of Nations to administer the colonies, what would be the attitude of the large nations, Japan, France, Great Britain, especially the British Dominions? It is clear that the most for which Wilson could hope was acceptance and application of his mandates principle by governments already in possession. They might conceivably agree to administer the former German colonies, which they had conquered and now possessed, on conditions formulated by the League of Nations, and to act as "trustees" subject to its supervision. To suppose that they would ever surrender these territories to the administration of, say, Switzerland, or even Portugal, Belgium, or Holland, was the sheerest fantasy. Indeed, the proposal to entrust colonial administration to small states was a desperate device to avoid even the semblance of a division of spoils at the Peace Conference. It had no support from the American expert chiefly concerned with the elaboration of the mandates idea, George Louis Beer, who would be well content if he could secure acceptance of the mandates principle from the powers in possession.[38]

Could Wilson claim that the Pre-Armistice Agreement bound the Allied Powers to acceptance of the principle? Two of his more general requirements which were part of that agreement certainly precluded merely division of spoils:

42

Peoples and provinces must not be bartered about from sovereignty to sovereignty as if they were chattels or pawns in a game.

Every territorial settlement must be in the interests of the populations concerned; and not as part of any mere adjustment or compromise of claims among rival states.[89]

But those are largely negative statements; they do not embody positive elaboration of the mandates principle. If such meaning can be found it is only among the Fourteen Points, and if it is there it is so thoroughly concealed under the language of sovereignty that only the sophistication of Walter Lippmann can reveal it. The text of Point Five reads:

A free, open-minded, and absolutely impartial *adjustment of all colonial claims,* based upon a strict observance of the principle that in *determining all such questions of sovereignty,* the interests of the populations concerned must have equal weight with the *equitable claims of the government whose title is to be determined.*

To be sure, the well-being of native populations is accorded equal status with equitable claims in determining what particular colonial power shall receive title and thereby acquire sovereign rights. Presumably, therefore, the reputation of any particular claimant for enlightened treatment of its natives in other colonies should double the weight of its claim based upon other grounds. Possibly also the prospective heir to German sovereign rights in the colonial sphere might be required to promise certain specific measures in the interests of its new subjects, though it is difficult to perceive any such condition in the language of Point Five. In any case, once title has been determined full sovereign rights go with it, and sovereignty is not conditional. But Frank Cobb of the New York *World* and Walter Lippmann—chiefly the latter—wrote an elaborate commentary on the Fourteen Points which left little to the imagi-

43

nation. Their own imaginative insight reveals the true meaning of Point Five:

> . . . It would seem as if the principle involved in this proposition is that a colonial power acts not as owner of its colonies, but as trustee for the natives and for the interests of the society of nations, that the terms on which the colonial administration is conducted are a matter of international concern and may legitimately be the subject of international inquiry and that the peace conference may, therefore, write a code of colonial conduct binding upon all colonial powers.[40]

Now this commentary did acquire a semiofficial status, for it was undertaken at Colonel House's request and it secured President Wilson's general approval as "a satisfactory interpretation of the principles involved," though details of application were to be regarded as "merely illustrative suggestions." Moreover, House testifies: "These interpretations were on the table day after day when we sat in conference in Paris while the Armistice was in the making. Many times they (Clemenceau, Orlando, Lloyd George) asked the meaning of this or that point and I would read from the accepted interpretation." [41] But there is no record of any discussion of the colonial question during the negotiation of the Pre-Armistice Agreement. There was certainly no "code of colonial conduct binding upon all colonial powers" actually in existence and it seems impossible to argue that the Pre-Armistice Agreement bound the Allied Powers in advance to the acceptance of any such code. It is, therefore, difficult to find the reason for President Wilson's optimism about the colonial settlement when he addressed the American Delegation aboard the *George Washington*. Possibly it lay in his belief that *"England herself was against further extension of the British Empire."* [42]

So far as the British Cabinet was concerned, that belief was well founded. A majority even favored the surrender of German East Africa to the United States ". . . if the United States

44

were prepared to take their share of responsibility in a mandatory capacity." [43] But as to larger issues of war and peace the British Cabinet had merged in a greater directorate, the Imperial War Cabinet, including the premiers of the British Dominions. The latter had clearly defined national objectives of their own which required the most respectful consideration from members of the British Cabinet. In the spring of 1917 it was settled by the Imperial War Cabinet that the Union of South Africa should annex German Southwest Africa, that Australia should annex New Guinea, and New Zealand should annex Samoa. [44] So much Lloyd George tells us: he might have added that the British Government exchanged promises with the Japanese Government reserving to the former complete rights of disposal as to German Pacific islands south of the equator, and to the latter equal freedom north of the equator. [45] There were certain, then, to be serious reservations in any acceptance of the mandatory principle by the British Cabinet. They were deeply committed to annexationist aims of their own Dominions a year and a half before the armistice negotiations.

6 : *Buckingham Palace—German Colonies*

President Wilson arrived in Paris on December 13, 1918, where his conversations with Clemenceau during the next ten days revealed a serious divergence of views that was inevitable. While the former talked of making the League of Nations "the center of the whole programme," the most he could get out of Clemenceau was a very mild agreement. "He thought a League of Nations should be attempted, but he was not confident of success, either of forming it or of its being workable after it was formed. . . ." [46] To the Chamber of Deputies he was frankly contemptuous of the *noble candeur* of President Wilson in expressing his own preference for the old international system of the balance of power based upon military alliances. He did not yet reveal the French program for the Rhineland, but his general principles received a four to one vote of endorsement from the Chamber. "About as bad an augury for the success of progressive principles at the Peace Conference as we could have," wrote House. "Coming on the heels of the English elections, and taking into consideration the result of the recent elections in the United States, the situation strategically could not be worse." [47]

Meantime, President Wilson had been to England—only to encounter much the same sort of discouragement. In anticipation of his visit, Lloyd George held further meetings of the Imperial War Cabinet to canvass some of the larger questions that he and Wilson were to discuss prior to the Peace Conference. Among these questions the German Colonies bulked large. The Cabinet accepted Wilson's mandatory principle in respect to former enemy possessions—except Southwest Africa and the Pacific islands, New Guinea and Samoa. [48]

Premier Hughes said he had already made it perfectly clear to Wilson ". . . that the demand for the Pacific Islands was being put forward in the interests of Australian security and not in the interests of the British Empire." General Smuts, who had just elaborated the first comprehensive constitution to embody the mandates principle, confined its application chiefly to former Russian, Austro-Hungarian, and Turkish territories. In any case it was not to apply to Southwest Africa, which the Union of South Africa claimed in outright sovereignty. [49]

Premier Borden of Canada made it clear that Canada had not gone to war in order to add territory to the British Empire, but as to the territories conquered by South Africa, Australia, and New Zealand, he would support their retention on the one condition that they were essential to the future security of the Empire. For the rest of the conquered territory, he favored ". . . entrusting their control and dominion to whichever state was appointed as mandatory for that purpose by the League of Nations, on the lines suggested in General Smuts' paper." [50] Lord Milner agreed that Southwest Africa and the Pacific Islands should be excepted from the treatment accorded other occupied colonies, and regarded as the property of the Dominions which had conquered them. [51]

Lloyd George was now ready to receive President Wilson, who arrived in England on Boxing Day, the day after Christmas. He arranged a Bank Holiday in Wilson's honor to accord him the largest possible popular demonstration in the London streets. There followed a Royal Banquet in Buckingham Palace, "a scene of unsurpassed splendor," where Wilson's speech of "measured emphasis and cold tones" produced a "chill of disappointment." . . . "There was no glow of friendship or of gladness at meeting men who had been partners in a common enterprise and had so narrowly escaped a common danger." Worst of all, the speech made no reference to the part played by the British Empire in the mighty struggle just concluded. [52] Nor did the President atone for his sins of omission at the subsequent ceremony in the London Guildhall—even after Lloyd George's gentle hint conveyed via Lord Reading. Lloyd George was anxious to create "a better atmosphere for coöperation at the coming Peace Conference, especially on subjects where we might have to take a more liberal view of the Treaty than Clemenceau was likely to adopt." [53]

While the tone of the recent British elections certainly cannot excuse Wilson's disregard of the amenities, it may partially explain it. He may have entertained quite natural doubts as to the extent to which Lloyd George was really prepared "to take a more liberal view of the Treaty than Clemenceau was likely to adopt." His conversations with

Lloyd George at Buckingham Palace were not such as to dispel those doubts.

There was complete agreement by Balfour and Lloyd George on the establishment of the League of Nations, and even complete acceptance of the President's proposal that this be "the first subject discussed at the Peace Conference." Lloyd George presented him with a copy of the Smuts paper; Wilson had prepared no document, of his own, for he preferred to establish agreement on general principles before drafting any plan. It is quite clear that such ready acceptance of Wilson's plan to put the League in the forefront of the work on the treaty came from anxiety to settle the disposition of the German Colonies as quickly as possible. If a League of Nations was to distribute mandates, the sooner there was a League of Nations to do the distributing, the better.[54]

Finally, there was no question of returning any of her colonies to Germany. President Wilson was as decided on that point as any of the Allied leaders. Germany stood convicted by Allied publicists of inhumane treatment of her native populations through economic exploitation and militarization, and ironically in this as in other instances, the anti-German "propaganda" was based on evidence from German sources, very largely the attacks by Social Democrats on German Imperial administration in Southwest Africa at the time of the Herrero Rebellion. The American expert, George Louis Beer, joined in the general verdict, while pointing out that Germany had too limited experience as an imperial power to develop the high standards of imperial administration which a century or more of educated public opinion had forced upon the British Government. He had found evidences of such trend in Germany shortly before the war.[55] But, meantime, Allied publicists had seized on official wartime pronouncements of German leaders of their colonial aims, as additional proof that Germany could not be trusted with colonial responsibility. They cited Zimmermann's program for a German Mittel-Afrika, with a black conscript army of 1,000,000 men, equipped with naval and air bases on both the Atlantic and Indian oceans.[56] To protect natives from militarization and equally to protect Allied Powers from the constant menace of German aggression, President Wilson agreed that none of her former colonies would be returned to Germany.[57] But this was as far as agreement went.

The President said that without exception, former German Colonies must be administered on the mandates principle under the supervision of the League of Nations, though he wisely did not insist on his earlier idea of selecting the small countries to act in mandatory capacity.[58] Lloyd George attempted to draw the familiar distinction between "the German colonies conquered by the British Dominions and adjacent to them, and those in the conquest of which the forces of the Empire as a whole had shared."[59] In the latter category he was willing to leave German East Africa to the disposal of the League of Nations, and to commit Great Britain—if chosen as mandatory power—to acceptance of all conditions imposed by the League.[60] But he made the strongest possible argument for leaving German Southwest Africa in outright sovereignty to the Union of South Africa which had conquered it, since "it would be quite impossible to separate from the South African Union what was essentially part of the same country."[61]

While Wilson was not at that moment prepared to argue the point, he did retort "that the position of Australia with regard to the Pacific colonies was not quite the same." When Balfour and Lloyd George both put the case for Australia as strongly as possible on the ground of security, Wilson warned them that similar arguments could be made for all captured territory. When they revealed their promise to Japan of all

49

German islands north of the equator, to convince him that what they had promised Japan they could hardly withhold from Australia and New Zealand, Wilson said emphatically that "he was by no means prepared to accept the Japanese treaty, and was doubtful whether Japan could be admitted there even in the capacity of a mandatory Power." They had not succeeded in moving him from that position. All Lloyd George could do was to leave the matter "to be fought out at the Conference, where the Dominions would be able to present their case." [62] There was certain to be a conflict.

Yet, if Wilson was unbending on the mandates principle, despite the vagueness of the Pre-Armistice Agreement concerning it, he was even more unyielding on "indemnity"—"stiffer than on any other question," Lloyd George reports. He insisted that initial claims be limited to "pure reparation"—that is, to claims for "damage to the civilian population of the Allies, and their property," in the language of the Pre-Armistice Agreement. When Lloyd George complained that such procedure would practically rule out the British Empire and would give practically everything to France and Belgium, the most that Wilson would concede was that after "pure reparation" other claims might possibly be considered. Far from undoing the impression of British intransigence created by the recent elections, Lloyd George clearly revealed to Wilson his own insistence on the principle of War Costs in defiance of his prior acceptance of the Pre-Armistice Agreement. It is small wonder that he "failed to make any impression on the President." [63]

There were many other miscellaneous matters, few of which created any difficulty. Lloyd George was gratified that the President was in no mood to tolerate French schemes for the control of the west bank of the Rhine, but he was uneasy at his hostility to Italian claims, for here, as in the case of Japanese annexationist demands, the British Government

50

had treaty commitments. Lloyd George feared that "the President would strongly support the Yugoslavs against Italy." [64]

The real storm broke at the Imperial War Cabinet meeting convened to hear Lloyd George's report of his Buckingham Palace conversations with President Wilson; and, characteristically, it was Premier Hughes of Australia who led the attack. Lloyd George was essentially a politician of Liberal tendencies who trimmed his sails to the winds of public opinion and steered with a discriminating eye to the shoals and rocks of political forces. Few politicians were keener in estimating the combined effects of weather and hidden shallows on his course. His attitude on indemnity and the German colonies was clearly not the result of any personal conviction; it was determined by the exigency of public opinion and of Dominion pressure, and Hughes was intransigent on both subjects.

Hughes had played a prominent part in the formulation of British demands for war costs and he was the leading exponent of annexationist aims among the Dominion premiers. A man "of frail physique, defective hearing, and eccentric gesticulations," he had a gift for mordant phrase, and a hide like a rhinoceros. He was the living embodiment of everything that was anti-Wilsonian; he gloried in savage attacks on the President's plans for a new world order; he was as hard-boiled a nationalist as any at the Paris Peace Conference. Lloyd George, though he found him difficult, admired him greatly; and Clemenceau fairly doted on him. Clemenceau later heard from Lloyd George the Dominion claims in the Pacific, and wanted to hear more from the premiers concerned. "Bring your cannibals here this afternoon," he said, and when they arrived he challenged Hughes, "I hear that you are a cannibal," to which Hughes replied that "the report is grossly exaggerated." From that time they were close friends, sharing a common view of Wilson's program.[65] Hughes was not popular with the more liberal members of the British Empire Delegation, and Lord Robert Cecil, who took the League of Nations very seriously, referred to him in obvious irritation as "that shrimp Hughes." [66] Even the suave Lord Balfour was heard to remark on one occasion, "How I detest him!" [67]

Lloyd George's report of Wilson's program provoked Hughes to fury. He took about one-third of the time in a savage attack on the President's "intolerable" claim "to dictate to us how the world should be governed." The British Empire must not permit itself to be dragged "behind the wheels of President Wilson's chariot," for he "had no claim to speak even for his own country," whereas both Clemenceau and Lloyd George enjoyed an overwhelming popular mandate. They "could settle the peace of the world as they liked." As to a League of Nations, that was to Wilson as a toy to a child—"he would not be happy till he got it."

Wilson's one idea seemed to be to establish the League so that he could go home with the proud boast that he had achieved it, leaving all practical matters to the determination of the League. Hughes did not believe that the peace of the world could be settled on any such terms. He wanted to know what Australia, what the British Empire, was to get out of it for all the sacrifices they had made. Once there were adequate guarantees for "reparation and indemnities," once there were safeguards of security in the possession of New Guinea—only eighty miles from Australia—he would have no objection to handing over other matters to a League of Nations. He insisted that "in any case we should not commit ourselves to the League of Nations until the Conference had completed its labors. . . ." He asked, "above all things, that the Prime Minister who now stood clothed with all power by the recent vote of the people, should resolutely insist upon such terms of peace as were necessary for the safety of the Empire. . . ."[68]

Despite some counsels of moderation, the Hughes attack undoubtedly struck the keynote of the meeting. Premier Borden might caution the Empire representatives that Canada put coöperation with the United States in the forefront of her policy, that Canada could not approve nor support an Empire policy of collaborating with any European nation against the United States—yet he agreed that the Empire policy on the Pacific Islands and indemnity must be stoutly maintained.[69] Lord Robert Cecil might warn them that a good understanding with the United States was the greatest guarantee of a settled peace, and that such an understanding could be had only by British support of the League of Nations idea. Yet Lord Curzon, though approving generally of Anglo-American coöperation, said that "if President Wilson persisted in the line reported it might be necessary, on some issues at any rate, for Mr. Lloyd George to work at the Conference in alliance with M. Clemenceau."[70]

Lloyd George testifies that President Wilson's views evidently made a worse impression on his colleagues of the Imperial War Cabinet than they had made directly on him in his conference with the President. He credits much of this impression to the critical power of Hughes' speech, and characterizes the speech as "a fine specimen of ruthless and pungent analysis of President Wilson's claim to dictate to the countries that had borne the brunt of the fighting." Under the spell of its "stabbing sentences" they all—speaker and listeners alike—forgot the existence of the Pre-Armistice Agreement. Like Clemenceau, they were willing enough to apply its provisions to questions in which they had no stake, but like him were equally determined to achieve national objectives at variance with their pledges.

President Wilson could scarcely have carried to Paris much

53

assurance from his conversations with Lloyd George at Buckingham Palace, even if he had no way of knowing what had been said about them in the Imperial War Cabinet.

7 : *Eve of the Peace Conference—The League of Nations*

On one point, despite objections in both French and British circles, Wilson could scarcely be denied. He had Lloyd George's promise to support his program of putting the League of Nations first on the agenda, and the French, though skeptical, were not likely to make serious objections, particularly if they could endow their acceptance with bargaining value. They would, after all, be represented in the commission which would negotiate the actual constitution of the League, where they might press for provisions adequate to French security. In default of such provisions in the League itself, they might block English and American proposals until they had extracted adequate guarantees of French security in other matters, as, for instance, in the Rhineland.

Lord Balfour arrived in Paris at the very end of the year and on December 31, 1918, reported to Colonel House the fairly general agreement which he, Lloyd George, and Wilson had reached concerning the League during their London conversations. House outlined his views, which Balfour regarded as "practical and satisfactory." [71] But only two days before, Clemenceau's cynicism about the League had received the overwhelming approval of the French Chamber of Deputies. It was some time before Colonel House could approach Clemenceau directly, and he spent most of the first week of January 1919 in fruitless efforts to induce Allied representatives to accept the Pre-Armistice Agreement as the sole basis for reparation demands on Germany. He reported on January 6 that there must be a "show-down" soon, for not only did he encounter excessive indemnity demands, but an increasing

54

disposition to look to the United States for cancellation of Inter-Allied debts and additional contributions toward reconstruction finance. "I am sure the devil will be to pay," said House.[72]

Up to this time Colonel House had been President Wilson's personally accredited agent to the Allies in Europe, and as such, he outranked all others. He was the official and personal repository of Wilson's views, and he had become their interpreter to the Allies. He had already established intimate relations with Clemenceau, which steadily grew more intimate. To be sure, the President had arrived in Europe in the middle of December to become his own plenipotentiary, but after several conversations with Clemenceau, he had gone to England for his conversations with Lloyd George, and now on January 7, 1919, he had just returned from a state visit to Italy. He would remain in Paris to negotiate until the middle of February—not much over a month—when he must return to the United States to wind up the present session of Congress and sign its bills.

Nothing was more natural than that Colonel House should continue to act as the President's spokesman, interpreter, intermediary; the President undoubtedly trusted him, and so did Clemenceau. There is, none the less, something a little ominous about the tone that creeps into the Colonel's diary for this period; a hint of complacency about the intimacy of his relations with Clemenceau, a touch of satisfaction in his own superior diplomatic abilities in handling difficult problems. There is no question that he utilized both of these advantages at this time to forward the President's program. The danger of the complacency was that he might at any time be tempted—out of his superior wisdom as a negotiator—to whittle or explain away awkward obstacles to successful negotiation, even when those obstacles were some of Wilson's most cherished principles. But on this occasion he secured Cle-

55

menceau's support for the President's program of the League of Nations.

January 7, 1919: Clemenceau and the President both sent word they would call on me at five. The President came first to my reception room and met the other Commissioners. We had hardly begun our conversation before the Prime Minister arrived. *I asked President Wilson and the Commissioners to excuse me and took Clemenceau into another room, where we had one of our heart-to-heart talks. I convinced him, I think, for the first time that a League of Nations was for the best interests of France. . . .*[73]

He argued simply that in the last war both Great Britain and the United States had voluntarily supported France without any treaty obligation to do so. Would not France feel safer if England and America were bound by covenant of the League of Nations to protect her in the event of another attack by any nation? "The old Tiger seemed to see it all and became enthusiastic. He placed both hands on my shoulders and said, 'You are right. I am for the League of Nations as you have it in mind and you may count upon me to work with you.' "

House was encouraged to ask Clemenceau to use his influence with Frenchmen like Ribot to check their advocacy of silly proprosals, such as American cancellation of war debts, German payment of the costs of the war, French control of the left bank of the Rhine. Such claims were doing harm to France in American eyes. He begged Clemenceau's pardon for "bringing up the internal affairs of France." Clemenceau granted full forgiveness: "I think of you as a brother and I want you to tell me everything that is in your mind, and we will work together just as if we were parts of the same Government."[74] It is clear from the earlier record that Clemenceau was not telling everything that was in his mind, though there was no reason to doubt the good faith of his promise to put the League of Nations into the treaty.

The Peace Conference opened in plenary session on January 18, 1919. The Supreme Council, an executive Council of Ten representing the five Principal Powers, Great Britain, France, Italy, Japan, and the United States, wasted nearly a week in disorganized attention to the executive problems of Europe and a "rough and tumble of discussions" about details of the peace settlement.[75] The second plenary session convened on January 25 to adopt several resolutions to establish a League of Nations "as an integral part of the general Treaty of Peace." It proceeded to the appointment of a committee "to work out the details of the constitution and functions of the League." [76] The chairman of the League of Nations Commission, as it came to be called, was President Wilson himself. He had thus begun his work at the Peace Conference with an initial victory for his program.

It was certain to be very much less than half of the battle.

★ 3 ★

THE GERMAN COLONIES AND THE MANDATES PRINCIPLE

1 : *Annexationist Demands—January 23-28*

LLOYD GEORGE HAD warned President Wilson that the colonial question would have to be fought out at the Peace Conference. Since Wilson insisted that the Covenant of the League incorporate some arrangement for administering former German Colonies, his own success in committing the Conference to the immediate adoption of the League of Nations precipitated the fight. Even General Smuts had incorporated the mandatory principle in his draft League of December 1918, though he had excluded the German Colonies from its operation. If Wilson insisted on applying the mandatory principle of trusteeship more widely, he could scarcely avoid an argument with the actual possessors of German territory as to the nature of their title, if any, under the League.

The two questions simply could not be separated, as Colonel House's own record clearly shows. "During the interval between the endorsement of the League's principles by the Peace Conference on January 25, 1919, and the first meeting of the Committee on February 3, strenuous efforts were made by the Americans and British especially interested in the fortunes of the League, to reach an agreement upon its outstanding features. The chief problem came in the discussion of the mandates." [1]

To be sure, Lloyd George raised the colonial question two days before the Conference endorsed the League, but both Lloyd George and Clemenceau had guaranteed that endorsement much earlier. It may have been sinister, but it was scarcely surprising, that on January 23, 1919, Lloyd George proposed to give precedence to "Oriental and Colonial Questions" over purely European problems. He argued that the former were inherently much less complicated because there were no problems of boundary involved, whereas new states in Europe, like Poland and Czechoslovakia, would need a long time to formulate their claims. His plea was in the interest of convenience and efficiency. It was a difficult argument to meet, even if it did conceal his real purpose of getting the Dominions what they wanted before they were confronted by a fully developed League of Nations to restrict their colonial rights.

Wilson can scarcely have been deceived about Lloyd George's purpose, but he had difficulty in meeting the argument. He much preferred to deal with European questions first because they were more *important*. It was the unsettled condition of Europe that was the cause of world unrest. Lloyd George did not in the least deny the greater importance of European problems, but stuck to his argument about convenience. Wilson rather lamely replied that he was anxious only to set in motion everything essential to speedy decision, and the Council of Ten resolved ". . . that the Secretary General ask all delegations representing Powers with territorial claims to send to the Secretariat written statements in ten days." [2] There was nothing in the resolution to prevent the submission of territorial claims in the colonial field as soon as they were ready. Wilson's anxiety to expedite decision on purely European questions was met by the requirement that *all* territorial claims be presented within ten days. He could scarcely refuse to consider claims in the order in which they appeared, and those made by the Dominions were ready the next day, as they had been for nearly two years.

The next day is pure melodrama in the account given by Ray Stannard Baker, who sees it as the dénouement of a villainous plot. He records that the Allied premiers planned a concerted drive to secure immediate distribution of colonial spoils, so as to wreck Wilson's program at the outset and to facilitate the later achievement of their annexationist ambitions in Europe. He is sure that Wilson felt he had foiled their strategy on January 23; that he had successfully postponed discussion on colonial claims. But ". . . he had not counted on the mercurial Lloyd George. At the afternoon session of January 24 there was a great stir in the outer room of the French Foreign Office." Suddenly, the Dominion premiers came into the room.[3] Certainly Lloyd George had discussed the matter that morning with Clemenceau, who had cordially invited the "Cannibals" to be present at the afternoon session of the Council of Ten, but Wilson knew they were coming. The minutes for the afternoon session record that Clemenceau proposed to keep the Dominion premiers waiting outside while the Council discussed other matters of urgency, chiefly the Polish situation. These matters were dispatched, and "At this stage the Dominion Premiers entered the room."[4] Which is hardly the movie scenario of Mr. Baker.

Lloyd George had three points to make before introducing the Dominion leaders to state their case. He had with him a memorandum to prove Germany's unfitness for colonial rule, but he was not required to produce it, because Wilson at once agreed that none of her colonies was to be restored to Germany. Baron Makino of Japan and Signor Orlando of Italy promptly concurred, and this principle was adopted by the Council.

Secondly, Lloyd George accepted the mandatory principle on behalf of Great Britain. Traditionally, said Lloyd George, Great Britain had administered her own colonies as a "trustee" for the resident natives and for the whole civilized world. She had refrained from economic and military exploitation of the natives, and she had maintained full equality of economic opportunity for all nations within her colonies. Great Britain, therefore, had no objection to acceptance of mandatory responsibility for any of the former German Colonies that fell to her lot under the League. The whole mandates principle was virtually a codification of existing British practice. But thirdly, and finally, Lloyd George explained, he must ask that British Dominions be excused, because the Union of South Africa, Australia, and New Zealand each had an irrefutable case for annexation of former German Colonies on grounds both of military security and of administrative efficiency. He would request each in turn to state the case.[5] Lloyd George's own gloss on this record in his recent memoirs is admirable for its simplicity. His marginal summary of his remarks reads, "I propose Mandates." [6]

Smuts and Botha for South Africa, Massey for New Zealand, and above all, Hughes for Australia, each spoke his familiar piece with the dominant note of "security." It was Friday afternoon, and the meeting adjourned after the presentation of Dominion claims. Saturday, January 25, was devoted to the plenary session of the Conference which adopted the League of Nations in principle. It was Monday before discussion of colonial claims could be resumed, and then it was in direct relation to the League of Nations.

On January 27, Baron Makino followed the beaten track of Dominion claims by presenting Japanese demands for "unconditional cession" of former German rights in the Shantung peninsula, and of all former German Pacific Islands north of the equator. If the Dominion arguments about security were good for the Dominions, they were equally good for Japan.

President Wilson at length met the problem head on, urging the universal application of the mandatory principle to all former German Colonies wherever located, in Africa and in the Pacific Ocean. The military argument for absolute annexation he repudiated as showing lack of faith in the League of Nations. Hughes and Botha dissented on the ground that the League of Nations "was a long way off." Wilson then revealed that he was prepared to make one inevitable concession. The Powers with claims to former German Colonies—and they were all in a state of actual possession—must be permitted to administer the conquered territory. There could be no question of wresting the territory from them and turning it over to the "small nations" to administer as mandates. The sole problem now concerned what limitations on their sovereign rights of administration the possessor states could be induced to accept. Could they be forced or cajoled into acceptance of the principle that they administered conquered territory solely as agents of the League of Nations, under conditions prescribed by the League, and subject to its constant supervision? This solution seemed highly unlikely.[7]

On the same day the same issue emerged as part of the problem of drafting a covenant for the League of Nations. There was an informal meeting of English and American experts who were engaged in that task; these were Lord Robert Cecil, Sir William Wiseman (who acted as chief liaison official between the English and American delegations), Colonel House, and David Hunter Miller. The wires got badly crossed both ways.

Colonel House, in his anxiety to conciliate, offered a very "free translation of the President's ideas" by suggesting that if the British Dominions would only accept the mandatory principle in the first place, there need be no difficulty in persuading their natives to vote for annexation later.[8] The President would thus secure the adoption of his principle and the Dominions could get their annexation. Lord Robert Cecil, not to be outdone in the courtesies, accepted the idea that the Dominions should act as mandatories of the League of Nations, and thought the Dominion premiers would also accept this status provided they were assured there would be no cancellation of the mandate.

Colonel House certainly got the impression that there would be no difficulty with anyone except possibly Hughes of Australia.[9] It was only later that Wiseman and House discovered what different lines both Wilson and Lloyd George were taking at their meeting at the Quai d'Orsay.

Next day the battle was resumed with a tightening of the lines and with no progress on any front. The French Colonial Minister, Simon, ranged himself solidly on the side of Dominion and Japanese annexationist principles. He even offered to produce the text of Grey-Cambon correspondence concerning the partition of Togoland and the Cameroons between France and Great Britain, but Lloyd George assured him that it was unnecessary. The latter repeated the assurances of the British Government with regard to the mandatory principle, but renewed his plea for an exception in the case of the Dominions. This provoked Wilson to remark that, so far, he had been more impressed by a general "negation in detail" than by any acceptance of his principle.

Anxious conciliators thought they saw a way out, and Borden of Canada suggested that the appointment of mandatories need not await the actual constitution of the League of Nations. The Powers there represented were actually a League

63

of Nations, and why should they not at once proceed to the distribution of mandates? Lloyd George said, "This Council practically is the League of Nations which was born Saturday," and expressed the hope that Wilson would not postpone the selection of mandatories till the League was more fully formed.

Wilson understood the maneuver perfectly. From his point of view it amounted to the thinnest disguise for annexation. There was as yet no constitution for his League of Nations, much less any formal code of mandatory responsibilities. He insisted, therefore, on the immediate acceptance of the principle by all Powers with colonial claims, the details of application to be worked out later by the League. The acceptance of the mandatory principle must *precede* distribution of the mandates. "They must consider how the treaty would look to the world. The world would say that the Powers first portioned out the helpless parts of the world and then formed the League." His great difficulty, he confessed, was "to prevent the assignment of mandatories, if they are to be the Great Powers, from appearing to the world as a mere distribution of spoils." [10]

Wilson gained one advantage from Lloyd George's acceptance of the Mandates principle on behalf of Great Britain: it undermined the French claim to annex their share of Togoland and the Cameroons. Under a war-time agreement, which Lloyd George excused Simon from producing, the two states were to divide between themselves both these former German Colonies in west central Africa. If the British Government were to accept mandatory responsibilities in their portion, it would be awkward for the French to refuse a similar status in their share of the same area. Clemenceau virtually admitted that Lloyd George had cut the ground from under his feet. He had been impressed by the Dominion claims, but since Lloyd George was prepared to accept a League

64

mandate for Britain, he would not block a general agreement merely for the sake of the Cameroons and Togoland. He did not approve of trusteeship, but he would be guided by his colleagues.

Still the Dominions refused to yield and Wilson's refusal to purchase their acceptance of his principle by an immediate award of mandatory title prevented him from capitalizing on Clemenceau's concession. At the end of the debate Makino asked if the mandatory principle had been accepted. Clemenceau replied: "No—it is adjourned." [11] The deadlock was so complete that it was idle to continue debate in the Council of Ten and the following day had to be spent in negotiations behind the scenes.

2 : Veiled Annexation—January 29

Now there were two who were prepared for a first-class row. President Wilson and Premier Hughes had at last seen each other face to face, and neither liked what he had seen and heard. Wilson reported his wrath in a twenty-minute telephone call to Colonel House at 9:30 P.M. on January 28. He complained of the British and French demand that "if the 'Mandatory' is used by the League of Nations as to German Colonies, it shall be used immediately and the different powers designated now rather than later." He threatened to give the widest publicity to this maneuver, but apparently yielded to the Colonel's advice to wait and warn his opponents that they did not represent the Conference as a whole, holding in abeyance an appeal to a plenary session of the Conference.[12]

Hughes was less diffident. He promptly gave an *ex parte* version of the January 28th discussion to some Australian journalists who printed it. President Wilson was depicted as a doctrinaire scholastic who was forcing Utopian ideals on the world, and the British Delegation was accused of "kowtowing

65

to Wilson." The Home Government was accused of giving away the case of the Colonies, which the Colonies resented. If this kind of thing continued it would lead to disruption of the British Empire.[18] Lloyd George and Smuts were trying to work out a compromise the very day before this article appeared. It did not facilitate their task.

General Smuts first codified the Mandates principle in a way to serve as a basis of agreement, and in a form substantially incorporated later in the League of Nations Covenant. The first four clauses of his January 29 draft put at the disposal of the League of Nations as a "sacred trust of Civilization" not only all former German Colonies—which Germany was held unfit to administer—but also the Arab regions of the former Turkish Empire. The fifth clause established the principle that the character of the mandate must vary according to the stage of development of its population, the geographical situation of its territory, economic conditions, etc. The last three clauses distinguish three types of mandate to meet these different conditions. Clause six treats the Arab populations of Syria, Mesopotamia, and Palestine as capable of eventual independence, which limits the rôle of the mandatory power to the rendering of "administrative advice and assistance" until such time as the native state can stand alone.

"The wishes of these communities must be a principal consideration in the selection of the mandatory power." This constitutes the Class "A" Mandate. Class "B", outlined in clause seven, applies to the peoples of Central Africa who are at a stage where the mandatory must be responsible for the administration of the territory "subject to conditions which will guarantee the prohibition of abuses such as the slave trade, the arms traffic, and the liquor traffic, and the prevention of the military training of the natives for other than police purposes, and the establishment of fortifications or military and naval bases, and will also secure equal oppor-

66

tunities for the trade and commerce of other members of the League of Nations."

So far, this was a genuine embodiment of President Wilson's ideals. However, this was not true of German Southwest Africa and the islands in the Pacific. They are dealt with in clause eight, which was the very essence of the compromise. It reads:

Finally, they consider that there are territories, such as *South-West Africa and certain of the islands of the South Pacific,* which owing to the sparseness of their population, or their small size, or their remoteness from the centers of civilization, or *their geographical contiguity to the mandatory State,* and other circumstances, *can best be administered under the laws of the mandatory State as integral portions thereof,* subject to the safeguards abovementioned in the interests of the indigenous population.[14]

In this case, the Class "C" Mandate, mandatory obligation is pared to the bone. It is limited to the specific guarantees for the welfare of the native, listed in clause seven, and the Class "C" mandatory power must report annually on this phase of its trusteeship to the League of Nations just like any other mandatory.[15] But the other aspect of trusteeship, the maintenance of equality of economic opportunity in the interest of the whole civilized world, is entirely omitted. Moreover, the provision for direct administration "under the laws of the mandatory State as integral portions thereof" looked too much like sovereignty.

But chiefly, clause eight meant immediate distribution of former German territory to the Dominions which claimed them. It named and described the territory and selected the mandatory state on the basis of "contiguity." It required no large store of geographical knowledge to determine the propinquity of certain of the Dominions to the territories named. Unqualified acceptance of clause eight meant the immediate award of mandates to the Dominions, the immediate division of "spoils" which Wilson was determined to prevent. The exclusive concern of clause eight with the Dominion claims is further seen in the omission of any reference to the islands of the *North* Pacific which Japan claimed. The only territories mentioned in this clause are those which the Dominions claimed.

Smuts, with Lloyd George's approval, at once sought out Colonel House to see if they "could not get together on the colonies question." He had shown his draft resolutions to Lloyd George and a few others of the British Empire Delegation, but no one had as yet tackled Hughes and Massey. There was no use submitting the compromise for their approval until it was known whether Wilson would accept it. Colonel House apparently committed the President. His diary records: "When I read it I saw they had made great concessions from the position they took yesterday and I told them with a few slight verbal changes *I was ready to accept it.*" He promptly sent it on to Wilson at the Quai d'Orsay with his own comment: "Lloyd George and the Colonials are meeting at 11:30 and this is a draft of resolutions Smuts hopes to get passed. He wants to know if it is satisfactory to you. It seems to me a fair compromise." [16] Lloyd George was sufficiently encouraged to miss the meeting at the Quai d' Orsay in order to proceed with his negotiations with the Dominion premiers.

Lloyd George found both Massey and Hughes difficult, the latter particularly so. Though General Botha of South Africa and Premier Borden of Canada did all they could to abate the pugnacity of those two gentlemen, Lloyd George complained bitterly to Borden that Hughes wanted to stretch Australia from island to island across the Pacific, and that he had warned Hughes that he would not quarrel with Wilson merely to put Australia in possession of New Guinea. He urged the Dominion premiers not to take the responsibility

68

of wrecking the Conference "on a refusāl to accept a principle which Great Britain was quite ready to see applied to much more extensive and important territories in East Africa."

Lloyd George argued with Hughes, particularly, that the proposed Class "C" Mandate provided Australia with practical ownership of New Guinea, subject only to certain conditions on behalf of the natives. What was the difference between outright ownership and ownership under the League of Nations subject to such conditions? Did Mr. Hughes object to the prohibition of both slavery and the sale of strong drink to the natives? Mr. Hughes did not object. "Are you prepared to receive missionaries?" Lloyd George asked him. "Of course," said Hughes, "the natives are very short of food and for some time past they have not had enough of missionaries," [17] to eat. Lloyd George secured the adoption of the Smuts resolutions, or thought he had, and was prepared for renewed negotiations with President Wilson in the Council of Ten the following morning.

Would the President follow the line indicated for him by Colonel House and accept the resolutions as a satisfactory embodiment of his principles?

3 : Hughes—January 30

Premier Hughes' anonymous attack on President Wilson —and on the British Government for its compliance with his wishes—appeared in an English newspaper early in the morning before the Council of Ten convened. Wilson arrived thoroughly indignant. It was not an atmosphere conducive to calm deliberation on the Smuts resolutions. When Lloyd George introduced them, Hughes said he could not agree until he had a chance for further discussion with his colleagues that afternoon.

It is clear that Wilson suspected Hughes as the source of the press attack, for he at once delivered an angry speech on that subject, threatening to make disclosures to the press himself. He all but threatened to break up the Conference. Lloyd George later confessed to the leading British press representative, Lord Riddell, that Hughes' action had made his own task extremely difficult, for Wilson had actually threatened to break off the Conference and go home to America.[18] It is an interesting detail that Lloyd George's recently published memoirs of the Peace Conference are silent as to the identity of Wilson's assailant. The article is ascribed to an English newspaper "unfriendly to the Government," without revealing the source of the information which it published, though clearly it had been someone present in the Council of Ten on January 28.[19]

When finally Wilson was asked if he accepted the draft resolutions as a satisfactory charter of his principles, the most that could be got from him was an acceptance of the document as "a precursor of agreement." It could not be "a rock foundation, because the League of Nations was not yet fixed as the basis for this mandatory superstructure." Meantime he must ask the Council to get on with European questions. The League of Nations was to be an integral part of the peace, and the peace itself must be quickly made in order to validate the League of Nations. The question of peace was the question of Europe.

Read into the context of the whole diplomatic situation, Wilson's words were primarily a refusal to award the mandates at once, which would have been the consequence of accepting the Smuts draft at once and without qualification. That is why Lloyd George said that Wilson's remarks "filled him with despair," for Lloyd George knew that the only possible means of securing Dominions' acceptance of the mandatory principle was immediate distribution of the mandates on the lines of Smuts' proposals. Wilson was willing that the Council accept these proposals, but only subject to reconsideration when the full covenant of the League of Nations was drawn up.

Hughes angrily accused Wilson of upsetting the whole basis of compromise (which Hughes himself had been very careful not to accept up to this point) by saying that acceptance of the resolutions would settle nothing "until the League had been created and clothed with authority." What was he to say to the Australian people? "This is the League here in this room; let them act," Hughes said. On this note the Council adjourned until afternoon.[20]

The morning meeting had been bad enough; the afternoon session was even worse. Though the official minutes have been edited to tone down asperities, the heat of controversy still glows through the muffled words. Massey of New Zealand and Hughes of Australia repeated their arguments in favor of annexation, but the former gave a grudging assent to the Smuts resolutions, provided Wilson accepted them also. "But does President Wilson accept them?" Massey asked. That is, does Wilson agree now to the award of New Guinea and Samoa as mandates to Australia and New Zealand respectively? The official minutes give the following version of Wilson's reply:

> Is he to understand that New Zealand and Australia have presented an ultimatum to the Conference? They had come and presented cases for annexation. After discussion among themselves they agreed to present that proposal [the Smuts resolutions]. Was he now to understand that that was the maximum of their concession? That their agreement upon a plan depended upon that concession? And that *if they could not get that now,* they proposed to do what they could to stop the whole agreement?[21]

Massey denied delivering any ultimatum, but the deaf Mr.

Hughes had not heard Wilson's question. Wilson repeated it:

> Is this an ultimatum? . . . finding the Conference probably disinclined to agree upon annexation of New Guinea and Samoa, they had reluctantly agreed to the modification of Clause 8, and that was the maximum of what they would concede, and *if that was not conceded definitely now*, they could not take part in any agreement at all?
>
> Hughes said that Wilson put it fairly well . . . They are in favor of direct control, but have fallen in with Lloyd George's suggestion. That is the maximum of concession. . . .[22]

Fortunately we have the original version of the encounter between Hughes and Wilson. One eyewitness describes Wilson's manner toward Hughes as "dictatorial and somewhat arrogant," and the tone of his remarks "a heated allocution rather than an appeal." Wilson inquired, "Mr. Hughes, am I to understand that if the whole civilized world asks Australia to agree to a mandate in respect of these islands, Australia is prepared to defy the appeal of the whole civilized world?" Hughes replied, "That's about the size of it, President Wilson," and Massey grunted his approval of the defiance.[23]

General Botha of South Africa poured oil on the troubled waters. He realized the damage that the press attack had done and he began by deploring it. He heartily supported the President "with regard to what was in the papers that morning." It had caused infinite harm, for the contents of the paper had been cabled all over the world. He himself had hoped to have a peaceful lunch, but had been interrupted by a cable from South Africa insisting that he return at once. Negotiators were assembled as gentlemen and must keep these things out of the papers, "or it would be impossible for other people to remain here." He favored an investigation as to the source of the leak, in order to put a stop to it. He proceeded to a conciliatory and statesmanlike speech, stressing the degree of concession already made by the Dominions and appealing for moderation on Wilson's part.

The latter was undoubtedly impressed by the power of Botha's appeal. It was followed by renewed assurances from Massey that he intended no ultimatum and took upon himself full responsibility for acceptance of the compromise proposals, though he realized Premier Hughes must consult his Australian colleagues before finally committing himself. But beyond doubt the final obstacle to agreement was removed by Lloyd George himself, when he withdrew his insistence that Wilson accept the Smuts resolutions at once and without qualification, and so commit himself to immediate distribution of the mandates. He proposed "that this be taken as a *provisional decision*," subject to reconsideration if the covenant of the League of Nations as finally drafted did not exactly fit.[24] This was exactly what Wilson had proposed that very morning—an acceptance of the resolutions "subject to reconsideration when the full scheme of the League of Nations is drawn." Early in the day that suggestion had filled Lloyd George with despair, but after the burden and heat of the day he was at length prepared to advocate it himself. It is clear that the Council of Ten accepted the Mandates principle as defined in the Smuts resolutions without as yet awarding mandates to the interested powers.

That President Wilson made great concessions cannot be denied. There was never any hope of vesting the League of Nations with free rights of disposal of conquered colonial territory, and Wilson was fully aware of the situation. French, British, Dominion, and Japanese troops were in actual possession of the territories concerned and the respective governments had accepted no precise commitments to deliver them up. It is even arguable as to how far these governments were committed by the Pre-Armistice Agreement to accept any limitations on their sovereignty. There was as yet no League of Nations and no constitution of the Mandates principle.

Wilson certainly agreed, implicitly, to an eventual grant of some sort of title to the possessor nations. There was an implied distribution of mandates in even the provisional acceptance of the Smuts resolutions, and there were considerable concessions to the Dominions' demand for direct administrative rights and exclusive economic privileges. But it was an accomplishment to have extracted an unwilling assent to the universality of the trusteeship principle—even narrowed as it was in the case of the Class "C" Mandates—and to have endowed the League of Nations with rights of supervision. The requirement of annual reports from the mandatory powers on their stewardship was an assurance of some degree of publicity. It was even more to have achieved this much recognition of principle without paying a price which would have extracted most of the force from the recognition —a price originally demanded by the entire British Empire Delegation, supported by the French and by the Japanese— the price of an immediate distribution of the spoils. Actual division did not begin until after the main body of the Treaty of Versailles had been drafted, including the text of the League of Nations. The first mandates were assigned on May 7, 1919.

Wilson himself was disappointed with his accomplishment, partly because Japan would have to be granted the same type of mandate for the north Pacific which Australia and New Zealand secured in the south Pacific, and he was especially distrustful of Japan. But this very disappointment only served to emphasize the extent of his success, because it proved to be beyond anything that other members of the American Delegation would have fought for. David Hunter Miller told Wilson that the "A" and "B" Mandates were a

74

remarkable achievement which far outweighed any concessions in the "C" class.[25] Wilson seemed convinced and remarked that he had not thought of the resolutions as going so far.

They certainly went much farther than anything contemplated in the numerous memoranda compiled by the chief American expert on colonial questions, George Louis Beer, who had done more to elaborate the Mandates principle than any other American publicist. Beer frankly derived the principle from his studies of British colonial administration, which to him seemed an actual embodiment of trusteeship. He was apparently willing to trust the British and Dominion governments to administer former German territories without binding them to any very precise commitments. He frankly recognized that "factors of national power and prestige, as well as those of national economic advantage, cannot be wholly eliminated" from the selection of mandatory states, and he fully supported the Dominion thesis that extremely backward areas, like Southwest Africa and some of the Pacific islands, had best be annexed and administered directly by the contiguous states. Also he advocated annexation of Southwest Africa by the Union of South Africa and of New Guinea by Australia. Other Pacific islands he would mandate to Australia and New Zealand, less because it was advisable or necessary to do so than because Japan must be tied tightly by mandatory commitments in her islands, and it would be easier to deal with Japan if the principle were generalized. He was even willing that Togoland be partitioned between France and Great Britain, on condition that the Open Door be maintained, a condition he expected to be observed in all the former German Colonies.[26]

In the light of such recommendations by the leading American expert, even the Class "C" Mandate was a considerable achievement. If it did not guarantee the Open

75

Door, it at least submitted both Japanese and Dominion administration to League supervision in all their mandated territory.

But Wilson's isolation within his own delegation became even more marked as a consequence of Colonel House's attitude. House clearly felt that the President had gone too far. He and Lord Robert Cecil that day had discussed the colonial question in connection with the League Covenant, and had "agreed absolutely." House recorded: "Strangely enough at the same time the President was having a 'first-class row' with Clemenceau, Lloyd George, Hughes, and Massey. It looked as if the whole thing had 'gone to pot.' However the row may do good. It will teach them all a lesson. The President was angry, Lloyd George was angry, and so was Clemenceau. It is the first time the President has shown temper in his dealings with them—the British had come a long way, and *had I been in his place I should have congratulated them over their willingness to meet us half way*." [27]

If House had had his way, the deal would have been settled at once the day before on the basis of an immediate award of the Mandates. He had virtually said as much to Smuts, so that by this time the British Empire Delegation fully realized the more flexible character of the Colonel's mind—which is possibly what Harold Nicolson means by his description of that mind as "the best diplomatic brain that America has produced." Sir William Wiseman, who had exceptionally close relations with House, was quick to point the moral to Lloyd George. After the acrimonious session of January 30, he suggested to Lloyd George the "necessity of coming to agreement on these questions with the President *through House* and not discuss them at the Conference." Lloyd George was anxious for his part that House should actually attend the sessions as delegate. Wiseman went to see

House to explain the situation and found him "as usual intensely helpful." [28] The Colonel's relations with members of both French and British delegations had by this time become intimate, but the President, at the cost of personal popularity, was still winning the diplomatic battles in spite of House's affability.

4 : *The French and "Nigger Armies"—January 30*

Even President Wilson found it difficult to be disagreeable all the time. Harold Nicolson, an expert commentator on diplomacy, says that one of the persistent disadvantages of diplomacy by conference was the anxiety not to offend, the "human difficulty of remaining disagreeable to the same set of people" continuously.[29] Wilson had mastered the difficulty remarkably well during the week of controversy over his Mandates principle, and he had reaped the fruits of his discourtesy in a surprisingly extensive diplomatic victory. It was only after his "ruffled and irritable" behavior had achieved the provisional acceptance of the Smuts resolutions on January 30 that the French raised an apparently innocent question as to their interpretation.

The question itself was an interesting illustration of the ubiquity of the French Security problem. To scratch the surface of any problem at the Peace Conference was to reveal a question of French security *vis-à-vis* Germany. George Louis Beer had foreseen the difficulty of securing any French agreement to a Mandates scheme which would forbid the French Government to raise large native armies in mandated territory. He saw clearly that the French had treated their African empire before the war as a reservoir of man-power to make up their deficiency as compared with German military effectives in Europe, and he noted that the French had raised larger armies in West Africa than would be required for purely local needs. The Belgian and French native levies had out-numbered both British and German. He did not find the French guilty of the German practice of deliberately creating a soldier caste among their natives to prey on the rest of the native population, but he foretold accurately enough the French objections to any restraint on their military policy in Africa.[30]

One most vital part of trusteeship was protection of the natives, not merely from economic exploitation but from military exploitation. Another equally vital aspect of trustee-ship prevented the use of mandated territory as a vast military or naval base to threaten the territory or possessions of another state. Clause seven of the Smuts resolutions embod-ied guarantees on both points, by forbidding fortifications and naval bases, and by forbidding "the military training of natives for other than police purposes and for the defense of territory."

The French Foreign Minister, Pichon, wanted to know the precise bearing of this provision on French rights in man-dated territory, and he stated flatly: "France cannot renounce the right of raising volunteers in the countries under her administration." But for the assistance from her colonial troops, the French situation in the last war would have been very critical. It was a matter of absolute necessity that she be empowered to "recruit, not conscripts but volunteers, from all Colonial territories under French control." It was "abso-lutely necessary for the future security of French territory."

Wilson wanted to know if the French were insisting on this right in mandated territory as well as in their existing co-lonial empire, and Clemenceau made it clear that the French people would demand the right equally in French mandates, for the French were "the nearest neighbors to Germany and at all times can be suddenly attacked."

Lloyd George said there was nothing in the present clause

78

to prevent the raising of volunteer forces in mandated areas; ". . . what the document did prevent was the kind of thing the Germans were likely to do, namely, organize great black armies in Africa, which they could use for the purpose of clearing everybody else out of that country." . . . "There was nothing in this document which prevented France from doing what she did before. The defense of territory was provided for."

Clemenceau said if he could raise troops that was all he wanted; he needed troops in the event of a general war. Lloyd George said that was perfectly permissible so long as Clemenceau does not "train big Nigger armies for purposes of aggression." The latter disclaimed any such purpose; he just wanted to be insured against charges of breaking his pledges if he raised native troops for a general war. He was fully satisfied with Lloyd George's interpretation. Wilson, who had been strangely silent after his one question, then said that such interpretation fully accorded with the language of Clause seven.[81]

That was a very considerable concession, which further restricted the conception of trusteeship, but Clemenceau did not long remain content with mere oral assurances. The logical precision of the French mind did not consort happily with the bumbling ambiguities of Anglo-Saxon phrases. If France were conceded the right to recruit native "volunteers" in mandated territory, let the language of the Mandates article say so specifically, instead of leaving it to interpretation of vague generalities. There followed a veritable battle of words, the French fighting for precision, the English and American for their general phrases.

The League of Nations Commission on February 8, 1919, adopted the Smuts resolutions virtually intact as Article XVII of the League Covenant (it eventually became Article

XXII) despite the efforts of the French member, Léon Bourgeois, to amend it by omitting all restrictions on military service in mandated territory.[32] On May 1, 1919, Clemenceau sent orders to the Drafting Committee via Fromageot to alter the wording of the Mandates Article to permit specifically the recruitment of native troops, not merely "for the defense of territory," but for service in the homeland as well. House and Cecil, failing to block the change in committee, appealed to the Supreme Council, where on May 5 it appeared that the alteration in Article XXII of the Covenant had been "made under instructions given personally to Fromageot by Clemenceau, the President of the Conference." The latter justified himself by saying that it was very important to France "that some words be put in to enable her to utilize native troops for the defense of French territory, just as in this war." He denied responsibility for the actual wording employed by Fromageot! Wilson repeated the argument of January 30th that the general words, "for the defense of territory," covered French needs, and the Council then decided to restore the original wording.[33]

French persistence is fully equal to French logic, and the contest of verbiage continued for years. They were soon at work on the draft of their own mandatory charters for Togoland and the Cameroons, and House reported to Washington on July 9, 1919, that they were insisting on the words, "for the defense of (French) territory, *whether colonial or metropolitan.*" House was refusing to budge despite the French use of the January 30th minutes to justify their text.[34] In August David Hunter Miller found cause to complain of the same difficulty. He felt that the "whole idea of training black troops in mandate territory to fight in Europe is contrary to the principle of mandates." [35]

In September, House reported that American "good offices

for the French reservations concerning black armies in Togoland and the Cameroons are quite finished." [86] and more than a year later the French presented their draft mandates to the League of Nations Council with the words: "It is understood, however, that troops thus raised may in the event of a general war be utilized to repulse attack or for the defense of territory outside the mandate." The League Secretariat appended a comment calling attention to the language of Article XXII of the League Covenant as "inconsistent with the foregoing permission." [87] Echoes of this wordy struggle continued in the Permanent Mandates Commission of the League of Nations as late as 1926.[88] This contest is a good example of what Harold Nicolson calls the chief bane of the Conference of Paris, the fatal lack of precision in diplomatic dealings. In this case both English and American negotiators clung to their imprecisions as to a holy principle. It was perhaps their only means of pretending to salvage something of their promise that the native population of mandated territory would not be subjected to military exploitation.

The significance of this episode, however, went far beyond the immediate question of the Mandates principle. If the French could be so logical and persistent in pursuit of military security in apparently non-European questions, how much more concentration of purpose were they likely to show in areas nearer home? If they could show more concern for the military capacity of the African native than for his capacity for civilized development in the pursuits of peace, how much more willingly would they override principles of self-determination in Europe in order to destroy German military power? Almost every territorial question, as well as largely economic problems, was bound to affect French security at one point or another. The Polish boundaries, Austria, Rhineland, Saar, and Reparation—all were certain to bring out the traditional elements of French national policy,

81

whose simple goal was the reduction of the German state east of the Rhine to a condition of military impotence.

Yet there remained some non-European questions sufficiently related to the Mandates question to obtrude themselves at an early stage of the Conference. Their solution did not precede—in fact, it followed—that of many of the European questions. At some stages the problems ran concurrently, but both convenience and logic require consideration of the Japanese claims in the next chapter.

★ 4 ★

JAPANESE STRATEGY

1 : *Two Pounds of Flesh and One Ounce of Prestige*

"Baron Makino and Viscount Chinda were there for Japan: silent, unemotional, but watchful; rising with power only when their own interests were affected." Such was Colonel House's description of Japan's delegates in the League of Nations Commission. It may well serve to characterize Japan's rôle throughout the Peace Conference.

Their interests were directly affected in only three questions, two of them imperialist claims to territorial and economic rights, the third a claim to explicit equality of treatment in the League of Nations, clearly a matter of prestige. Makino and Chinda concentrated unceasingly on the attainment of these material and moral rights.

They, too, asked for direct and immediate cession of former German islands in the Pacific which they had conquered and now occupied. Possession was nine points of the law, and British treaty obligation was the tenth. The same treaty which bound Japan to support Dominion claims to South Pacific islands bound Great Britain equally to support Japanese claims to North Pacific islands. Lloyd George could hardly press Dominion claims for annexation without mak-

83

ing an equivalent case for Japanese annexation. Japan could expect no better treatment than the Dominions, and need fear no worse. Hence her delegates could afford to play a passive rôle during the controversy over the Mandates principle.

Japan did not secure outright annexation, but neither did the British Dominions. Both the Dominions and Japan were assured of Class "C" Mandates for the former German territory they coveted, and if they did not secure an immediate grant of mandatory authority, again Japan was no worse off than the Dominions in this respect. Meantime they had saved their diplomatic shot and shell while Lloyd George had depleted his artillery reserves.

Secondly, Japan wanted extensive rights in the Shantung peninsula on the mainland of China. These rights formerly were exercised by Germany, but had been seized by Japan early in 1915, and Great Britain was also treaty-bound to support this claim. China was equally bound. Moreover, the Japanese Government had promised, under certain conditions, to restore Chinese sovereignty in the Shantung province. What objection could Wilson offer to the Japanese demand for "unconditional cession" of former German rights in Shantung?

In 1898, the Imperial German Government had extracted from China by threat of force a "ninety-nine year lease" of the harbor of Kiao-Chow with a fifty-mile radius of territory around it. Such a deal in real estate could not affect Chinese sovereignty in theory; it merely suspended the exercise of Chinese sovereignty within that area for that period of time, and permitted Germany to fill the vacuum with military and naval forces and a civil administration. In addition China promised Germany that German capital and materials would be used for the construction of railways and the development of mining throughout the Shantung peninsula beyond the

84

confines of the leased territory. The railways were ultimately to become Chinese property.

Japan entered the World War as Britain's ally. There is nothing more ironic than the diplomatic exchanges of these two Powers immediately preceding Japan's decision to enter the war. Sir Edward Grey, British Foreign Secretary at the time, repeatedly assured Japan that Britain did not need her assistance; Japan as often protested the strong sense of honor that kept her true to her treaty obligations. Japan saw her opportunity to dominate China with Europe in a turmoil. Sir Edward Grey saw as clearly that the British Dominions and the United States would object to a Japanese Monroe Doctrine in Asia, and would blame Japan's ally, Great Britain, for making it possible.

Japanese troops conquered Kiao-Chow and overran the entire Shantung province, 250 miles inland to the terminus of the Tsingtao-Tsinan Railway. They established civil government bureaus to replace Chinese authorities. In the spring of 1915 the Japanese Government imposed upon China the notorious Twenty-One Demands, composed of five groups of articles. One of these groups gave Japan free rights of disposal of German privileges in Shantung. Three others gave her extensive economic rights in other parts of China. The fifth established a virtual Japanese protectorate over the whole of China. Not again until 1937 has Japan's policy of a Monroe Doctrine for Asia been so explicit.

China seemed successfully to escape from the extensive political vassalage that Japan forced upon her. By violating a pledge of secrecy the Chinese got the United States to protest against the fifth category of the Twenty-One Demands, and Japan ostensibly relinquished it while quietly warning the Chinese that Japan still held to its validity. China's declaration of war against Germany in 1917 would at any rate gain her powerful friends and entitle her to a seat at the Peace Conference alongside Japan's delegates.

Japan met the changed diplomatic situation by a new series of negotiations with China in September, 1918. The Shantung articles of the Twenty-One Demands were presumably still valid, and they became the basis of the exchange of notes on September 24, 1918. Japan would anticipate the demands of China and her friends by promising to restore Chinese sovereignty in Shantung, but there would be no express limit of time and the promise would be made solely to China on a matter concerning China and Japan alone. Moreover, the promise would be conditional on certain arrangements to protect Japanese economic rights. Specifically, there must be adequate policing of the Tsingtao-Tsinan Railway as a joint Sino-Japanese undertaking. The "police" provisions of the Sino-Japanese agreement of September 24, 1918, seemed to involve the presence of Japanese soldiers in Shantung all the way from Kiao-Chow on the coast up to Tsinan, 250 miles inland.

Japanese strategy received one severe reverse in the opening days of the Peace Conference. When Lloyd George raised the colonial question which also affected Japan, her delegates tried to couple with their strictly colonial claims to Pacific islands their somewhat more complicated claims in Shantung. These claims seemed justified on two counts. Lloyd George had asked immediate consideration of "Oriental and Colonial Questions" on January 23, which would certainly cover Shantung, but even more important, Britain was bound by the same treaty to support Japanese claims both to the islands and to Shantung. Wilson was equally anxious to postpone both questions for fear of anything like a distribution of spoils. He could not evade the colonial question because it was directly related to the Mandates principle, which again was in itself directly related to the League of Nations. He

86

could not gain general acceptance of the trusteeship principle without discussing its application to the particular German colonies which France, the Dominions, and Japan wanted to annex outright. Eventually he had to give implicit assurances that these Powers should have mandatory authority over the areas they claimed, but he did postpone the actual grant of that authority. Therefore, when Baron Makino on January 27 pressed Japanese claims both in the Pacific and on the mainland of China, Wilson "suggested that the question of the Pacific should first be taken up and a decision reached as to whether the mandatory principle should or should not apply in that area." That effectively separated the Shantung question from the colonial question.

It was one thing to isolate the Shantung question; it was quite another to stall, and postpone the Japanese claims. Here Wilson's method was to confront Japanese claims with Chinese counterclaims. Since Shantung was a province of China, he insisted that China's delegates be heard. At the end of the morning session of the Council of Ten on January 27 Makino asked for a hearing on the Japanese case that afternoon. Wilson agreed, but proposed that it be heard in the presence of the Chinese delegates. Makino squirmed. The suggestion offended his delicate sense of the proprieties. He "did not wish to discuss in the presence of Chinese delegates *Japan's relations with Germany*," as if there were something indecent about them. Wilson was sure that Makino did not mean "to contend that the disposition of Kiao-Chow did not affect China," and the Council supported his view by inviting Chinese delegates to participate in the discussion of Shantung.[1]

The Sino-Japanese debate of that afternoon and the next morning was only a dress-rehearsal and it ended in complete deadlock. Makino asked direct and unconditional cession of Germany's rights in Shantung to Japan. Wellington Koo

87

asked direct retrocession to China. Germany had extorted these rights from China in the first instance, and China as one of the victorious coalition against Germany could with justice take them back. The Wilsonian principles adopted by the Peace Conference supported the justice of the claim. It was a moving appeal, but Makino remained a stickler for etiquette.

Japan recognized the justice of China's claim and had promised that the leased territory be restored eventually to China, but there were legal technicalities to be attended to. Japan was in possession and before disposing to any third party of what she had conquered from Germany it was essential that she *"obtain free right of disposal from Germany."* Makino reminded the Chinese delegates that China herself had assented to the fullest discretion for Japan in Shantung. Koo needed no reminder of the Twenty-One Demands and their sequel. He bluntly demanded that they be wiped from the slate by maintaining that China's declaration of war against Germany in 1917 had released her from any treaty commitments to Japan. If Japan were really sincere in her promise to restore the leased territory, the simplest way of fulfilling the promise was direct cession to China. It was "always easier to take one step than two, if it led to the same place." Makino held to his original demand that the treaty provide direct cession to Japan; "what should take place thereafter had already been the subject of an interchange of views between Japan and China." [2]

The real issue was the validity of the Sino-Japanese agreements of 1915 and 1918. For Japan the maintenance of these treaties was essential for reasons of both prestige and power. They were the symbol of a Japanese Monroe Doctrine for Asia, an expression of Japan's right to do what she liked in China, a denial that third parties—much less an international tribunal—had any right to review or modify Sino-Japanese

88

relations. For these very reasons China was bound to oppose Japan's policy. China's declaration of war against Germany entitled her to a place in the Peace Conference, which she immediately used in an endeavor to secure cancellation of her treaties with Japan by international agreement. China's only hope lay in internationalizing her relations with Japan. In the face of these realities there is something a little absurd in the offended tone of Japan's delegates when they complained that China's failure to accept Japan's promises at face value was an insult to the national honor.

Yet it was a more tangible and material aspect of Sino-Japanese treaties that eventually became the basis of negotiation. Reference has already been made to the treaty of September 24, 1918, prescribing the conditions for the reestablishment of Chinese sovereignty in Shantung. There was real question whether the provision for Japanese troops to "police" the Tsingtao-Tsinan Railway, besides being in excess of German privileges in Shantung, would not effectively perpetuate Japanese military control of the province under a very thin disguise. This question did not emerge, however, until the middle of April. Wilson had achieved his primary purpose of postponing the real negotiation, of forestalling a division of the spoils of war.

The Japanese realized that Wilson had frustrated their strategy by confronting them with the Chinese delegates. Secretary of State Lansing, who heard them, said that Koo "simply overwhelmed the Japanese with his argument." The next day, January 29, one of the Japanese delegates called on Lansing "to offset the overwhelming effect of the Koo presentation" by an "indirect threat" of what might happen to the friendly relations between Japan and the United States because of the intensity of feeling in Japan on the subject of Shantung.[8]

Partially satisfied by the Mandates settlement, but completely stalled in Shantung, the Japanese turned their full energy to the attainment of a clause in the League of Nations Covenant to guarantee explicit recognition of the equality of races. This was their third and final objective at the Peace Conference, and it was almost entirely a matter of prestige. It seemed to bear no relation to their aims in Shantung, but the strategic genius of Baron Makino and the shock tactics of Viscount Chinda could combine to give the racial issue a nuisance value far beyond its intrinsic importance. Important in itself to the Japanese as a matter of "face," it might be traded for something more tangible in Shantung.

For many years both the British Dominions and the United States had discriminated against Asiatic peoples in their immigration policies. The American Exclusion Acts are too well known to require comment, but the Australian policy was equally stringent. In fact, when Premier Hughes was arguing for annexation of certain Pacific islands he said, "whatever else the people of Australia differed on, they were united on two things: firstly, their attitude toward Japan and the White Australia policy; and secondly, the retention of these islands." [4] The Japanese had always cared less about the fact of exclusion than about the symbol of discrimination, the label of an inferior people. They had willingly enough negotiated the "Gentlemen's Agreement" with Theodore Roosevelt in 1907, binding the Japanese Government to prevent emigration of its people to the United States in the absence of American legislation to prevent it. The Japanese were certainly justified in taking President Wilson at his word when they insisted that if the League of Nations meant anything it meant full equality of the member states, a "Gentlemen's Agreement" on a universal scale. Express provision for equality of races could reasonably be urged as essential in the Covenant of the League of Nations. It would be embarrassing for advocates of a new world order to refuse such

90

a request, and that very embarrassment could be exploited by skilful diplomacy.

No one—probably least of all the Japanese themselves— supposed that the League of Nations could adopt provisions forbidding member states to do what they liked with regard to immigration. That was still a matter of domestic legislation. Influential sections of American opinion were demanding the exclusion of such questions from the jurisdiction of the League. Yet both President Wilson and Colonel House were hopeful of finding some formula which would satisfy Japanese susceptibilities. It is even possible that House had made some commitment to Ambassador Ishii in the summer of 1918, for when Makino and Chinda came to solicit his good offices on February 4, 1919, they said, "on July 8 at Magnolia you expressed to Viscount Ishii sentiments which pleased the Japanese Government, therefore we look upon you as a friend and we have come for your advice." [5] The number of Colonel House's friends who sought his advice was becoming embarrassing.

In any case there was no way of putting off the Japanese claims to consideration in the Covenant of the League of Nations, since the drafting of the Covenant had become, by Wilson's own command, the first order of business. The sessions of the League of Nations Commission under the chairmanship of the President began on February 3, 1919.

2 : *Hughes Opposes Racial Equality—February 4-April 28*

"The Japs never speak," Colonel House wrote after the session on February 4. Outside the meetings of the Commission, however, the Japanese actively negotiated with House. House describes his own function as that of "troubleshooter." "My province is to keep things running smoothly, . . . to find out in advance where trouble lies and to smooth it out before it goes too far."[6] His advice to Makino and Chinda was to prepare two resolutions, "one which they desired and another which they would be willing to accept in lieu of the one they prefer."[7] One would obviously be a provision of legal effect, forbidding members of the League of Nations to discriminate, in their immigration policies, against the members of any race. The other would be some purely general and "pallid" formula endorsing the principle of racial equality without giving it any legal effect. It is clear that the Japanese would have agreed at once to the latter if they had gained any assurance of its general acceptance. They had said to House on February 4, "there is a demand in Japan that the Peace Conference through the League of Nations should express *some broad principle of racial equality*," without putting insistence on anything more specific.

On February 5 Makino and Chinda brought their two draft resolutions, and House showed them to the President. Their preferred draft was rejected at once, but their compromise draft "the President thought might do by making a slight change, which he did in his own handwriting." Viscount Chinda seemed to be satisfied, though he would have to consult his colleagues before definitely committing himself.[8]

Something happened before his next meeting with Colonel House, for when he appeared on the next evening, February 6, it was to announce that the compromise draft would not be accepted. He had consulted his legal advisers, who had assured him that the draft had no legal effect, which he must clearly have recognized the day before. He therefore brought a draft with real legal effect on immigration policies, which House said, quite flatly, neither the United States nor the British Dominions could possibly accept. And again, Chinda unquestionably must have recognized this defeat. Yet, as House records, "The Japs are making the adoption of a clause

92

regarding immigration a *sine qua non* of their adhesion to the League of Nations," which was certainly a much stiffer position than they had taken at the beginning. House remained hopeful of a "satisfactory compromise which will in no way weaken the American or British Dominions' position and yet will satisfy the *amour-propre* of the Japanese." [9]

What had happened to stiffen the Japanese soon became clear. They had discovered that not even the good offices of President Wilson and Colonel House could achieve any satisfaction of their desires. The obstreperous Hughes of Australia had his back up. He was out for trouble, and during the next two months put on one of his most characteristic displays of intransigence and effrontery. House records for February 9: "I had a good many callers to-day, including Viscount Chinda and Baron Makino, who came again upon the inevitable race question. I have placed them 'on the backs' of the British, for *every solution which the Japanese and I have proposed, Hughes of the British Delegation objects to.*" [10] The most embarrassed people in Paris were Hughes' own colleagues of the same delegation, and it was only a few days later that the imperturbable Lord Balfour exploded at the mention of Hughes' name, "How I detest him!" [11] Lord Robert Cecil came to regard Hughes as an inveterate trouble-maker.[12]

Under these circumstances the Japanese course becomes perfectly clear. They had nothing to gain from pressing the compromise resolution, because Hughes refused any concession to their desires. They might just as well match intransigence with intransigence, either as a means of getting the other delegations to put pressure on Hughes, or as a manifestation to their own people. Chinda was completely frank with Colonel House. On February 12, he reported that he could get nothing from the British and therefore he intended to present in the League of Nations Commission a more drastic resolution than the one which Wilson had agreed to accept. He was well aware that it would not be adopted, but "it will be an explanation to his people in Japan." At the same time he thanked House warmly for his interest and promised him that the Japanese people would always remember his "considerate sympathy." [18]

The Commission finished its preliminary labors with a completed draft of the Covenant on February 13, and that day saw the end of the first phase of the race question. Baron Makino presented the Japanese amendment with a conciliatory speech. He proposed to amend Article XXI (dealing with religious equality) by adding the clause: "The equality of nations being a basic principle of the League of Nations, the High Contracting Parties agree to accord, as soon as possible, to all alien nationals of States members of the League, equal and just treatment in every respect, making no distinction, either in law or fact, on account of their race or nationality." [14] He disclaimed any intention of requiring immediate and complete realization of the principle in all its details. He fully recognized that the question of race prejudice was a very delicate and complicated matter. He would ask the adoption of his clause as an enunciation of principle and "an invitation to the governments and peoples concerned to examine the question more seriously and closely, and to devise some acceptable means to meet a deadlock which at present confronts different peoples." [15]

Lord Robert Cecil had the thankless task of rejecting the proposal on behalf of the British Empire Delegation, and his words reveal why it was rejected. He said there had been long and difficult discussions of the race question within the British Empire Delegation; that it raised "extremely serious problems within the British Empire." He admired the nobility of thought which inspired Makino's proposal, but the matter was so highly controversial that "he thought it wiser for the moment to postpone examination." Colonel House accord-

94

ingly withdrew Article XXI entirely, since with the removal of the religious equality clause, there was no basis for the Japanese amendment.[16] The Colonel's diary provides the epitaph:

Makino agreed upon a form the other day which the President accepted and which was as mild and inoffensive as possible, but even that the British refused. . . . I understand that all the British Delegation were willing to accept the form the President, Makino, and Chinda agreed on, excepting Hughes. He has been the stumbling-block.[17]

The next day, February 14, President Wilson read the completed Covenant to a plenary meeting of the Peace Conference, which adopted it. That evening the President departed for the United States. The leave-taking was impressive, for all official France and much of the Peace Conference personnel was at the station to see him off. "From the curb to the train itself . . . a beautiful red carpet was spread with palms and other evergreens on each side, making a corridor of some fifteen to twenty feet wide and extending several hundred feet. The President and Madame Poincaré, M. Clemenceau, and his entire Cabinet, the British Ambassador, and everybody else of prominence was there." Colonel House describes it as a fitting tribute for a great achievement.[18]

During the month of Wilson's absence the racial question did not sleep. In Washington the President received a formal note of thanks from the Japanese Government for his past efforts, but neatly blended with expressions of gratitude were inducements to further effort. Japan feared that lack of attention to the racial question would gravely hamper the smooth functioning of the League of Nations, and the government was therefore disposed to continue its efforts. It permitted itself confidently to hope "that the President will give further friendly support." It did not in the least insist on the original draft and would gladly entertain any suggestion from the President.[19]

By an irony of circumstance it was President Wilson himself who had to insist on a revision of the League of Nations Covenant which had been adopted by the plenary session of February 14. He discovered in Washington that his only chance of getting the Senate to ratify the Covenant lay in substantial amendments. The story of those amendments is vitally important in another connection and must be reserved for a later chapter, but one of them was directly related to the race question. The Senate opposition insisted on explicit recognition that matters of domestic legislation lay outside the competence of the League of Nations. If, for example, there should at some later date arise a serious dispute between the United States and Japan which turned on American immigration policies, the League Council must be expressly forbidden to take any cognizance of the case. The President returned to Paris on March 14, and within the week he had renewed the sittings of the League of Nations Commission to press his own amendments.

There was no good reason why delegations other than the American should not propose amendments of their own, and the Japanese took full advantage of the opportunity.

The last two weeks of March were a repetition of the first two weeks of February, behind-the-scenes negotiation with Premier Hughes wrecking every effort at accommodation. Not content with the rôle of *saboteur,* he had the effrontery to deceive the Japanese by pretending that the American Delegation was the real source of opposition. There can be no other explanation for the confusing and contradictory reports of his attitude. When the Japanese approached him directly, the report invariably came back that "they were getting on very well with him." [20] Yet at the very same time Hughes made it clear to his British colleagues that if they and the

96

Americans agreed even to the mildest formula of racial equality, he would publicly raise the whole question at a plenary session of the Peace Conference. He threatened to appeal deliberately to the racial prejudices of the Dominions and the United States, to "raise a storm of protest not only in the Dominions but in the western part of the United States." [21] Lord Robert Cecil, General Smuts, and Colonel House did not dare run that risk. The Colonel dealt frankly with Makino, telling him that while he and Wilson would willingly accept the pallid formula which would satisfy the Japanese, they dared not agree to it unless Hughes promised not to make trouble. House took occasion to complain to Makino of the violent abuse that the Japanese press was heaping on the American Delegation. Makino was sorry, but explained that there was an impression in Japan that the United States was blocking the race clause. He himself knew better and would certainly inform his people where the real trouble lay.[22]

About two weeks later David Hunter Miller saw the evidence of an interview given by Hughes to a representative of the Japanese press which blamed the United States for its opposition to Japan's just claim for recognition of the principle of racial equality.[23]

The final meeting of the League of Nations Commission was held on the evening of April 11 and that was the last chance to alter the completed draft of the Covenant. The Japanese courteously waited to the last moment before injecting their demands into the Commission. House had begged them to drop the whole question, for the time being, but neither he nor Cecil had been able to do anything for them. They were certainly entitled to their day in court, and they made the most of it. It was a most embarrassing experience for both Cecil and House.

All that Makino asked was the insertion in the preamble to the Covenant of the simple words: ". . . by the endorsement of the principle of the equality of *nations* and just treatment of their *nationals*."[24] The dangerous word *race* did not appear, and the principle itself was the merest generality of the most harmless kind, separated entirely from the specific provisions of the body of the Covenant itself. If there remained the slightest chance that it could be interpreted to affect immigration policies, that danger was entirely removed by adoption of the American amendment which removed such questions from the competence of the League. Makino said he had no intention that his amendment "encroach on the internal affairs of any nation." It fell far short of Japanese desires, but it was an honest attempt to compose differences of viewpoint.

Cecil, whose hands were tied, made a pathetic speech. He personally agreed with the Japanese proposal, but "regretted that he was not in a position to vote for this amendment." The rest of his speech was a deliberate evasion of the issue. In effect, he said that any race clause adopted by the Commission was bound to encroach upon the sovereignty of states. He thereupon stated the profound truth that either the Japanese proposal meant something, or it did not. If it had legal effect it was unacceptable. He left it at that, without ever meeting the Japanese offer to accept what they admitted was meaningless for the sake of prestige and to satisfy the people at home. The recorded words of the speech betray perplexity and embarrassment, and David Hunter Miller, who heard it, says that after Cecil spoke he looked fixedly at the table in front of him without ever once raising his eyes.[25]

President Wilson wanted to accept the amendment, and Colonel House had to intervene actively to prevent his doing so. The Colonel knew that Cecil was under instruction from his government to oppose it. He also knew that if the amendment were adopted, Hughes would carry out his threat to make an inflammatory speech at the plenary session. He therefore scribbled a note to Wilson, "the trouble is that if this Commission passes it, it would raise the race issue throughout the world," and Wilson took the hint. He warned the Commission that there was danger of controversy outside the Commission; that it was unwise, therefore, to accept the Japanese proposal. He relied on the implicit equality of nations in the League to meet all reasonable desires.[26]

Conciliation having failed, the Japanese delegates tried threats. Viscount Chinda said that if the amendment failed, the League of Nations would be very unpopular in Japan. There were some people in Japan who went so far as to say that Japan would not even join the League in that event. In any case, he must insist that the Commission vote, so that if the amendment were rejected on a formal vote the Japanese people would understand that the Commission had refused to endorse the principle of the equality of nations. Baron Makino supported the demand in rather more honeyed phrases. He ". . . could not avoid the necessity of asking the Commission to make a definite decision, and he had the honor to ask his fellow-members to vote."[27]

It was a very skilful maneuver. The request for a vote was reasonable, and Wilson as chairman could not refuse it. The amendment itself was so innocuous a statement of an entirely just principle that no delegate could afford to be on record as opposing it. Actually no one voted against it, for no one dared. The sole vote recorded was affirmative, including a total of eleven members representing all but the British and American delegations. The last two did not vote and Wilson declared the amendment not adopted because it had failed of unanimous approval. A French legalist, Larnaude, argued for adoption by majority vote, but Wilson, while admitting the majority, insisted that decisions were not valid unless

99

unanimous, and his ruling stood. Baron Makino quietly urged that the vote be recorded in the official minutes. It was.[28]

The Japanese had one more opportunity to press their demands. The final version of the Covenant of the League of Nations had to be approved by a plenary session of the Peace Conference scheduled for April 28, 1919. If Premier Hughes could effectively threaten to make trouble on this occasion, why should not the Japanese try the same threat? The sole reason for their defeat on April 11 was fear in English and American quarters of what Hughes would say publicly in the plenary session. What if the Japanese were to inspire an equal fear of what they might do?

Baron Makino did make a speech on April 28, and for a while he seemed to be leading up to renewed—and this time, public—demands. He summarized the history of the question, emphasizing the conciliatory disposition of the Japanese, who had receded from their original request to the modest proposal put forward on April 11. Since even this had failed of adoption in spite of a majority vote in its favor, Makino said, "I feel constrained to revert to our original proposition and to avail myself of this occasion to declare clearly our position. . . ." He then quoted the stringent formula of February 13, deliberately devised to affect immigration policies. It looked like a serious threat, which might well break open the Peace Conference, or at the very least, lead to a Japanese rejection of the League of Nations Covenant. But Makino promptly removed the sting by saying, "We will not, however, press for adoption of our proposal at this moment. . . . I feel it my duty to declare clearly on this occasion that the Japanese Government and people feel poignant regret at the failure of the Commission to approve of their just demand. . . . They will continue in their insist-

100

ence for adoption of this principle by the League of Nations." [29]

So this was only a speech for the record, after all, a manifesto to the Japanese people, for home consumption, and not a challenge to the Peace Conference, or even a threat to the League. None of his auditors was in the least disturbed, because they knew in advance just about what he would say.

It was simply a deal in diplomacy. Japan's claims in Shantung had not been met until the very eve of the plenary session of April 28, and the Japanese delegates were restive. Baron Makino made numerous visits to the British Foreign Secretary, Lord Balfour, and the latter's account of one of these visits is so revealing that it deserves to be presented in full:

. . . Makino came to see him again Sunday evening. With great delicacy but perfect clearness he had indicated that Japan wanted a decision on Japanese claims *as a whole*. He had pointed out that Japan was asked to agree to the League of Nations although she could not obtain recognition of her claims for equality of treatment. He had said that public opinion in Japan was much concerned on this question, that if Japan was to receive one check as regards Shantung, and another check as regards the League of Nations, the position would be very serious. Consequently, *it was very important to obtain a decision on the question of Shantung before the Plenary Session to be held the same afternoon on the subject of the League of Nations. He understood that if Japan received what she wanted in regard to Shantung, her representatives at the Plenary Meeting would content themselves with a survey of the inequality of races and move some abstract resolution which would probably be rejected. Japan then would merely make a protest. If, however, she regarded herself as ill-treated over Shantung, he was unable to say what line the Jap Delegates might take.*[30]

Makino certainly fulfilled his part of the bargain. He did not make a row, but what did he get in return? The answer is to be found in the Shantung settlement.

It is a mistake to underestimate the complexity of the Shantung issue. To do so is to misunderstand the diplomatic problem. It is also to join the company of propagandists who assailed the settlement as an outrageous betrayal of China and a cynical support of Japanese imperialism. "Shantung" and the "League of Nations" were the war cries of the Senate "Irreconcilables" who overthrew the whole Versailles settlement.

Japan had a strong legal case in her agreements with China, and assurance of unqualified diplomatic support in her treaty with Great Britain. She enjoyed, moreover, an impregnable defense against appeals to sentiment or principle. Wilson could postpone attention to Japanese demands, but he could not shake either their purpose or their position. By the middle of April, when all the other problems of the German treaty had been settled, it was no longer possible to avoid discussion of Shantung.

On April 11, Makino and Chinda suffered defeat in the League of Nations Commission on their racial equality amendment. On April 15, they were invited to surrender Shantung. Wilson gave up his idea of requiring direct restitution to China, but still refused to have it ceded directly to Japan. He therefore proposed that Germany cede all her Shantung rights directly to neither China nor Japan, but to the Allied and Associated Powers. Makino declined to agree. When Secretary Lansing, acting as Wilson's agent, reminded Makino of China's claim for direct restoration, the Baron repeated his argument that Sino-Japanese agreements already prescribed the conditions of the return of Shantung to China. He still demanded direct cession to Japan. He still insisted on the validity of Sino-Japanese treaties.[31]

Nearly a week later, April 21, Makino and Chinda paid

102

calls on Lansing and on Wilson. Lansing merely lectured them: it was up to them to prove the justice of their claim, which they had not done and which Lansing frankly doubted their ability to do.[32] They remained impassive and imperturbable. Wilson was more sympathetic. He reported to Lloyd George that they had been "very stiff" in their demand for direct cession of Shantung rights, but when Lloyd George suggested cession to the League of Nations, Wilson said, "Japan is too proud to accept this solution . . . to be perfectly fair to Japan, he thought they would interpret this as a challenge to their good faith."

Wilson tried an appeal to sentiment and principle. He maintained that all special spheres of influence in China ought to be abandoned. The Japanese politely agreed to take their part in any such laudable policy, but remarked that neither Lloyd George nor Clemenceau had as yet responded to that idea. To suggest that Japan act upon the principle of China's right to abrogate all the "Unequal Treaties" forced upon her was to raise the whole question of the status of foreign concessions in China. There were few converts to the idea of extinguishing these rights, and Japan's offer to participate in any general conversion was quite safe. At the same time it was unreasonable to expect the Japanese heart to melt at an appeal which left other hearts stony. It is fair to say that for this reason Japan's moral case was as impregnable as her purely legal and diplomatic position. All Wilson could obtain from her delegates was an expression of "benevolent intentions." [33]

The very next day Makino presented his demands officially to the Supreme Council of the Peace Conference, and Chinda supported them by a characteristic threat. He and Makino were under express instructions from the Japanese Government to secure direct cession of Shantung rights. They could neither postpone the question, nor sign a treaty which failed to meet their demands. During the remainder of the morning of April 22 they successfully answered every attack on their position. In the first place, they claimed and secured the diplomatic support promised them by the treaties of 1917. Lloyd George even produced the exchange of notes between Japan and Great Britain. Secondly, they made a good legal case for the validity of their arrangements with China. The "Twenty-One Demands" of 1915 gave Japan free disposal of German rights in Shantung. If the Chinese delegates maintained that China's declaration of war against Germany, a full two years later, invalidated that treaty, then how explain the Sino-Japanese notes of September 24, 1918, which established the conditions on which Japan agreed to restore Shantung to China? The 1918 agreement presupposed the validity of the 1915 treaty; it was both a supplement and a sequel.

Finally, the Japanese met Wilson's renewed appeal, on moral grounds, to forgo their legal rights for the sake of a better world. The appeal itself was a clear admission that Japan's diplomatic and legal position was impregnable. Wilson said he had no wish to interfere with treaties, but there were treaties which ought never to have been made. "He had hoped that by pooling their interests, the several nations that had gained a foothold in China (to the detriment of the Chinese position in the world) might forgo the special position they had acquired in China." Makino again expressed Japan's readiness to take her full share in any general renunciation of special advantages in China.[34]

There was only one way out. When Wilson perceived the futility of his general attack on Japanese claims, he began to inquire into the specific nature of the Sino-Japanese agreement of September 24, 1918. What conditions did it prescribe for Japan's restoration of Shantung to China? Makino's draft articles presented that morning included provisions that would seem to give Japan military control of the whole Shantung province. Japanese troops could be posted at the termini of the Tsingtao-Tsinan Railway, at the seacoast and far in the interior of the province, as well as at important stations between.

These provisions raised two very serious questions in Wilson's mind. Had Germany ever exercised any such military rights outside the fifty-mile radius of her Kiao-Chow lease? Secondly, if Japan were to secure such rights directly from the Peace Conference, would she give them back to China? Wilson asked Chinda to define more exactly the nature of Sino-Japanese agreements on this subject.

Chinda replied that the railway was to be a joint Sino-Japanese undertaking, which would contribute to the establishment of a police force with Japanese "instructors." The Japanese army officers employed as instructors were to be present in the training school and at stations along the railway. Wilson was perplexed about the status of these Japanese officers, who were to remain in Shantung even after the leased territory was restored to China, and began to wonder just what Japan had promised to give back to China. He was not reassured by Makino's statement that Japan had promised to China the withdrawal of the Japanese civil administration throughout the Shantung peninsula.

This was more a revelation of the complete nature of Japanese domination at the moment than any assurance of its extinction in the future. It was clear, for the first time, that the Japanese Government had more at stake than merely prestige in their insistence on the validity of their treaties with China. There was no possibility of denying Japan's claim to direct cession of former *German rights*. It would certainly meet all reasonable Japanese claims to consideration on the ground of prestige. There was no good reason for giving Japan more than Germany had ever enjoyed,

105

and there must be absolute assurance that Japan would restore full Chinese sovereignty in Shantung.

That is what Wilson meant when he said at the end of the morning session that "he realized the situation in a fuller light than ever before." [35]

In the afternoon the Supreme Council held a discussion with the Chinese Delegation. Wilson had again insisted that they be heard, even though Makino decided not to exercise his right to be present. On this occasion Wilson's attitude toward the Chinese claims was less favorable than previously. He frankly told them that their legal and diplomatic position was weak. He read extracts from the Sino-Japanese notes and reminded them that Lloyd George and Clemenceau were bound by treaty to support Japanese claims. He asked the Chinese representatives to realize "the embarrassing position which had been reached." He felt constrained to agree with Japan that China's declaration of war against Germany in 1917 could not invalidate Sino-Japanese treaties of 1915, and he warned Wellington Koo not to entertain the idea that "there is injustice in arrangements based on treaties which Japan has entered into," because "unjust treatment of China in the past has been by no means confined to Japan."

Wilson himself had proposed that all governments renounce their special rights in China, and Japan had agreed to take her part in any such general agreement. So far this was an almost verbatim repetition of the arguments of Makino and Chinda that morning. Wilson concluded this part of his address by saying that he had put the Chinese case to Japan as strongly as he could. What he sought now was "only a means of getting out of a position that was extremely difficult." England, France, China, and Japan were all bound by treaties, and the United States was the only power not so bound.[36]

106

During the morning discussion with the Japanese, Wilson had seen a possible way out and he now proposed it to the Chinese. Let China decide whether Japan shall receive directly only former *German rights* in Shantung, or the rights China herself agreed to in the Sino-Japanese notes of September 24, 1918. Both Wilson and Lloyd George thought the German rights more limited, and under close questioning Wellington Koo agreed with them. Lloyd George and Clemenceau were bound to support Japan's claims to what Germany had possessed—but no more. Within the limits of English and French treaty engagements to Japan the two premiers were willing to protect China to the utmost. They would join Wilson and the Chinese in asking Japan to forgo the extra privileges provided by the Sino-Japanese agreement.[37]

Here was a new basis of negotiation, and the only realistic one to meet the circumstances. Neither Japan nor China agreed to it. Japan enacted the rôle of Shylock and insisted on the bond, the full letter of the agreements with China, which prompted one American to describe Chinda as demanding his "pound of flesh." Nor were the Chinese any more reasonable in their insistence on complete cancellation of all Sino-Japanese agreements made during the war. The Supreme Council, nevertheless, adopted the compromise as its working basis, and charged its experts to examine and report.[38]

Before the Supreme Council could reconvene to consider the report, the worst crisis in the history of the Peace Conference occurred. President Wilson came to an open breach with the Italian Delegation over its Adriatic claims. On April 23, the day following the Shantung discussion, the President addressed a public appeal to the Italian people over the heads of the Italian delegates to the Peace Conference. The next day Premier Orlando and Foreign Minister

Sonnino packed up and returned to Italy. Defection from the Peace Conference probably would mean boycott of the League of Nations. It was the worst blow Wilson had received, and it occurred when success had almost been achieved.

A magnificent opportunity was thus supplied for the Japanese to apply pressure. On April 24, the day of the Italians' departure, Wilson received a letter from the Japanese Delegation demanding "definite settlement" of the Shantung question "with the least possible delay," and Wilson said to Ray Stannard Baker, "they are not bluffers and they will go home unless we give them what they should not have." [39] He still would not concede what he felt they should not have.

The experts' report to the Supreme Council the following day made it clear that the Sino-Japanese agreement of September 24, 1918, gave Japan rights far in excess of German rights. Germany had never been permitted to exercise either rights of civil administration or of military and police control outside the fifty-mile radius of her leased territory. There had never been provision for German soldiers or police to guard the whole length of the Tsingtao-Tsinan Railway, which in any case was to be constructed as a purely Chinese Government railway.[40] It now appeared that for the past four years since the capture of Kiao-Chow, Japanese troops had penetrated 250 miles up the railway into the interior of the province of Shantung, and on the basis of their military occupation had established civil government bureaus to exercise fiscal and judicial authority over the Chinese population.[41]

Clearly the Japanese promise to restore the civil administration to China, while retaining military rights along the entire length of the railway, justified Koo's statement that the restoration of Chinese sovereignty on such terms would be more nominal than real. Therefore President Wilson suggested Japan be told that the Supreme Council could not consent to the terms of the Sino-Japanese agreement for the retrocession of Shantung. He asked Lloyd George and Balfour to see the Japanese, and Lloyd George agreed that Balfour would talk to them.[42]

The deadlock was so complete the next day, April 26, that President Wilson held a conference with all the American Peace Commissioners. Colonel House felt that both Wilson and Lansing were so pro-Chinese that they risked driving Japan out of the Peace Conference. The Colonel's own feelings were about evenly divided on the merits of the case, but he felt strongly it would be a mistake to reach any decision likely to result in the Japanese departing from Paris. He argued the matter at some length with the President without, however, shaking his determination.[43] Wilson stated: "If the Japanese will return Kiao-Chow and Shantung to China, and relinquish all sovereign rights, and reduce their claims to economic concessions, forgoing all military rights, I would regard it as returning these possessions to China on better terms (for China) than Germany held them."[44] He even asked Lansing to try the Japanese once more with his earlier proposal that all Shantung rights be ceded directly to the Allied and Associated Powers to act as trustees. Lansing did this, but found the Japanese insistent on the letter of their agreements with China. In desperation Wilson again sounded Lloyd George on the proposal that all powers forgo special rights in China, but "The British Government could not agree."[45]

Once again Chinda resorted to threats designed to play upon Wilson's fears for his League of Nations. He reported instructions from his home government not to sign any treaty which failed to incorporate Japanese demands.[46] On Sunday evening, April 27, Makino called on Balfour to remind him of the plenary session scheduled for the following afternoon to adopt the League of Nations Covenant. This was the occasion on which "with great delicacy but perfect clearness" Makino promised not to make a public row about the race question, provided Japan gained her point in Shantung.[47]

Time was short and the Supreme Council convened hastily next morning. The session proved to be a contest between Wilson and Balfour, with Balfour, or more accurately the Japanese, holding the trump cards. Wilson again said he should agree to direct cession of former *German rights*, if Japan would give up all military rights which Germany never even temporarily possessed. He could not consent to putting Japan in a more dominant position than Germany had enjoyed. Balfour tried to argue that such was not the effect of Japan's draft articles, but Wilson said his own experts did not agree. Wilson undoubtedly had the better of this argument, but there was another argument that he could not meet—the danger of a public conflict with Japan in the plenary session that afternoon. Before it convened the Japanese had a message from Balfour expressing, on behalf of the Supreme Council, "general approval" of their Shantung articles, despite some anxiety concerning "the temporary arrangements with regard to the guarding of the railway line and the garrisoning of Tsinan." Balfour hoped the Japanese would forgive the *inevitable postponement of final decision until after the plenary session*.[48]

Makino was sufficiently satisfied with this assurance to feel he could safely relinquish Japan's demand for explicit recognition of the principle of racial equality in the League of Nations Covenant. His moderate speech on that subject at the plenary session has already been reported. The British, however, were afraid that Wilson might still prove difficult. After the session Lloyd George took Colonel House aside

110

and asked him to get the President "in a more amenable state of mind." Both he and Balfour thought President Wilson unfair to the Japanese. He admitted very candidly that he regarded Japanese insistence on spoils of war as no worse than the doubtful transactions now going on in Europe. After all, the Japanese had promised to return their concessions to China provided the Allies let Japan save face by taking them over directly in the first instance.[49]

Yet it took two more days of haggling over details and formulae to satisfy the President's conscience. He undoubtedly secured some concessions from Japan, and it is remarkable that he secured any.

On April 29, the Japanese agreed to the declaration of a promise to return Shantung in full sovereignty to China, retaining only economic privileges. The declaration was further to "explain" the arrangements for guarding the railway as solely for the purpose of giving security to traffic on the line. They were even willing that the railway company appoint the Japanese "instructors" for the police force; but Wilson still balked at any scheme which would station Japanese troops along the railway far into the interior of the province.[50]

Colonel House begged Wilson to make no further difficulties. He reported his discussion with Lloyd George and Balfour, and pressed their view of the reasonable nature of the Japanese claims. He urged acceptance of Japanese assurances. "My feeling," he said, "is that while it is all bad, it is no worse than the things we are doing in many of the settlements in which the Western Powers are interested. I feel, too, that we had best clean up a lot of old rubbish with the least friction and let the League of Nations and the new era do the rest. England, France, and Japan ought to get out of China, and perhaps they will later, if enough pressure is brought through public opinion as expressed in the League of Nations." [51]

On April 30, the Japanese made one further slight concession. They agreed that both the Shantung articles in the treaty and their own declaration should pay a little more lip-service to the principle of Chinese sovereignty. The declaration as amended read:

> The policy of Japan is to hand back the Shantung Peninsula in full sovereignty to China retaining only the economic privileges granted to Germany and the right to establish a settlement under the usual conditions at Tsingtao.
> The owners of the railway will use special Police only to ensure security for traffic. They will be used for no other purpose.
> The Police Force will be composed of Chinese and such Japanese instructors as the Directors of the Railway may select and *will be appointed by the Chinese Government.*[52]

This was the limit of Japanese concession to Chinese sovereignty, and it was largely verbal. It might conceal, but it did not alter, the fact that Japan was acquiring military rights in Shantung in excess of former German rights, and that she did so by insisting on the validity of her agreements with China.

Wilson grimaced, but he swallowed the formula. He could scarcely do anything else. Yet he could not yield without an acrimonious dispute with Chinda over the Sino-Japanese agreements which lay at the basis of the settlement. He might argue their validity with the Chinese, but that was because he knew that in the end he would have to accept them himself. He loathed them as part and parcel of war-time imperialism, and he did not hesitate to tell the Japanese exactly what he thought.

He told them he intended to make the most of their general promise to restore Chinese sovereignty, in order to justify his own concessions, to the American people. Chinda objected strongly, and maintained that the Japanese declaration must appear clearly "as the voluntary expression of the Japanese Delegates' interpretation of the policy of their government, that no impression be given that the decision had been forced." Wilson was equally insistent that nothing in the agreement be construed as any "admission of recognition of the Notes between China and Japan." Chinda said that here was the root of the difficulty: Wilson did not acknowledge the validity of these agreements, while Japan insisted upon it. He reserved the right to invoke the full letter of these agreements in case China made any difficulty about carrying out her more limited obligations under the present arrangement for the policing of the railway.

Wilson hoped that Japan would have recourse to the League of Nations, in the event of any such dispute with China. He warned Chinda of American distress over the "Twenty-One Demands," and said that "the less the present transactions were related to that incident, the better." As a friend of Japan he would not like to see any reference to the Sino-Japanese notes of the past few years.[58]

Critics of Wilson have not spared his handling of the Shantung question. Most of them regard it as an outrageous repudiation of his principles. It was so interpreted in the United States by opponents of the whole Versailles settlement. Others, including Colonel House, felt that his surrender was reasonable and necessary, but lacking in grace. House, Lloyd George, and Balfour apologized to the Japanese for what seemed to them unnecessary and discourteous postponement of the agreement a full two days beyond the plenary session on April 28.

The difficulties of the President's position were increased by the split in his own delegation. While House urged capitulation in order to save the League of Nations, Secretary Lansing, General Bliss, and Henry White unanimously opposed Japanese claims and stiffened Wilson's own disposition

113

to support the Chinese. On April 29 General Bliss wrote a strong letter of protest against any concession.[54] Wilson himself may well have had the last word in this controversy, and it is best said in the account he gave Ray Stannard Baker at 6:30 p.m. April 30:

> He said he had been unable to sleep the night before for thinking of it (the Shantung Settlement). Anything he might do was wrong. He said the settlement was the best that could be had out of a dirty past. . . . The only hope was to keep the world together, get the League of Nations with Japan in it, and then try to secure justice for the Chinese, not as regarding Japan alone, but England, France, and Russia, all of whom had concessions in China. If Japan went home there was danger of a Japanese-Russian-German alliance and a return to the old "Balance of Power" system in the world. . . . He knew his decision would be unpopular in America, that the Chinese would be bitterly disappointed, that Japan would feel triumphant, that he would be accused of violating our principles, but nevertheless he must work for world order and organization against anarchy and the return of the old militarism.[55]

Wilson told Baker quite frankly that with Italy already out of the Peace Conference, the defection of Japan might well break up the Conference and destroy the League of Nations.[56] He asked him to explain to the Chinese how sorry he was that he could not do more for them, but he had to grant Japan's wishes in order to save the League.[57] On the same day the President cabled a statement for the American press, expressing satisfaction with the settlement and accepting Japanese assurances "as very satisfactory *in view of the complicated circumstances.*"[58] The statement was essential, the qualification was important.

The following August in Washington, Senator Johnson of the Senate Foreign Relations Committee asked the President, "And the decision ultimately reached at the Peace Confer-

114

ence was a disappointment to you?" Wilson replied, "Yes, sir; I may frankly say that it was." [59]

Henry White blames Colonel House for the settlement, but his accusation goes far beyond the limits of the Shantung question. He charges the Colonel with a disposition to compromise on principle for the sake of maintaining agreeable relations with the delegates of other powers and thereby assuring their acceptance of the League of Nations. He finds evidences of actual "intrigue" in the Colonel's frequent assurances to foreign delegates behind Wilson's back that their wishes would be met, and even more in his tampering with American experts to influence their recommendations, in order to ensure "that no decision should be attempted, much less reached, which would in any way be likely to cause jeopardy to the adoption of the League Covenant." In his letter to Secretary Lansing of November 8, 1919, White added: "I am afraid the Shantung decision which, as you, the General (Bliss), and I felt, would arouse such serious opposition to the Treaty at home, besides being wrong, was another case in point." [60]

The Colonel's anxiety that Wilson yield to Japan in order to save the League is plain enough. He enacted his familiar rôle of errand-boy and intermediary on behalf of the British, who in turn interceded for the Japanese. It is even possible that he made Wilson's position more difficult by giving private assurances of sympathy to the Japanese, but there is no positive evidence to support Henry White's charge of intrigue in this case. [61] The legal and diplomatic strength of the Japanese claim, fortified by their bargaining advantage on the race question, is sufficient to account for Wilson's surrender.

★ 5 ★

LEAGUE OF NATIONS — FRENCH STYLE

1 : *The Higher Strategy*

THE FRENCH TRADITION in politics is military, an honest inheritance from Louis XIV and Napoleon. Aggressive in those earlier periods of military conquest, it has necessarily assumed the defensive in the last two generations. Yet military it has remained, and necessarily so in the face of German military strength. A German philosopher of war, von Clausewitz, symbolized the shifting balance of power when he defined war as an extension of policy. It is not surprising that Clemenceau should have regarded diplomacy as the legitimate means for exacting the utmost in military guarantee for French security. France had miraculously beaten Germany by the aid of a powerful coalition. The victory must be used to make Germany powerless for all time to come.

The French program was certain to challenge Wilson's program at every fundamental point; an imposed peace as against a negotiated peace on the basis of agreed terms; a permanent Grand Alliance of military domination as against the voluntary coöperation of all Powers, victors and vanquished alike, in a League of Nations; dismemberment of Germany as against "self-determination"; crippling indemnities as against

116

just "reparation"; disarmament of Germany as against general disarmament. Centuries of French military tradition were face to face with a made-to-order world newly exported from a new country in a remote continent. On one occasion Clemenceau made claims to territory which France had held one hundred years before, and Wilson objected: "That was a hundred years ago—a hundred years is a very long time." "Yes," said Clemenceau, "a very long time in the history of the Etats-Unis."[1]

Wilson had the great advantage that his program had been accepted as the basis for the peace settlement. He enjoyed the further advantage that Lloyd George was deeply committed by vital British interests in continental stability to oppose the creation of new "Alsace-Lorraines." He had already frowned on General Foch's plan of tearing the Left Bank away from the German Reich to incorporate it into the French military system. How, then, could Clemenceau hope to persevere in military projects against the united opposition of American and British delegations?

Clemenceau was aptly named the "Tiger" for his ferocious defense of French interests. Passionate in the cause of his country's military security, he was cynical about everything else, including most Frenchmen. Nothing could match his savage remarks about his own colleagues: that Klotz was the only Jew he had ever met who knew nothing about finance; that Léon Bourgeois once achieved the French premiership only because he (Clemenceau) had already overturned so many ministries that the Chamber had run out of first-rate talent. The man who could treat his own countrymen with such contempt was not likely to be sparing of the principles or feelings of the new Messiah, who, according to Clemenceau, talked like Jesus Christ. Before the Peace Conference formally convened, he had spoken contemptuously of the President's *noble candeur* and had openly championed a mil-

117

itary peace in preference to the President's program of a League of Nations.

Moreover, knowing simply and directly what he wanted, he organized his delegation effectively to get it. With essentially military objectives he adopted virtually military methods of organization to achieve them. The Peace delegation was a General Staff with Clemenceau as Chief of Staff. He coördinated perfectly the activities of the several members, so that each knew precisely the status of negotiations as a whole. Tardieu, for example, "did not take part in the discussion of the financial clauses of peace. But the close unity between Clemenceau and his coworkers kept each of them informed of the negotiations as a whole and enabled him to formulate suggestions concerning matters for which he was not responsible." [2] Perhaps the best description of his organization is that of Ray Stannard Baker:

> Foch had a military plan of safety, Bourgeois a diplomatic plan, Loucheur and Klotz an economic plan (but the coördination between them was perfect), and Clemenceau was the supreme strategist of the entire campaign. . . . The French had their entire programme worked out before the Peace conference met. They were the first to place their memoranda in the President's hands. No other nation approached them—unless it was the Japanese—in diplomatic preparedness or singleness of purpose.[3]

Finally, Wilson himself provided Clemenceau with the opportunity to extract maximum advantage from his superior diplomatic organization. The League of Nations was the central feature of the Wilsonian program. The French, and other delegations, had accepted it in principle when they subscribed to the Fourteen Points. Moreover, on January 25, 1919, they agreed to incorporate a covenant of the League in the peace treaties. But there was no ready-made covenant to adopt and the precise structure of this document was as much

118

a matter of arduous negotiation as any other section of the treaty. One of the first acts of the Peace Conference was to organize a Commission for this particular purpose. At its very first session on February 3, the French members, Bourgeois and Larnaude, appeared with a complete French constitution for a League of Nations. From this moment, until the League of Nations Commission completed its labors on the 11th of April, it is perfectly clear that Bourgeois and Larnaude acted under instructions from Clemenceau.

2 : *Anglo-Saxon Moralism*

Nothing could have revealed more clearly the deep gulf in the experience, and therefore in the habits of thought, between the French and the English-speaking countries than discussion of an international organization to prevent war. Both Great Britain and America, enjoying relative detachment from continental struggles, have kept their institutions remarkably free from the influence of militaristic-coercive ideas. "The Reign of Law" is a peculiarly Anglo-Saxon concept and it rests on the habits of voluntary obedience and judicial arbitrament. One citizen is as free from coercion by the state as is compatible with the rights of the next citizen. The moments of national emergency have been so infrequent that the regimentation of the entire citizenry by the state has been the exception, rather than the rule, in both countries.

Rarely has either state resorted to conscription of its subjects for military purposes and then only as an emergency measure promptly abandoned once the emergency is over. The same community of ideas and experience and the same relative immunity from constant military danger have led Great Britain and the United States to develop the practice of judicial arbitrament of their international disputes with each other, which is the projection of the reign of law and the principle of voluntaryism from the national to the international sphere. And the final unity of Anglo-American thinking on international affairs was achieved under the pressure of the World War. Theodore Marburg, as Corresponding Secretary for the American League to Enforce Peace, has published two volumes of correspondence between English and American publicists interested in international organization. These years of correspondence produced practical unanimity of program and deeply influenced the official British and American peace delegations, who paid the utmost attention to them.[4] Nothing is more significant in this whole collection than the paucity of correspondence with the French League of Nations Society.

The Anglo-American principles were in the main negative. They rested upon the notions of voluntaryism and the self-denying ordinance. The root of all evil was the European conscript system with nations-in-arms always ready to fly at each other's throats. Germany was, of course, to blame for introducing this most pernicious form of militarism and forcing other nations to adopt it in self-defense. Germany must, therefore, be required to abandon the system and to adopt the more virtuous Anglo-American device of a small professional *volunteer* force adequate for defense but not for aggression. But this was to be merely preliminary and preparatory to a general destruction of the conscript system. All members of the League of Nations were to pledge themselves to its abandonment and to a reduction of even their volunteer armies to a police force.

In much the same spirit, nations must deny themselves the indulgence of territorial appetite and pledge themselves to the judicial arbitrament of all their disputes, or, at the very least, to the processes of political conciliation. To be sure, there were to be some positive guarantees, a pledge to guarantee the territorial integrity and political independence of

120

all members of the League, and a pledge to apply economic, military, and naval sanctions to coerce a covenant-breaking state. These more positive guarantees were the source of much heartburning to some members of both British and American delegations who dreaded anything beyond the most negative type of self-denying ordinance. Yet the French were bound to see the positive guarantees as no real advance beyond the principle of voluntaryism which saturated the entire program.

In the last analysis, national sovereignty remained unimpaired. There were many paper promises, but when the League Council should decide to apply sanctions to an aggressor it could only recommend to the member states what forces they should employ in common action, and the final decision as to what forces, if any, should be employed rested with the sovereign state. These were not the ironclad guarantees of military security for which the French were looking. To the logical French mind they embodied characteristic Anglo-Saxon moralism, high-sounding phrases devoid of content and reality—vague, theoretical.

3 : "They Can Christen It The Society of Nations"

There was a type of League which Frenchmen could understand and value. The great coalition of the Allied and Associated Powers had proved its military value by vanquishing the Central Powers. A binding military covenant to perpetuate the coalition against Germany would provide an excellent guarantee of French security. The text of such a treaty could be drafted in such general terms as to make it appear a universal charter of a new world order, not a mere alliance aimed at Germany. Practically all sections of the French press were agreed that the League of Nations should be an alliance of the five victorious Powers, and one

French newspaper, the Democratic *Nouvelle,* said, "They can christen it the Society of Nations to please Mr. Wilson. That will hurt no one." [5] That is just about what Léon Bourgeois did when he presented his official draft covenant at the first meeting of the League of Nations Commission on February 3, 1919.

Section III of the Bourgeois document was devoted to "Military Sanctions" and reveals the true nature of French purposes. It provides an international army to enforce the decisions of the "International Body," and an international general staff to prepare and direct the military operations of this army. The authority and functions of the staff can only be described as supernational, since its word is law to the International Body and to the sovereign states which compose it. The staff can override both the legal and territorial boundaries of national sovereignty. Its activities strike at the roots of Anglo-Saxon notions of independence and voluntary action, and penetrate deep into the sacred precincts of both domestic and foreign policy.

The staff is to inspect the international army and its equipment. But the army itself is composed of national contingents and the inspection must therefore be conducted at the point where each of these national units is originally recruited, trained, and equipped; that is, within the territorial boundaries of the national state. Lest there be any doubt about the matter, paragraph iv of Section III provides that the inspection shall be carried out "in agreement with the military authorities of each state." The purpose of investigating national military organization at its source becomes clearer still from the authority given the staff to recommend improvement "either in the international military organization or *in the constitution, composition, and methods of recruiting of the forces of each state."* After such recommendations have been made to the International Body,

122

"Military instructions shall be given in each member state in accordance with rules designed to procure, as far as possible, uniformity in the armament and training of the troops destined to act in concert." Finally, "The International Body shall be entitled at any time *to require that the member states introduce any alteration into THEIR NATIONAL SYSTEM OF RECRUITING which the staff may report to be necessary.*" [6]

Granting the desirability of "uniformity in the armaments and training of the troops destined to act in concert," why interfere with the methods by which the individual state sees fit to recruit its soldiers? And what type of recruitment shall be taken as the norm? It is reasonably clear that the French were thinking in terms of their own military organization, which was essentially that of the continental European pattern, and the most fundamental element of that system was conscription. The chief nucleus of the international army would obviously be European, probably French. It would certainly help if English and American units in the international force had training and equipment like that of the European units with which they were to serve, but did it matter whether they were volunteer professionals or conscripts? In the light of World War history, one can only suppose that the French here intended to force Great Britain to adopt conscription in order to have available larger reserves of man-power than were immediately ready in 1914.

The "Old Contemptibles" proved a magnificent and highly professional force, but their numbers were too few to help much in stemming the German advance, and it took the British Government two years of desperate conflict to throw off the habits of centuries, to abandon the volunteer system, and to adopt coercion and conscription as an emergency measure. Already in 1919 the English were relapsing into their hopelessly civilian attitudes and clamoring daily for demobilization of their troops.

The French notion of using the principles of the League of Nations, not merely to perpetuate the vicious conscript system in Europe, but to force it upon the remaining "free" peoples of the world, was the supreme irony. It was a challenge to the deepest instincts of the Anglo-Saxon race. The attack on the voluntary principle and free association could hardly go further.

There is no record of any discussion of the Bourgeois Draft League. It was not even granted the distinction of a funeral *"de première classe."* It lies buried as an "Annex" to the minutes of the first session of the League of Nations Commission.[7] So completely did the Anglo-American delegations intend to dominate the League Commission—President Wilson was its chairman—that they presented a joint draft, named the "Hurst-Miller Draft" from the British and American legal experts who concocted it, and by sheer weight of numbers and prestige got the Commission to adopt it as the basis of discussion. To complete the humiliation of Bourgeois, they had not even prepared a French text of this peculiarly Anglo-Saxon document, and exacted his consent to its adoption while refusing his request for time to study it. Professor Noble, to whom Louis Aubert told this story in 1931, scarcely exaggerates when he says, "It was a bad diplomatic beginning and Bourgeois experienced no little embarrassment and pique over this episode." [8]

Bourgeois had his revenge. He had to confine his attention to the Anglo-American draft, but he had every right to object to some of its particulars as unacceptable to France, and he had an equal right to insist on the adoption of amendments to make it adequate to the requirements of French security. He received the fullest instructions from Clemenceau on both points, and he had very personal reasons for complying with them. There was scarcely a session of the League Commission at which Bourgeois did not either press for the adoption of French proposals, or object to Anglo-American proposals. Everyone got very tired of Bourgeois before the end.

4 : *French Amendments—Act One*

Act One began with discussion of Article VIII of the Hurst-Miller Draft on February 6. This was the article which was to eradicate the evils of militarism throughout the world by destroying the conscript system and reducing all armies to the level of a domestic police force. Anyone who recalled the privileged position which Bourgeois had accorded conscription in his draft League could have predicted his attack on Article VIII. He might refrain from the attempt to force conscription on Anglo-Saxon peoples, but he would scarcely abandon conscription for France at their dictation. His remarks reveal strikingly the apparently unbridgeable gulf between the mentalities of these peoples. "Bourgeois pointed out the inability of France to agree to the abolition of compulsory military service which appeared to *France to be the fundamental issue of democracy and the corollary of universal suffrage.*" [9]

To associate democracy with compulsion of the individual and his regimentation for warlike purposes must have seemed sacrilege to Anglo-Saxons, yet here again unique historical experience supplies the explanation of habits of thinking. Traditionally, the French professional army was the agency of the *coup d'état* and dictatorship, and nothing is more significant for the force of Bourgeois' remarks than the efforts of the *Third* Republic to democratize its armies, efforts symbolized by transition from essentially a volunteer to a conscript system. The buttresses of that system, there-

125

fore, were rooted deep in the French consciousness that compulsory universal service was the best guarantee of French democracy from internal as well as from external aggression. President Wilson saw no choice but to yield to Bourgeois' objection and he eliminated from the draft the offensive phrase that "the Executive Council . . . shall also enquire into the feasibility of abolishing compulsory military service and the substitution therefor of forces enrolled upon a voluntary basis. . . ." [10]

Article VIII still contained the principle of reducing armaments "to the lowest point consistent with domestic safety," i.e., to the level of a police force, but not even this much of the Hurst-Miller Draft survived the session of February 6. Baron Makino, one of the Japanese delegates, insisted that national armaments must be measured, not by requirements of mere domestic safety, but by the necessities of *national security*. The minutes record no discussion of the proposed change, which probably seemed innocent enough. The words, "national safety," were simply substituted for the words, "domestic safety," [11] and Article VIII was adopted as amended. Before the next meeting of the Commission on February 11 Bourgeois had ample time to confer with Clemenceau on how best to utilize this change of text in the interests of French national security.

On the morning of the 11th Bourgeois suggested a reëxamination of the text of Article VIII. The new emphasis given the principle of "national safety" required measures to give it effect. It was well that the League Council should study how best to effect a reduction in armaments, but if it were to consider this problem in relation to *national* security, it must also consider positive guarantees of that security. He recalled Wilson's own words, that for the League to be successful "force must be created, force so superior that no nation or combination of nations can challenge or resist it." He would, therefore, amend Article VIII by adding that the League Council "will establish *international control of troops and arms* and the High Contracting Parties agree to submit themselves to it in good faith. It will fix the conditions under which *the permanent existence and organization of an international force is assured.*" [12] Here, in a few words, is the essence of the French proposals for an international army and an international general staff embodied in the original Bourgeois draft. In one form or another, Bourgeois resurrected them at almost every session of the League Commission, from mid-February until the plenary session of April 28 which finally adopted the League Covenant.

The ensuing debate again revealed the conflict of mentalities, French notions of rigid control, coercion by supernational authority, military regimentation against Anglo-Saxon concepts of voluntary action undertaken in good faith in compliance with the voluntary pledge. Wilson said:

We must distinguish between what is possible and what is not. *No nation will consent to control.* As for us Americans, we cannot consent to control because of our Constitution. . . . [Agrees to reasonable national forces for safety] . . . but the construction of a unified military machine in time of peace is quite another matter . . . unity of command in time of peace . . . no nation would accept. . . .[18]

Bourgeois attempted to explain away the force of the word "control." In the first place, when he spoke of the "control of troops and arms," he meant simply that the League was to have adequate means of verifying the quantities of arms which each nation possessed. He meant only "surveillance" or "verification." Moreover, he did not suggest a permanent international army, "but simply some provision for military organization to be given national contingents so that they can be rapidly coördinated against an aggressive state." "He

127

did not hold in any way to his wording, but simply to the double idea of . . . the verification or surveillance of armaments and a certain organization to provide for cases in which the utilization of national contingents might be required."

Lord Robert Cecil emphasized the unanimity of Anglo-Saxon conceptions by describing the French proposals as a real departure from "our conception of a League," and when Bourgeois retorted that in that case France was presented with a real dilemma—whether to enter such a League at all or to stand alone—Wilson once again appealed to the principle of voluntary action and mutual trust:

The only method . . . lies in our having confidence in the good faith of the nations who belong to the League . . . for I think any control, by whatever name . . . called . . . too offensive to be adopted. . . . When danger comes, we too will come, but you must trust us.[14]

Anglo-American refusal to concede positive guarantees made it all the more difficult to insist on full French coöperation in a genuine program of disarmament. Not only did France protect her right to conscript armies—her delegates sought and obtained the regulation of armaments with "special regard to the situation and circumstances of certain states." It was clear France could argue that her situation was one of special danger, requiring more than the normal complement of armed force for adequate protection.[15] The later French thesis that "Security Precedes Disarmament" was born at the Peace Conference, and appeals to good faith and mutual trust were powerless against it. This was a dilemma which Great Britain and the United States never solved.

Cecil, indeed, proposed some attempt to meet the French demand for a permanent military organization by adding to Article VIII "A permanent Commission shall be constituted

128

to advise the League in military and naval matters." It was not adopted and the whole task of satisfying French demands was relegated to the drafting committee, which was to meet the next day.[16]

The session of February 11 had lasted till nearly midnight and when it was finally broken off, it left the situation very strained. The sitting of the drafting committee consumed nearly the whole of the next day—Sunday, February 12—without reducing the tension. Rather, it drew the lines of conflict even more sharply and consolidated the Anglo-American united front. Bourgeois became so insistent that, shortly before lunch, the mild-mannered Cecil resorted to threats:

> . . . Finally Cecil, saying that he was speaking very frankly but in private, said: that America had nothing to gain from the League of Nations; that she could let European affairs go and take care of her own; the offer that was made by America was practically a present to France . . . to a certain but to a lesser extent this was the position of Great Britain . . . he wished to say very frankly to the French delegates that in his view they were saying to America, and to a lesser extent Great Britain, that because more was not offered they would not take the gift that was at hand, and he warned them very frankly that the alternative offer which we have made, if the League of Nations was not successful, was an alliance between Great Britain and the United States. He asked them to consider this before they made any final conclusion. . . .[17]

Neither passive resistance nor threats made any difference to Bourgeois, who renewed his insistence the next day for the dual principles of "verification" and a permanent military organization at the disposal of the League. The drafting committee had agreed to require that members of the League "exchange information" with regard to their military establishments, but had balked at giving any League Commission the right to verify the facts, emphasizing once more the principle that the League must be founded on the good faith of its members. Bourgeois held out for thoroughgoing supervision and, to avoid the appearance of challenging the good faith of those present, warned them of the danger from Germany. It was necessary to anticipate the time when other nations would join the League and safeguard the present Allies from having their good faith taken advantage of. French public opinion was unanimous in its demand and Bourgeois must insist on an amendment to provide the proper security. His amendment was rejected by a vote of 12 to 3, and Article VIII was adopted in the form in which it emerged from the drafting committee.[18]

Cecil then offered a new Article IX which he thought might meet French requirements on two points. It provided a Permanent Commission "to advise the League of the execution of Article VIII and on military and naval questions generally." It ought to satisfy the French anxiety for some sort of supervision of national military establishments and it ought equally to provide the League with all the military information necessary for its purposes. Naturally it satisfied Bourgeois on neither count. This was still the voluntary principle. What was essential was not advice, but authority and power. Bourgeois suggested an amendment to create a "permanent body . . . *to plan and prepare the military and naval program* by which obligations imposed upon the High Contracting Parties by the present Covenant shall be enforced, and in order to give effect to it in any urgent situation. . . ." Cecil said, rightly enough, that this was neither more nor less than an international general staff, and he warned Bourgeois that the League was not a military alliance against Germany. Nothing would more quickly imperil peace, and no country would agree. Both Bourgeois and Cecil said that they were at the limits of their own public opinion. Bourgeois' amendment was defeated; Article IX was adopted as drafted. Bourgeois reserved both his amendments for later insistence.[19]

The first draft of the Covenant was complete and the League of Nations Commission had therefore finished its labors. What further opportunity could Bourgeois find to make trouble? The Anglo-American bloc had proved too strong to resist and the completed covenant enshrined Anglo-Saxon principles of international organization.

There still remained the formal session of the whole body of peace delegates—the Plenary Session of February 14—to adopt the Covenant of the League of Nations as an essential part of the treaty of peace with Germany. The directorate of Great Powers could be counted upon to attempt arrangements in advance that would make this session the purest formality, but Colonel House records their failure to silence the indomitable and persistent Bourgeois. The program was carefully arranged and it was "literally carried out with the exception that Bourgeois spoke for France. We tried to get Bourgeois not to mention any of the reservations he had made concerning the Covenant, but our efforts were futile." [20] During Bourgeois' dreary and threadbare speech, General Tasker Bliss, noting its effect on those present, scribbled a note to President Wilson:

I think it would be a good time to put the League to a vote as soon as Bourgeois is through. Everyone will be so afraid that they will have to hear about it again that all will vote "Yes." [21]

They did vote "Yes" and Bourgeois was silenced for the time being. President Wilson left Paris that evening with the completed and adopted text of the Covenant to justify to skeptical senators and congressmen in Washington, and he was gone a month. But memories of Bourgeois did not fade. It was only shortly before Wilson's return to Paris that Colonel House was further instructed in the methods of

French diplomacy. On March 8, 1919, he received the following letter from Cecil:

> I saw Clemenceau this morning. If all Frenchmen were like him how easy our business would be.
> He said to me . . . that Bourgeois' insistence on the military amendments was by his orders, and that he did it merely to be able to say that he had tried every means to obtain security for his country before asking for guarantees on the frontier. If it had been possible for the League to guarantee to him military assistance in an effective way that would have been a great security for him. But if not, then he was quite satisfied to accept that refusal and to use it as an argument in favour of guarantees of another nature. That seemed to me a perfectly legitimate attitude. It is only a pity that it was not made clear at the outset. I told him that I had guessed that that was the real meaning of Bourgeois' amendments, and that I felt sure that if he (Clemenceau) had been a member of the Commission he would have put them forward in a very different way. He laughed and said that in this case he had acted at his (Clemenceau's) instigation. . . .[22]

It was a very revealing letter and it had just as much significance for the diplomatic campaigns still to come as for Act One of the French amendments.

5 : *American Amendments*

Meantime President Wilson encountered people more difficult to deal with than French diplomats. The latter found his covenant meaningless, but United States senators saw in it a sinister attack on the independence of the United States, an abandonment of traditional American policies. Before sailing, the President had cabled an invitation to members of the Senate and House of Representatives committees on foreign relations to dine with him at the White House on February 26. He would then go over with them, article by article, the text of the Covenant, but until that time he requested that Congress refrain from debate on the League of Nations. The very day he sailed from Brest, Senator Borah attacked the Covenant as a "renunciation of the Monroe Doctrine," and, by February 18, debate on the principles of the League was in full swing on the floor of the Senate.

Senator Borah declined to dine at the White House on February 26. Senator Lodge attended but complained that, whereas the President was perfectly civil and answered questions, he gave out no real information. Lodge and his fellow "Irreconcilables" promptly renewed their attack in the Senate, and, on March 2, Senator Brandegee circulated a "round-robin" resolution as a statement of their policy, demanding that the Peace Conference first attend to its real business of making peace and defer the construction of a League of Nations until that job had been completed.

Thirty-nine senators signed the resolution and the next day Senator Lodge got it read into the *Congressional Record* so that it could be franked throughout the country as propagandist attack on the Wilsonian program. Wilson answered defiance with defiance and the night before sailing from New York, March 4, made a fighting speech in Madison Square Garden. He warned his foes that, when the treaty of peace came back from Paris for ratification, the "gentlemen will find the Covenant not only tied to it, but so many threads of the treaty tied to the Covenant, that you cannot dissect the Covenant from the treaty without destroying the whole vital structure," a challenge that the "Irreconcilables" were quite ready to accept.[28]

Wilson remained in a defiant mood for some time after his return to Paris on March 14, but the need for some concession to Senate opposition was obvious. Colonel House, in his anxiety, even talked privately with his son-in-law, Gordon Auchincloss, about extricating the Covenant from the treaty

133

of peace entirely and putting it in a separate treaty "to concede something to the Senate." [24] That would have yielded one of Wilson's chief principles, but, despite earlier charges that House deliberately plotted such action during Wilson's absence, there is nothing to indicate that this was more than passing panic. On the contrary, the Colonel even entertained ideas of setting up provisional machinery for a League of Nations *before* the treaty of peace had been settled, ideas which Wilson discouraged as a dangerous challenge to the Senate's constitutional authority in foreign affairs.[25]

The course suggested by both Democratic and moderate Republican friends of the League, and urged by Colonel House, was amendment of the Covenant to quiet the genuine fears of many Americans about the dangers to national independence contained in it. Specifically, three amendments would probably satisfy even some of the "Irreconcilables"; exclusion of matters of domestic legislation—i.e., tariff and immigration laws—from the competence of the League; explicit recognition of the Monroe Doctrine in the Covenant; and provision for the withdrawal of any member state from the League of Nations.

On March 16, two days after the President's arrival in Paris, Colonel House spent an hour and a half going over the Covenant with him and Cecil and discussing the proposed amendments, but the President was still stiff, arguing that any concession would be hailed as a sign of weakness and would, in the end, lessen the chances of ratification.[26]

Two days later, he was more amenable, but other difficulties appeared. House and Cecil had a long conference, and then, after dinner, the Colonel conferred with President Wilson and David Hunter Miller. It was one thing to agree on the desirability of the amendments; it was quite another to devise any practicable means of achieving them. House said, "We are perfectly willing to adopt them *if the balance of*

134

the world would accept them, and if they do not cause more difficulties than they cure." [27] In other words, if the United States is to press amendments to the Covenant, it must reassemble the League of Nations Commission and give an opportunity to other states to renew their amendments which the Anglo-American delegates had so stoutly resisted during the February sessions of the Commission. As Henry White wrote confidentially to Elihu Root the next day, ". . . after much time devoted to the subject, it has appeared very difficult, if not impossible, to get any of these amendments adopted without having to accede to claims for exceptions on the part of other countries which the Senate would not accept for a moment." He also foresaw that the French would regard at least two of the American amendments as weakening the security which France might expect from the League guarantees. If the United States were able to withdraw from the League within a few years, what remained of even the inadequate pledges taken by the United States under the Covenant? And of what possible value to European nations could these pledges be, even during the period of their legal duration, when they were contradicted by the Monroe Doctrine which enshrined the principle of American disinterest in the European continent? [28]

David Hunter Miller saw even further implications in the American dilemma, and underlined the effect of the American amendments, not merely on the Covenant, but on the treaty of peace as a whole:

. . . France does not think that our interest in a future attack of Germany on France is secondary, but primary, and feels that that possibility should be the first concern of the world in general and of America in particular . . . whether this feeling on the part of France is right or wrong is not the question, for it exists in a degree which it is almost impossible to overstate, and any attempt to limit our responsibility in the matter would defeat

135

the whole Covenant, for France would prefer then to make a different kind of peace with Germany and not to have a League. *Certainly without the League we could hardly refuse her the right to make a peace with Germany which would let her feel secure, but such a peace would then be made as would be contrary to everything we have stood for. . . .*[29]

Moreover, at this very moment, Clemenceau was asking Colonel House for specific pledges of Anglo-American military assistance within the text of the Covenant. He had received such general pledges, but they were to form the substance of a special treaty outside the framework of both the Covenant and of the general treaty of peace. They were the price paid for Clemenceau's abandonment of the more extreme French designs in the Rhineland and must be more fully discussed in a subsequent chapter dealing with those designs. They were already the cause of much misgiving in the American Delegation as incompatible with the concept of a universal League which should relegate the vicious system of pre-war alliance to the scrapheap of discarded militarism. Clemenceau's desire to corrupt the universal guarantees of political independence and territorial integrity contained in Article X of the League Covenant into an old-fashioned treaty of alliance seemed monstrous and sinister. Miller described it as an attempt to make two plus two equal five. In principle, it was inconsistent with the Covenant and, in practice, it would never get by the American Senate. Miller tried his hand at one or two drafts to embody the proposal and there the matter ended, but it was not a hopeful augury for the American amendments.[30]

6 : *"Lest Old Acquaintance Be Forgot"*

There was nothing to do but to reconvene the League of Nations Commission. The threat from the American Senate was immediate and pressing, the risk of French obstruction at worst was hypothetical. French demands had already been met and overcome by an Anglo-American united front, and Clemenceau had as much as admitted that those demands had never been meant seriously. They were a demonstration to the French public and an argument for tangible guarantees of French security on the frontier, i.e., on the Rhine. Lord Robert Cecil certainly had the impression that Clemenceau would cause no further trouble for the League of Nations Commission.

There were five sessions of the Commission at the most critical period of the Conference, March 22, 24, 26, April 10, 11. The first meeting barely reached Article VIII before hearing the familiar voice of Léon Bourgeois chanting a familiar refrain concerning the inadequacy of that article in its present form and suggesting that it be amended to provide an international commission with authority to inspect the scale of national armaments. The arguments were threadbare and the inevitable Anglo-American steam-roller secured the adoption of Article VIII as it stood. The full measure of repetition required that Bourgeois persist in his amendment, reserving the right to present it again not merely to the Commission but before a plenary session of the Peace Conference.[81]

There was just time left for Bourgeois to present his inevitable amendment to Article IX to transform the advisory body contemplated in that article into an international general staff, and, when that amendment was duly rejected, to say that he would present it again. Cecil, after the meeting, gave way to irritation. He told Miller that he felt very badly treated by the French, for Clemenceau had told him that the French really cared nothing about these amendments.[82] Yet presumably Bourgeois was here, as formerly, recording his master's voice.

At the very next meeting, March 24, Bourgeois renewed his

137

amendment to Article IX and, as in February, he tried to explain away its real significance. He had even modified the earlier draft somewhat, so that the permanent commission was no longer "to plan and prepare a military and naval program," but was to perform the task "of considering and providing for naval and military measures." [33] The idea was precisely the same even in this more tentative language and, while Bourgeois was making a speech to prove his amendment entirely compatible with the principle of national sovereignty, Miller scribbled a note to President Wilson:

> Regardless of the statements of the speech, the amendment
> . . . provides for an International General Staff *all but the*
> *name.* . . . The French amendment is with the idea, which is in
> the language, that the Commission shall prepare and make effec-
> tive the means, etc., *within the States.* It is not a question of draft
> but of idea.[34]

As was customary, Bourgeois reserved his amendment, and turned to an attempt to utilize the military and naval sanctions of Article XVI in the enforcement of at least four other articles of the Covenant. Cecil had no difficulty in showing the absurdity of using a blunderbuss to extract the information concerning military establishments which sovereign states had voluntarily pledged themselves to give in Article VIII and, finally, he confined the operation of sanctions to Article XV. Bourgeois desisted from his demand that they apply to Articles VIII, X, XIII.

The American Delegation had as yet had no opportunity to present their amendments, which were the real reason for reconsideration of the Covenant. French amendments applied almost entirely to the earlier articles of the Covenant, which must naturally be considered first, and French strategy utilized the opportunity to put the American delegation in the unhappy position of first denying the requests of others and then asking favors for themselves. Moreover, French amendments looked to a strengthening of the guarantees of the Covenant while American amendments weakened them. If the American Delegates persisted in a refusal to strengthen the Covenant, could they not at least refrain from attempts to weaken it?

Miller had drafts of all three American amendments ready for distribution at this session of March 24, and that which dealt with the Monroe Doctrine should have been the first to be considered. It would attach specific recognition of the Monroe Doctrine to Article X which embodied the general guarantee of political independence and territorial integrity, and Article X was due for consideration at this session. Yet, just before the meeting, House sent word that this amendment was not to be distributed.[35] There had undoubtedly been difficulty in achieving a suitable draft, but political obstacles from an unsuspected source turned out to be the real explanation. Meantime, the American delegation contented itself with the adoption of the least contentious of their three amendments, that which removed matters of domestic legislation (tariff and immigration) from the sphere of League competence. As to Article X, President Wilson merely served notice of his right to present an amendment at a later date.[36]

On March 26, Wilson proposed that, "After the expiration of ten years from the ratification of the Treaty of Peace . . . any State member of the League may, after giving one year's notice of its intention, withdraw from the League, provided all its international obligations and all its obligations under this Covenant have been fulfilled. . . ." The French at once saw a threat to their security, and Larnaude, Léon Bourgeois' colleague in the Commission, insisted that this would destroy the League before it had been established, by emphasizing its temporary character. The very essence of the League was its permanence as the corner stone of international peace.

139

If France thought the League was to last only ten years they would regard it as already a failure. He more than hinted that such a feeling would be disastrous for the future of disarmament for, at this very time, the French were anxiously discussing the possibility of abandoning compulsory military service. The implication was plain again that security precedes disarmament, and that security requires a powerful League equipped with supernational authority.

Wilson had again to emphasize the principles of national sovereignty and voluntary action rooted in good faith. He had "no idea of limiting the duration of the League, but sovereign states could not permanently be bound." As against the *legal right* of states to withdraw, which must be safeguarded, he would urge the force of *moral* compulsion to guarantee the permanence of the League. If the League were a success, it would be morally impossible for a state to withdraw. The French had once more to submit to Anglo-Saxon principles of international organization and the only concession they secured was abandonment of the time limit of ten years. Instead, any state was to be free to withdraw *at any time,* after two years' notice of its intention to withdraw. It is curious that France should have regarded such a provision as less dangerous to the permanence of the League than the minimum ten-year guarantee, and it is ironic to consider how this distinctively American amendment has been utilized by other nations.[37]

The American program was now complete, with the exception of the Monroe Doctrine. It surely ought not to require more than one more session of the Commission to attend to that; and yet, for two weeks, there was no session at all. To be sure there were serious difficulties with the French delegation on every phase of the peace negotiations, Rhineland, Saar, Polish boundaries, Reparation. On March 28, Clemenceau quarreled with Wilson and abruptly left the conference room at the President's hotel. Between March 25 and April 2, Clemenceau and Lloyd George carried on bitter polemics by way of memoranda. By April 7, things were no better and Wilson cabled for the *George Washington* to sail for Brest, presumably to take the American delegation home.

Yet, despite public clamor from outside that too much attention to this mystical nonsense called the League of Nations was delaying the essential business of making peace, the League of Nations Commission had regularly held its sessions in the evening so as not to delay the work on other matters, and there was no apparent reason why those sessions should not continue even during a deadlock in other negotiations. So far, the Anglo-American members had coöperated harmoniously in bringing the Covenant towards completion along lines determined by themselves. Continued coöperation at this critical juncture might have completed at least this section of the treaty.

It was exactly at this point that the harmony was broken by Lloyd George, who saw an opportunity to levy blackmail. He had decided to oppose the American amendment concerning the Monroe Doctrine, ostensibly because it localized the Covenant and gave the United States an unjustifiably privileged position, actually in order to force the United States to limit its naval building to a ratio of permanent inferiority to the British navy. Advance warning of his attitude probably explains why Miller did not present the American Monroe Doctrine amendment at the session of March 24, and why Wilson, on that occasion, merely served notice of his intention to amend Artice X at a future session.

In any case, there was no doubt where the difficulty lay when the American Peace Commissioners met on March 27 to discuss the problem. They recited Lloyd George's general objections but agreed that his failure to exact a naval agreement from President Wilson was undoubtedly "the fundamental objection." It was equally clear that Lloyd George's colleagues, Balfour and Cecil, were distressed at these tactics and wished to support the American amendment without making conditions,[38] but they were unable to handle their slippery premier.

The French were likely to cause trouble enough and, without assurances of British support, it would have been sheer folly to renew discussions in the League of Nations Commission. There were, consequently, no meetings during that critical period of early April, and it is significant of the crucial nature of that stage of the Peace Conference that Miller's diary, usually so full of matters relating to the League Covenant, became submerged in the Saar dispute.[39]

After the first week in April, the crisis over French demands abated in a series of compromises which adjusted the major disputes concerning the Saar, Poland, and Reparation, leaving only one important problem unsolved in the Rhineland area. The atmosphere was sufficiently improved to warrant renewed attempts to deal with Bourgeois and Larnaude in the League of Nations Commission, provided Lloyd George could be induced to restore the Anglo-American united front without making awkward conditions. There were three days of active correspondence and negotiation, April 8-10, for that purpose.

Lloyd George used Cecil to convey his view that American naval policy was one of expansion, "wholly inconsistent with the conception of a League," and to suggest that the American Delegation promise that, when the treaty of peace containing the League of Nations had been signed, the United States would abandon or modify its naval program.[40] Meantime, Colonel House wrote a fairly stiff letter to Lloyd George which he decided not to send, but, since it contains a statement of the actual American position, it must be quoted:

When I asked you yesterday what, if any, objection you had to the clause which I submitted regarding an affirmation of the Monroe Doctrine, you told me as you have told me before that you could not consent without first coming to an agreement with the United States regarding our naval building program. I cannot see what connection the two matters have. If the kind of peace is made for which we are both working and which will include a League of Nations it will be necessary for us all to live up to its spirit and to do this it will be inconsistent to continue to increase armaments by land or sea. Therefore it seems that your doubts answer themselves and to reach the objectives you have in mind it is only necessary to put into force as soon as possible a League of Nations. To do this it may be essential that specific reference be made to the Monroe Doctrine, otherwise there is danger that the Senate of the United States may reject it. I understand that no one but you has raised any objection to our proposal, and I hope, my dear Prime Minister, that you will not further insist upon the point you have raised.[41]

The utmost that the American Delegation would concede was a recognition of Britain's special naval needs, a willingness to negotiate future naval ratios before embarking on additional construction, and an assurance that the American administration had no intention of competitive building with Great Britain. On the essential point of Lloyd George's insistence that the United States abandon or modify its *present naval program*, already authorized by Congress, Colonel House had no authority to yield. He declined to bargain for the adoption of the Monroe Doctrine amendment. The unhappy Cecil, with whom he held a conference on April 10, said that Lloyd George was not satisfied, and that he himself was "upset and disposed to quit the whole thing." [42] There was to be a meeting of the League of Nations Commission that evening, and Cecil at least consented to discuss with Miller the draft of the Monroe Doctrine amendment. He even made the suggestion that it be separated entirely from Article X and brought in as an additional article toward the end of

143

the Covenant and, while he made it clear that he was discussing, not the question of the adoption of the article but merely its position *if it should be adopted,* Anglo-American collaboration had been tacitly resumed.[43] Lloyd George abandoned his efforts at blackmail, and a later conference was called in Washington to settle the problem of naval ratios.

It seems as if the unexpected rift in the Anglo-American lute had made both English and Americans forget all about the French, but they were quickly reminded that evening when the Monroe Doctrine amendment was offered to Article X in the League Commission. House's diary records it as "One of the stormiest meetings we have had." The French fought for an hour to block the amendment as destructive of their security under the Covenant.[44] Larnaude thought it would be very "unfortunate if the Monroe Doctrine were interpreted to mean that the United States cannot participate in the settlement of European affairs decided upon by the League," and, when he was assured that there was nothing in the Doctrine incompatible with the Covenant, he asked why in that case it should be mentioned at all. Wilson, in an "impassioned speech . . . full of eloquence and good sense," gave renewed assurances that the United States would live up to its obligations under the Covenant which "convinced everybody but the French delegates."[45] Larnaude continued his captious objections and Wilson finally asked him in some heat if he really doubted American assurances of good faith.[46]

Throughout the stormy session Cecil played a rôle of patient persuasiveness, consistently supporting the President's position as if to make up for the behavior of his chief. It was he who finally sought to turn the French position by suggesting that the amendment be taken entirely out of the context of Article X, on which the French relied so heavily for their security, and inserted as Article XX. Both Wilson and the French agreed, but even there Larnaude asked for some limiting definition, and Wilson again exploded, "Is it conceivable that M. Larnaude wants the United States to say that she will not repudiate her obligations?" Article XX was finally adopted as drafted.[47]

There was to be a final session the next evening, April 11, and House and Miller conferred on the probable strategy of the French delegates and on the best means of meeting it. Was the Monroe Doctrine to come up for further discussion, or was it to be regarded as fully adopted and settled? Miller thought the French would be unable to treat the amendment as not adopted, but they were more than likely to suggest further amendment of their own.

House was furious. Oscar Strauss had told him that Bourgeois frankly confessed that the French "*did not care anything about their amendment to the Monroe Doctrine clause, but simply that it was a good thing to trade with.*" [48] From start to finish, from early February to mid-April, French amendments to the Covenant and French objections to American amendments were thus confessedly spurious, solely for the sake of nuisance value and bargaining power. House said his plan was to ride over them regardless of what they did.

Promptly at 8:30 that evening, Larnaude presented an amendment to Article XX which would accord recognition to the Monroe Doctrine, *only in so far as it was compatible with the Covenant.* During the subsequent debate, Miller said to House, "I think they will withdraw the amendment and not press it," and House angrily replied that the French "could go to Hell seven thousand feet deep." [49] Wilson reminded them that the Commission had already adopted the American amendment on April 10 and, when Larnaude made the usual reservation on behalf of the French delegation, Wilson asked, "Will France, then, publicly oppose?" Bourgeois delicately remarked that he was anxious to avoid discussion in the plenary session of the Peace Conference and in the press and, therefore, urged adoption of the French amendment. Wilson declared it not adopted. "The proposed clause would raise objections in the United States and he thought it would be better not to insist on it."

Larnaude had the last word. He would reserve the right to bring the matter up again—at the plenary session—and meantime the French delegation would consult its government.[50] This was the final meeting of the League of Nations Commission.

Before the plenary session of the Peace Conference was convened on April 28 for the formal adoption of the League of Nations Covenant, all the main features of the peace treaty with Germany had been settled. Even the acrimonious dispute with the French concerning their Rhineland demands had been accommodated by compromise. There were no outstanding French demands and there was, therefore, no reason for making any further trouble about the League Covenant, which Clemenceau had always been willing to have constructed on Anglo-American principles, provided France received adequate guarantees in other ways. But the record must be kept straight, and if at the beginning Clemenceau was concerned to convince French public opinion of his earnest efforts to build the League into a binding military alliance against Germany, he was no less concerned that the official records of the Peace Conference should be a permanent monument to these efforts. Consequently, just as Baron Makino read into the record his efforts to achieve a racial equality amendment without making any formal demands of the conference, so Bourgeois made a dreary and threadbare speech about the French amendments. How little it all meant can be seen from Colonel House's notation in his diary:

Clemenceau put the "steam-roller" promptly to work as soon as those who wanted to make speeches for the procès-verbal had

146

finished. Everything passed almost before the Conference could catch its breath.[51]

But the accumulated tedium was too much and Bourgeois' speech was too long. It was while the speech was going on that Lloyd George bitterly asked Clemenceau how such a man could ever have become premier of France, and Clemenceau replied that the supply of first-rate talent had given out at that time.[52] House passed a note to Wilson, "Lest old acquaintance be forgot," and Wilson wearily replied, "I would rather forget speech and man." [53]

★ 6 ★

DISARMAMENT OF GERMANY

1 : *The Policy of Pin-Pricks*

THE ANGLO-AMERICAN program for general disarmament has already been described as an essential part of the League Covenant, but from the beginning it assumed a prior destruction of German militarism. Ten days before the League of Nations Commission began its deliberations, Lloyd George presented the Supreme Council with draft resolutions calling for, *first*, immediate and drastic reduction of enemy forces; *second*, a plan in connection with the League Covenant for the permanent and universal reduction of military burdens. The first part of his proposal Lloyd George described as a "matter of grave moment" for Great Britain. He must insist that within the month, when the armistice was to be renewed, Germany's army was to be reduced to a force capable of maintaining internal order. Otherwise, according to War Office figures, Britain must maintain an army of 1,700,000 men, which simply could not be done except by compulsory service, and that the British electorate would never permit. Action was imperative.[1]

One would expect ready acquiescence from the French in any measures aimed directly at Germany's military strength, little as they liked the suggestions for general disarmament. Yet both Clemenceau and Marshal Foch showed singularly little interest in Lloyd George's proposal. The day it was made, January 23, Clemenceau quoted Foch's opinion that it would be difficult to enforce armistice provisions for German demobilization, and the next day the reasons behind the French attitude began to appear. Foch not only repeated his former statement but amplified it: "We can insert in the next Armistice a clause imposing on Germany a thorough-going demobilization of men and materials. But it will be very difficult to verify and enforce, and the results are more than doubtful. The only means of pressure is, first of all, *for us to keep strong forces mobilized,* and, second, the blockade." [2]

Foch cared chiefly to keep the armies of the Grand Alliance intact and on a war footing in Europe, better still in Germany. Lloyd George wanted German disarmament in order that British troops could go home, which was reason enough for Foch to find great practical difficulties in the way of German disarmament, so that British troops must stay. If this required conscription in England, so much the better. Léon Bourgeois had considered this possibility in his draft of a League covenant, and it was time that the British awoke to the realities of continental politics.

The French Delegation was not in the least reluctant to stiffen the armistice terms when they became due for renewal. They could even be used to achieve a measure of German disarmament, though characteristically in a way to require additional, not fewer, Allied troops, through extension of the areas of Allied military occupation within Germany. These already embraced the whole of the Left Bank of the Rhine and some four bridgeheads on the Right Bank. Loucheur now proposed to extend them to embrace the munitions factories of the Essen district in the Ruhr valley. President Wilson described this as a "panic program," expressed his strong

149

opposition to further occupation of German territory, and all the other delegations finally concurred.[3]

Meantime, the American delegation was becoming more and more concerned about the wisdom of adding new stipulations at each renewal of the armistice. On February 5, at a meeting of the Allied generals, General Bliss strongly urged the dangers of such a course, while Colonel House took up the matter with the French and British outside. Marshal Foch accepted the American position and supported it in the special commission of military and economic experts of which he was president. The committee's report of February 12 suggested that "Naval and Military terms of peace should be drawn up immediately by a Commission appointed for the purpose, and shall be imposed on the enemy." [4] The policy of pin-pricks was to be abandoned and the armistice terms were not to be the vehicle of German disarmament.

2 : *Preliminary or Final Treaty?*

In this way, the disarmament of Germany came to involve the large question of procedure in making the whole treaty with Germany. If the Supreme Council agreed to the committee recommendations, it would settle the order of procedure for the remainder of the Peace Conference; first, a simple renewal of the armistice without change; second, an immediate draft of final military and naval terms of peace to be imposed upon Germany as a *preliminary* treaty; finally, economic and political terms, presumably to be negotiated with German delegates, as the final treaty of peace.

As to the first of these proposals, renewal of the armistice unchanged, there was no difficulty, and the Supreme Council settled that question on February 12, but the rest of the program was certain to encounter French opposition on two counts. However sincere Foch may have been in supporting a preliminary treaty of final military and naval terms at this moment, Clemenceau at once objected, "What would happen when the military terms were signed and the Allied armies demobilized? What force would be left to impose the economic and political terms on Germany?" [5] He thus reëmphasized the French desire to keep the Allied armies on a war footing in Europe as long as possible, and he also made it clear that the French would insist on such stringent economic and political terms as would make such a force necessary. This was the French conception of an imposed peace from start to finish, not confined to military terms. Foch, too, soon supported this view, and it was not long before the entire French delegation took the position that the "military clauses cannot be separated from those which would fix the frontiers of Germany, the situation of the Rhenish provinces, occupation, etc." [6]

Technically, the American view prevailed in the resolution of February 12: "Detailed and final naval, military, and air conditions of peace shall be drawn up at once by a Committee to be presided over by Marshal Foch and submitted for the approval of the Supreme War Council; these, when approved, will be presented for signature to the Germans, and the Germans shall be at once informed that this is the policy of the Associated Governments." [7] Actually, the way was left open to French obstruction by the debate which preceded the adoption of the resolution.

Clemenceau, as a final attempt to stave off the unwelcome decision, said, "If the President had been staying, he would have raised no objection . . . but, as he was going, the difficulty arose, as he was quite unwilling to discuss the matter while President Wilson was away." [8] Wilson replied, in the indirect discourse of the official minutes:

In technical matters most of the brains he used were borrowed; the possessors of those brains were in Paris. He would, therefore, go away with an easy mind if he thought that his plan had been adopted in principle. He had complete confidence in the views of his Military Advisers. . . . If his plan were agreed on in principle, he would be prepared to go away and leave it to his colleagues to decide whether the programme drafted by the technical advisers was the right one. He did not wish to stop so important, essential, and urgent a work as the preparation of a Preliminary Peace. He hoped to return by the 13th or 15th of March, allowing himself only a week in America. *But he did not wish that during his unavoidable absence, such questions as the territorial question and questions of compensation should be held up. He had asked Colonel House to take his place while he was away.*[9]

The day of his departure from Paris, February 14, Wilson conferred with House on the meaning of this permission to proceed with territorial and economic questions during his absence. The Colonel said it was his understanding that he might proceed to "button up everything during the next four weeks" and, when that alarmed Wilson, he explained "that the plan was not to actually bring these matters to a final conclusion but to have them ready for him (Wilson) to do so when he returned." He intended to work out a program for a preliminary peace with Germany which should contain, in addition to military terms, delineation of German boundaries including cession of her colonies, the amount of Germany's Reparation burden, and an agreement concerning the economic treatment of Germany. When House asked Wilson if he had additional items to suggest, the latter thought these sufficient, and House warned him,

. . . to bear in mind while he was gone that it was sometimes necessary to compromise in order to get things through; not a compromise of principle but a compromise of detail; he had made many since he had been here. I did not wish him to leave expecting the impossible in all things.[10]

While Wilson was protected from any final decision on questions other than military, he had permitted the whittling away of his program for an immediate preliminary peace composed of final military terms. He had agreed in the Supreme Council meeting of February 12 that his absence was not to delay consideration of other matters, and he had apparently yielded to Colonel House's proposal of including *within the preliminary peace* broad items of territorial and economic settlement. The force of the Colonel's assurance that none of these other matters would be brought to a final conclusion during Wilson's absence, but were to be prepared for his decision when he returned, was weakened by the warning that compromise in detail was often necessary in order to get things through and that the President must not expect the impossible.

If the Colonel intended to insert only the broad outline of territorial and economic settlement in the preliminary treaty, what occasion was there for compromise of either principle or detail? There was left him a dangerous latitude of which the French were not slow to take advantage. They had only to obstruct the work of drafting military terms, on the familiar plea that those terms could not be considered apart from provisions for territorial and economic settlement; and by virtue of the same plea they could press for an immediate consideration of these other matters.

Marshal Foch, in his key position as chairman of the commission to draft the military terms, played an active rôle in both directions. By February 19, the day on which Clemenceau was incapacitated by a would-be assassin's bullet, Marshal Foch began to show signs of haste in all directions. He was sure that at the moment the Allies could dictate terms of peace, but there was no time to lose, and he suggested the immediate formulation of three principal conditions of peace to impose upon Germany: "1. The strength of her armed forces; 2. Her frontiers; 3. The indemnity she is to pay."

The task could be completed within the week, and he could guarantee Germany's signature the following day.

The reason for haste is apparent in Foch's proposal that this preliminary treaty shall specify that "under no circumstances will the German Empire extend beyond the Rhine," [11] a proposal President Wilson would certainly never sanction. No wonder that House cabled Wilson on this same day that the "French have changed their position and now desire to hurry the signing of peace." It was less reassuring when he added, "I am now doing everything possible to hasten the work of conference so that upon your return terms of preliminary peace will be ready for your consideration." [12]

Wilson was again alarmed, as in his final talk with Colonel House before leaving Paris on February 14, and cabled an immediate warning to withstand the French program for the Rhineland "immovably":

> . . . of course I am willing to have the strictly military and naval terms promptly decided and presented to the Germans. I am not willing to have anything beyond the military and naval terms (settled) and believe that the Conference of Ten would be going very much beyond its powers to attempt anything of this sort. The determination of the geographic boundaries of Germany involves the fortunes and interests of the other peoples, and we should not risk being hurried into a solution arrived at solely from the French official viewpoint. . . . Warm thanks for full information you are sending.[13]

It might be possible to resist the French pressure for immediate territorial and economic settlement; it was more difficult to push the military settlement without including the other. On February 23, House cabled Wilson again about Clemenceau's demand for a Rhenish Republic, and added that "Clemenceau thinks the entire terms should be given at once and that the military terms should not be made now

154

as at first planned. *There was afterwards common agreement on this point at our meeting at the Quai d'Orsay."* [14]

The resolutions adopted by the Supreme Council on February 24 were thus a compromise. They no longer specified a preliminary treaty composed solely of military terms, but envisaged "Preliminary Peace Terms, other than the Naval, Military and Air Conditions," which "should cover *inter alia* the following points: (a) the approximate future frontiers *(for Germany only*: and the renunciation of colonial territories and treaty rights outside Europe); (b) the financial conditions to be imposed on —— (name of enemy country); (c) the economic conditions to be accorded to ——; (d) the responsibility for breaches of the laws of war." They provided, finally, that the commissions set up to study these various matters should report not later than Saturday, March 8. [15]

It was still possible that, if the Military Commission completed its labors in time, Wilson's plan of a preliminary military treaty might yet be fulfilled, but it was no longer mandatory, and it became less and less likely. [16] Yet there is nothing to substantiate Ray Stannard Baker's charge that Colonel House deliberately sabotaged Wilson's program by conniving with Balfour to rush through a complete treaty of peace before Wilson's return. Wilson had himself agreed that his absence was not to delay progress on economic and territorial questions, provided final decision awaited his return, and Colonel House cabled him the fullest information concerning the resolutions on February 24:

At the present time the plan we are pursuing is as follows: the giving of priority to the work of the committees involving matters essential in the preparation of a peace treaty with Germany. Reports from these committees should be available by March 8th and should upon your arrival be in shape so that you can consider them without delay. After you have approved them they

155

should be submitted to a Plenary Session of the Conference and an agreement of all the powers reached respecting them. If this procedure is followed it ought to be possible to summon the Peace Conference for a date not later than the first week of April.[17]

In other words, the preliminary treaty was to deal in outline with all phases of peace settlement, and even this was to await Wilson's approval on his return. After his approval, would begin the formal work of the Peace Conference proper, the negotiation of a final treaty to fill in the details left blank in the preliminary outline treaty. In this way, it might still be possible to negotiate the details of the final treaty with German delegates.

Certainly the Colonel never intended to eliminate the League Covenant from either the preliminary or the final treaty, as Baker intended to prove. On the contrary, it was at his suggestion that Secretary Lansing inserted the words *inter alia* in the list of subjects which the resolution of February 24 adopted for inclusion in the preliminary treaty, and the purpose of those words was to cover the League Covenant.[18] The Colonel even went so far as to plan immediate establishment of provisional League of Nations machinery to start functioning at once, long before a preliminary peace treaty could be prepared. He reported to Wilson on February 27 that he had secured Balfour's and Cecil's approval of his scheme to authorize members of the League of Nations Commission to "act as the provisional executive council proposed in the Covenant." [19]

Neither House's plan "to start the League of Nations functioning at once" nor the program for a preliminary peace treaty in advance of the final and negotiated treaty ever came to fulfilment. Both had to be abandoned in deference to the constitutional rights of the United States Senate in respect to the ratification of treaties. Wilson cabled House

156

on March 3 that the plan for a provisional League made him uneasy for fear that it might appear "to forestall action by the Senate and commit the country in some practical way from which it would be impossible to withdraw." If anything of the sort were to be attempted, it must be with the most explicit and public understanding as to its purely provisional character.[20] House cabled the next day that he had so far found no satisfactory way of making his plan work. He promised to attempt nothing further until Wilson's return, and by that time there were so many other problems to attend to that the project died a natural death.[21]

When Wilson did return, discussion of military terms was at its height, and the problem of a preliminary peace had to be faced. The military terms were practically ready for final agreement on March 17 and the French legal expert, Fromageot, asked for a ruling by the Supreme Council on the legal character of these terms. Were they merely preliminary terms for immediate execution by the Germans, and not a final treaty of peace? If so, it was to be feared that when the final treaty was presented to the Germans, they might argue that the military terms had not been peace conditions and were, therefore, subject to reconsideration. On the other hand, if the military terms were final conditions of peace, they must be ratified by the legislators of the contracting powers. The logic was inescapable, but it hit Wilson very hard. He had assumed that the military convention "would only be temporary until the complete treaty was prepared," but "if this preliminary convention should have to be submitted to the Senate for a general discussion there, he knew from the usual slow processes of legislatures that it would be several months before it could be ratified."

Balfour regarded the President's statement as "most important and serious"; he had supposed that the conference could proceed with a preliminary peace, each clause of which

157

could be reënacted in the final treaty; but it now appeared "that the American Constitution made that full program impracticable." Wilson was not altogether sure of his ground and said he would consult his constitutional lawyers.[22]

The doom of the preliminary peace was sealed next day in a meeting of the American Commission where it was agreed "that the preliminary peace was in reality a complete and final declaration of peace which would have to be ratified by all the contracting states. The so-called final Peace Treaty would be merely a revision of this first Peace Treaty." [23]

The problem of dealing with the American Senate had again, as in the drafting of the League of Nations Covenant, worked to the advantage of the basic French strategy of obstructionism. From this time on, there was no doubt that the Peace Conference was elaborating final peace terms, of which the military terms adopted on March 17 were but the first instalment, not to become effective until the rest of the treaty had been drafted. While that did not achieve any of the positive aims of the French program, by rushing their schemes to completion in the Rhineland or elsewhere, negatively it did ensure them against rapid demobilization on the part of their Allies, and meantime the military terms themselves had been issued in the most drastic form. It is time, therefore, to study the strategy of Marshal Foch in achieving that result.

3 : *Conscription Again*

On February 6, the English and American members of the League of Nations Commission abandoned the clause in Article VIII of the Hurst-Miller draft of the Covenant which would empower the League Council to consider the universal extinction of the conscript system of recruiting national armies. While willing to yield to French objection on the general principle, no English or American delegate could conscientiously permit Germany, the arch-offender against international morality, ever again to enjoy the advantages of such a system, which they regarded as the root evil of international anarchy, the potent agent, if not the actual cause, of aggression. It was, therefore, a matter of bewilderment and alarm when, on March 3, Marshal Foch presented his report from the Military Commission, advocating that Germany be permitted an army of 200,000 men enrolled by the *conscript system* for a single year's service. It was a unanimous report concurred in by the military representatives of Great Britain and the United States, though the former at least with great reluctance abandoned their insistence on the voluntary principle.[24]

Balfour entered an immediate reservation on behalf of Lloyd George, who was absent. He personally wanted time to examine the report and was sure that Lloyd George would want to see it. There was also disagreement with regard to the duration of the provisions of the military report, Balfour suggesting that the limitation of German armaments last only "until Germany has fulfilled all the obligations imposed on her by the peace terms, and thereafter for as long, and with such modifications, as the League of Nations may determine," while Clemenceau was quite unwilling to set a time limit. He reminded the Supreme Council of Wilson's assertion of the moral right of the Allies to disarm Germany permanently; and clearly the Naval Commission had been proceeding on some such principle, for Admiral Benson gave it as his understanding that the German fleet was to be reduced to a fixed strength and kept there indefinitely, with the continuance of the régime to be assigned to the League of Nations. Clemenceau agreed that this might meet the case if the League turned out satisfactorily, and suggested that the principle be studied by the three commissions, military, naval and air, so that their reports might be coördinated.

This session of the Supreme Council ended after one more attempt by Marshal Foch to insist that the new German frontiers (i.e., Rhineland), be taken up in relation to the military terms, when Clemenceau himself said that it could not be done in the absence of both Lloyd George and Wilson.[25] While thus keeping the question out of the Supreme Council, Clemenceau did not relax his efforts to commit Colonel House to support of the French Rhineland proposals before Wilson's return.

By March 6, when Foch presented the coördinated military, naval and air terms without any substantial change in his earlier recommendations, Lloyd George was present, ready to fight the principle of conscription. He and Foch had it out, ostensibly on the ground of technical arguments concerning the proficiency of volunteer and conscript armies, each actually defending a political position. When Lloyd George warned Foch that the effect of permitting Germany a conscript army of 200,000 men on an annual service basis would be to produce a trained army of 4,000,000 men in twenty years, on the analogy of Napoleon's mistake after Jena, Foch replied that such a force would be worthless without trained officer *cadres*, whereas even a small professional volunteer army of long-term service represents ready-made *cadres* for training a vast force. As the French officer Bugeaud said, "better to have an army of sheep commanded by a lion, than a number of lions commanded by an ass."

Foch insisted that the real backbone of Germany's mighty pre-war army was the *cadre* of 120,000 professional non-commissioned officers. Lloyd George held to his view that Foch's proposals were dangerous even to France, in view of Germany's plentiful supply of trained officers ready to take

160

over command of a large conscript army. He asked for adjournment to give the British time to present counter-proposals, and, when Foch resisted on the ground of the unanimity of the Military Commission in behalf of the present recommendations, Lloyd George said that the question was not merely technical, but "partly political." Clemenceau was constrained to agree that such was the case and Lloyd George got his adjournment.[26]

Lloyd George had understated the case when he called the question partly political. He himself was under mandate from his own public to abolish conscription, at least in Germany, and said as much the next day when he warned the Supreme Council that England would never sign a peace permitting Germany to maintain a short-term conscript army.[27] With Foch, political considerations were at least as compelling, and Clemenceau had as much as admitted it. If the long-term professional army were really such a deadly weapon, why did France cling with fanatic fervor to the conscript system? It is hard to take seriously the technical arguments of an expert who declines to turn them to his own advantage.

It is worth remembering that the Anglo-American program had established a connection between conscription in Germany and conscription on the rest of the European continent. Germany was blamed for inaugurating the vicious system, the continent excused for adopting it in self-defense, yet it must be everywhere eliminated. If Germany led the way under compulsion of the treaty of peace, other nations might be invited to follow through the medium of the League Covenant. Great Britain and the United States had abandoned the second and more ambitious part of that program, but the connection remained in the French mind and was reflected in many sections of the French Press. Some groups of French opinion feared, others hoped, that a professional system in Germany would pave the way for a general abandonment of the conscript system all over Europe and, in general, the French press actually preferred the Lloyd George to the Foch program on the merits of the technical argument.[27] Foch may have believed profoundly in the truth of his technical arguments, but he appears to have been primarily concerned with preserving universal short-term compulsory service in France by perpetuating it in Germany.

In any case, Lloyd George was adamant and, on March 7, presented his own resolutions prescribing voluntary enlistment for a minimum twelve-year period as the sole basis of recruitment for Germany's military and naval forces, and fixing the maximum size of Germany's army at 200,000 men, and her navy at 15,000. He supported this program by the additional argument of the greater expense of such an establishment to Germany, and when Marshal Foch and General Desgouttes still opposed long-term enlistment, he declared flatly that Britain would not sign the treaty on any other basis.[28]

In the absence of support from Clemenceau, Foch had no choice but to yield on the principle of recruitment, but he declined to do so without drastically reducing the size of the army allotted to Germany. His revised draft of March 10 incorporated the British principle of voluntary long-term service but set the maximum figure for the army at 100,000 men. In the first place, he had assumed that 140,000 professional soldiers were the equivalent of 200,000 annual conscripts, because at least half the short-term conscripts would be undergoing training at any given time and could not be counted as effectives in a standing army. To this equation, Lloyd George offered no objection, even though it automatically reduced his figure of 200,000 to 140,000 in adopting his principle of enlistment. But Foch insisted on

162

a further mark-down from 140,000 to 100,000 because of the greater potential danger from a professional army.

At this point, Secretary Lansing, General Bliss, and Colonel House of the American delegation, and Lord Balfour of the British Delegation, became uneasy. There had been many reports of French military activity in central Europe, building an anti-German military bloc in the new Slavic states, Poland and Czechoslovakia, and English and American delegates began to feel that the limits of Germany's national, and even domestic security had been reached, if not actually passed.[29]

General Bliss expressed American opinion as opposed to further reduction and Lansing supported him, but it was Foch's turn to be adamant and Clemenceau supported him. Lloyd George, having won his point on enlistment, felt he must yield to Foch on figures and said that neither England nor the United States had the right to withstand French views if the French felt strongly about them. Lansing also submitted, but Balfour warned the Council that Germany's army would be reduced thereby to the level of a police force, that Germany like other states must be made secure against invasion, that Germany would have just cause to complain if her army were reduced to 100,000 men while her neighbors—France, Poland, and Bohemia—were free to have as many forces as they liked. In default of any provision for general disarmament, Balfour had no solution to propose to meet this danger.

When Clemenceau blandly assured Balfour that the League of Nations would provide an adequate solution by fulfilling its purpose of preventing aggression, his irony must have been deliberate, because by this time the French protests against the inadequacy of League guarantees were notorious. But Balfour merely said that if this were to be the solution, it must be communicated to the Germans.

163

When House reported Bliss' suggestion that the powers guarantee the neutrality of Germany on the Belgian model, Clemenceau said angrily that he would never guarantee Germany anything.[30]

The main provisions of the Foch draft were accepted, with some slight changes not affecting the principle of enlistment or the numbers of the German army. Germany was forbidden to maintain a general staff, provisions for the demilitarization of the whole Rhineland area were struck out of the military terms and reserved for special treaty arrangements regulating that area, and the difficult question of enforcement of the military terms was deferred to a later date. Yet the session of March 10 did not close without the familiar voice of the generals.

Foch had been momentarily silenced, but Generals Desgouttes and Weygand took up the refrain. The former attacked the enlistment principle, accusing the Supreme Council of insufficient consideration of the dangers involved, and when Clemenceau asked him why he had not said so at the appropriate moment when the relevant articles were under consideration, Weygand complained that the experts' hands had been tied by the assumptions furnished to them by the Council and he had not felt free to criticize those assumptions. The Italian General Cavallero, belatedly recalling his instructions as Italian military adviser, thought that the system of long-term voluntary service was unacceptable; and Clemenceau as chairman closed the debate with the remark that he recognized only the vote of the Italian delegation and not the views of the Italian military adviser. At the most, he would record General Cavallero's protest in the minutes.[31]

President Wilson had originally expected the Supreme Council to reach final conclusions on the military terms before his return to Paris, but the unforeseen difficulties led him to ask postponement. The French strategy of obstructing rapid completion of these terms in an effort to precipitate decision on other questions combined with the long struggle over conscription to delay the final draft of the military terms until the very eve of Wilson's return. The long session which tentatively adopted those terms took place on March 10, and Wilson returned to Paris on March 14. Moreover, he had left his military advisers and his representatives a wide discretion as to the approval of military terms, and clearly they were worried about the drastic character of the terms which finally emerged. It is probable they did not care to take responsibility for final decision and so informed the President. In any case, when the Supreme Council reconvened on March 15, Clemenceau reported a message from President Wilson asking that final discussion on military, naval and air terms be postponed until he could be present on March 17.[32]

4 : *Inspection Again*

When the Supreme Council met on March 17, Wilson showed the same anxiety about the extreme limits of German disarmament which had appeared in the session of March 10, but it was too late to reconsider the figures then tentatively adopted—connected as they were with Foch's resistance to the volunteer principle—and Foch gave the most explicit assurances that 100,000 men were adequate to all requirements of domestic order.[33] But Wilson was even more anxious about the Control Commissions which were to enforce Germany's execution of the military terms, and on this issue Lansing's reservation of March 10 had preserved him a free hand.[34]

The clauses of Chapter V, as drafted, seemed to establish indefinite supervision over Germany's military establishment

165

by essentially military agencies of the Allied High Command. Anyone familiar with Bourgeois' amendments to the League Covenant might see here a specific and partial application of his more general schemes which at different times he described, as "verification," "control," "inspection," "surveillance," "supervision"—and such arrangements were not likely to be more palatable to the Anglo-American delegates when removed from the context of the Covenant and applied specifically to Germany.

Wilson objected at once both to the military character of the agencies and to their apparently limitless duration:

> . . . they are instruments of the High Command, which seems to imply indefinite continuation of the High Command and of the army. If the Allied armies are to be maintained forever in order to control the carrying out of the peace terms, not peace, but the armed domination of the Allies will have been established. The United States Government would never agree to enter into any such arrangement.

Lloyd George supported Wilson's objections and the articles of Chapter V were considerably modified in a way to make control commissions apply only to those military, naval and air terms for which a time limit had been fixed, and to make even those commissions representative of the Inter-Allied Governments instead of the Military High Command.[85] There was surprisingly little resistance from Clemenceau and Foch, and the latter even said that he had never intended that control should operate for the disarmament provisions which were of indefinite duration. He was willing enough that the Allies should agree among themselves that control commissions were to cease after, roughly, three months; he only objected to making a contract with Germany to this effect; in other words, to putting it into the treaty.[86]

Yet the resources of French diplomacy were apparently

endless. We have seen that, when the League of Nations Commission renewed its sessions on March 22, Bourgeois reiterated the French demand for "inspection" in the League Covenant. On the same date, André Tardieu gave Colonel House a characteristic memorandum of impeccable logic, directing its appeal to American desire for a successful League of Nations. Starting from the assumption that Germany once disarmed might not be permitted to rearm, he insisted that the treaty grant to the League of Nations the authority to assure itself that Germany was not rearming— the persistent French proposal of "inspection" or "verification" in another guise.[87] When the Bourgeois amendments to the League Covenant, embodying this same principle had been defeated a second time in the sessions of March 22, 24 and 26, Tardieu produced a draft clause to be inserted in the treaty of peace:

If any of the signatory powers consider that Germany has violated any of the above clauses (the military terms and provision for demilitarization of the Rhineland area), it will have the right to bring the matter before the Executive Council of the League of Nations which will at once proceed to *verify* the facts stated. Germany undertakes to submit to said *verification* made in the interest of peace and to facilitate its execution.[88]

The period of acute tension and deadlock over all the major issues of the German treaty lasted from March 28 until April 10 or 11, beginning with Clemenceau's quarrel with President Wilson, and breaking with the storm of French protest in the League of Nations Commission against the American Monroe Doctrine amendment to the League Covenant. Tardieu consequently had no answer to his draft proposal until April 12, when Wilson replied that the League Covenant already granted the right to member states to notify the Council generally of any action "which threatens the peace of the world" and that it would be unfortunate to narrow this provision by tying it to these specific measures; that is, disarming Germany and demilitarizing her Rhineland provinces.

Tardieu, with a persistence worthy of Bourgeois, renewed his demand on April 15, arguing that Great Britain and the United States had already implemented the territorial guarantees contained in Article X of the League Covenant through their separate treaty of military guarantee of French security. This covered the case of an actual German attack, but not one of German preparations for such an attack, where he must ask for the same precision and strength. "In other words it is a matter of giving Article XIII of the Covenant as regards possible preparations by Germany, the same complement as the special treaty gives to Article X." He must insist that, "either in the Covenant of the League or in the military clauses of peace" this provision for verification appear; and with a final reference to French generosity to the Anglo-American views which shaped the League Covenant, he said: "The position of the French Government is identical with that which prompted the American Government to introduce an amendment to the Covenant with respect to the Monroe Docrine." This, too, was a question of public feeling, and the provision he sought was certain to assist ratification of the treaty by the French parliament.[39]

Two days later, April 17, Wilson granted a special formula without departing from the voluntary as compared to the coercive principle. He agreed that "Germany shall *pledge* herself to *respond* to inquiry whenever the Council of the League shall determine by majority vote that such inquiry is necessary."[40] French proposals for inspection and verification received as little recognition in the treaty of peace as in the Covenant of the League of Nations.

168

Both British and American delegates felt that disarmament of Germany had gone far enough, if indeed not too far, and the British delegates particularly were beginning to show symptoms of that guilt complex that has so profoundly affected post-Versailles British policy. The British members of the drafting committee were so worried about the drastic reduction of Germany's armed forces, while Poland remained free to build a large army and while Soviet Russia remained entirely outside the Peace Conference and the League of Nations, that they proposed a preamble to the military terms by which Germany's permanent disarmament could be linked with a general process of disarmament throughout the world. The Anglo-American program had always envisaged German disarmament as preliminary to, and the essential precondition of, general disarmament. The program had failed so far as the League of Nations Covenant was concerned, primarily because of French obstruction. Here was an opportunity to achieve the same result through the medium of the military terms of peace, by binding the signatories and the beneficiaries of German disarmament to recognize their own obligation to follow the German example.[41]

President Wilson gladly agreed to sponsor the proposal and, on April 26, "suggested that it would make the Military, Naval and Air terms more acceptable to the enemy if they were presented as preparing the way for a general limitation of armaments for all nations." Clemenceau wanted to see the formula before he agreed, but all delegates finally accepted the following clause:

In order to render possible the initiation of general limitation of the armaments of all nations Germany undertakes strictly to observe the military, naval, and air clauses which follow.[42]

169

When the sixth plenary session of the Peace Conference met on May 6 to adopt the terms of the German treaty, it was for merely formal approval of decisions already made by plenipotentiaries, but Foch could not resist the opportunity to make a speech protesting the military clauses as inadequate to the requirements of French security. Clemenceau, whose good faith was involved by his own agreement to the terms, rolled up to him in a passion at the conclusion of the session and inquired, "And why, M. le Maréchal, did you choose to make such a scene in public?" When Foch blandly replied, "It was merely to ease my conscience," it was not a hopeful augury for the cause of universal disarmament.[43] In France, the conscience of soldiers is apt to be taken more seriously than that of politicians, and the Foch views of the treaty enjoyed more popularity than Clemenceau's. Clemenceau himself could hardly have been called an advocate of universal, much less of French, disarmament.

Nor did it advance the cause of disarmament very far when the German Government signified its assent to the treaty provisions disarming Germany on condition of her immediate admission to the League of Nations.[44] French delegates had made it clear from the beginning of the Peace Conference that they would never entertain such proposals, even when British and Americans urged the wisdom of such a course. The refusal of the Powers to admit Germany at once to the benefits of League protection was bound to undermine the moral foundations of German disarmament, while the failure of the contracting Powers to live up to their own implied promise of disarmament presented Germany with a strong moral case for rearmament. It was clearly not a case of legal contract, but one of moral obligation, and provides one of the most striking examples to justify Keynes' general charge that a "Carthaginian" treaty was clothed in the language of hypocrisy and of "Jesuitical exegesis."

170

Winston Churchill has summarized the sole practical result of the general disarmament preamble in "the prolonged and, as they have proved, disturbing labors of the Disarmament Conference at Geneva." [45] They have proved as fruitless as they have been prolonged and disturbing.

★ 7 ★

DISMEMBERMENT OF GERMANY—
I THE EAST

---

1 : *"Poland Must Be Very Big and Strong"*

TRADITIONAL FRENCH POLICY bears down upon the Germanic states in Central Europe in three directions: on the west, on the east, and directly in the center. Germany's western boundaries are naturally of the most immediate concern to French leaders, but her eastern boundaries are of almost equal concern, and the actual political fabric of the German state which remains between the eastern and western boundaries is just as important. All three elements in French policy are so closely related that it is difficult to separate them, because they are merely different aspects of a single aim, the destruction of German military power. A powerful state on the east liberally endowed with German territory is the natural ally of France on the west, and if France can advance her frontiers to the Rhine, the Allies can exert a pulverizing pressure on what remains of the German state, to the point of its internal disruption.

It matters not so much to the French which particular state plays the rôle of eastern ally. His Most Christian Majesty Francis I did not hesitate to make common cause with the infidel Sultan of Turkey when it was a question of putting the Catholic Habsburg Empire in a vise, any more than he hesitated to deal with Lutheran German princes in that Empire to disrupt it from within. The Third French Republic and Czarist Russia joined hands against the new German Reich which had been founded on French military defeat in 1871, and as allies in the World War consecrated their bond by pledges to dismember the Reich east and west—in the event of victory, a free hand to Russia in the east and a free hand to France in the west.[1]

When the military collapse of Russia vitiated that arrangement, it almost automatically provided a substitute. A Soviet Russia which not only abandoned its allies but embraced heretical doctrines of social and political organization was an outlaw among nations. Moreover, Wilson's doctrine of self-determination branded Russia as a nation which had sinned against his principle by holding an unwilling Polish population in bondage. Since Russia had been the guilty accomplice of Prussia and Austria in the original partitions of the Polish state in the eighteenth century, the principle of self-determination could now be triumphantly vindicated at the expense of all three Empires by the re-creation of an independent Polish state. Such a rebirth would answer French purposes just as well as the original Russian alliance, because it would ensure the dismemberment of Germany's eastern provinces, and French policy was certain to support the most extravagant Polish demands for territory. Pichon made that plain when he said that resurrected Poland must be *"grande et forte, très forte."*

British and American delegates were equally committed to the reëstablishment of Poland, as was the German Government in accepting the armistice terms. The agreed basis of peace included both a general endorsement of the prin-

173

ciple of self-determination and its specific application to the Polish case. Point XIII of Wilson's Fourteen Points reads:

An independent Polish state should be erected which should include the territories inhabited by indisputably Polish populations, which should be assured a free and secure access to the sea, and whose political and economic independence and territorial integrity should be guaranteed by international covenant.[2]

The German Government unmistakably realized the general consequences of accepting such a provision as the price of armistice. The interim German chancellor, Prince Max of Baden, warned General Ludendorff that it would cost Germany the Polish provinces of the east, but the General insisted on the armistice as essential at any price. Prince Max thought that even then Ludendorff had no real conception of the consequences, probably hoping to exploit German occupation of Allied territory in a way to evade any real compliance with the Fourteen Points.[3] Yet Prince Max himself would probably have been surprised at the drastic application of Point XIII.

Despite the apparent clarity and precision with which the article had been drafted, there were ambiguities which Polish and French were certain to exploit to their own advantage, and there was no real unanimity in the American delegation about resisting such efforts. The uncertainties which plagued the delegation are well illustrated by the actual history of Point XIII. When the territorial and economic experts of the *Inquiry* first presented to President Wilson their recommendations early in January 1918 to assist him in the formulation of terms of peace, they had urged the importance of both economic and strategic consideration in the determination of boundaries for the Polish state. They suggested that "Its boundaries shall be based on a fair balance of national and economic considerations, giving due weight to the necessity for adequate access to the sea." [4] They

174

assumed, on the basis of their statistics, that even strict adherence to the ethnographic principle would award to Poland a corridor to the Baltic Sea, separating East Prussia from the rest of Germany, but doubted whether such a solution could ever enter the realm of practical politics because of Germany's enduring military strength. Failing this solution, Poland would have to depend on the Vistula river traffic and the canals which cross Germany to Hamburg and Bremen, which "would very probably involve both the economic subjection of Poland and the establishment of a new area of great friction." [5]

Wilson evidently preferred a less ambiguous statement of principle to govern Polish boundaries and, when he drafted Point XIII, changed the experts' phrase "fair balance of national and economic consideration, giving due weight to the necessity for adequate access to the sea," to:

It shall include territory inhabited by *indisputably* Polish populations, and *shall be granted free and secure access to the sea.*[6]

The sharper emphasis on ethnographic principle had both a restrictive and an expansive effect. On the assumption of the indisputably Polish character of the Corridor population—which German statistics supported [7]—it warranted Wilson's stronger language about Poland's access to the sea, presumably via the Polish Corridor. The experts themselves had suggested such an arrangement but, doubting its practicability, had phrased it in ambiguous and tentative form. Yet this very ambiguity opened up dangerous possibilities in the wide latitude given economic and strategic considerations, which Wilson's words were calculated to restrain. But his efforts at precision were fruitless, as can be seen in the semiofficial commentary on the Fourteen Points which Frank Cobb and Walter Lippmann compiled in October, 1918, to assist Colonel House, and which Wilson himself approved as a generally satisfactory interpretation of his principles.[8] The commentators wrote:

The chief problem is whether Poland is to obtain territory west of the Vistula which would cut off the Germans of East Prussia from the Empire, or whether Danzig can be made a free port and the Vistula internationalized. . . .
The principle on which frontiers will be delimited is contained in the President's word "indisputably." This *may* imply the taking of an impartial census before frontiers are marked.[9]

The experts' view that the Corridor was thoroughly Polish was never seriously challenged, and gradually doubts and hesitation about granting it to Poland for fear of separating East Prussia from the rest of Germany began to disappear. By the same token, there was no doubt that the city and area of Danzig at the mouth of the Vistula and the whole of the province of East Prussia were completely German, definitely to be excluded by Wilson's principles from the new Polish state. Yet Polish representatives, supported by French delegates, were clamoring for Danzig, most of East Prussia, and much else besides to which they had no shadow of right, on the grounds of ethnography. The Pole, Dmowski, and the French Foreign Minister, Pichon, mingled historical, strategic, and economic arguments in pressing these claims. The latter argued with Balfour in November 1918 for the Polish boundaries of 1772,[10] and the former had to go back several hundred years earlier to support his claim to Silesia. His proposals to the Supreme Council on January 29, 1919, incorporated Danzig and practically all of East Prussia in Poland, and left a small island of Germans to form a separate republic with a capital in Königsberg. He proposed an ingenious device for determining what was indisputably Polish territory by including any area which "had been oppressed by anti-Polish laws," in other words, any province where there were any Poles in residence.[11]

176

Meantime, the American experts of the *Inquiry*, re-christened *American Intelligence for Territorial, Political, and Economic Questions,* had prepared a tentative report on German boundaries for President Wilson's guidance.[12] This preliminary statement of January 20 became the basis for a more conclusive report in February, and the recommendations of these reports went very far toward satisfying Polish and French extreme demands for German territory.[13] They established the Polish Corridor to the Baltic through the former German provinces of Posen and West Prussia, as indisputably Polish in population and as essential for free and secure access to the sea. They admitted the difficulty of thus severing the 1,600,000 Germans of East Prussia from the rest of Germany, but considered it less serious than the sole alternative of leaving the 600,000 Poles of West Prussia under German rule and thus confining the bulk of Poland to a "hampered and precarious commercial outlet." An isolated East Prussia could still maintain its economic connection with the rest of Germany by rail transit through the Corridor and by water transport via Königsberg and the Baltic, and pre-war statistics proved that the bulk of East Prussian commerce with the rest of Germany was waterborne. "In either case a people is asked to entrust large interests to the League of Nations. In the case of Poland, they are vital interests; in the case of Germany, aside from Prussian sentiment, they are quite secondary." [14]

But the report pushed the logic of Poland's access to the sea well beyond ethnographic limits. The city and immediate area of Danzig was the chief Baltic port, the outlet for Poland's largest river, the Vistula, and the terminus for two railroads connecting central Poland with the Baltic. The city and its immediately surrounding area was indisputably German, yet the experts granted it to Poland on the ground of economic necessity.[15] The status of Danzig became a major test of Wilson's principles and the storm center of the Polish question.

2 : *The Battle of Danzig*

This was neither the first nor the last time that Wilson was embarrassed by the recommendations of his own experts. On the way to Paris he had enjoined them to tell him what was right and he would fight for it.[16] He had enunciated general principles with their assistance and was dependent upon their advice for the specific application of these principles in each instance. In the case of the Polish recommendations, he encountered the strong pro-Polish sympathies of Professor Robert H. Lord of Harvard University, sympathies which were generally shared by most of the members of the *Inquiry*, who, none the less, regarded his as excessive.[17]

When the first tentative report appeared late in January, Wilson declined to be committed to its recommendations, particularly in the matter of Danzig, which he said must remain an open question.[18] Yet Dmowski is certain that his speech to the Supreme Council on January 29 committed Wilson because, afterwards, House brought the message that Wilson was "convinced that Danzig must be Polish and that in this affair he would be with Poland."[19] That may be, but it seems unlikely that Wilson would depart from his general policy of avoiding all commitments on territorial questions at this stage of the Conference, when the territorial commissions were just beginning their studies. Later he made it very clear to Colonel House that he was willing to have only military terms settled during his absence from Paris. Territorial and economic commissions by all means should speed up their work, but only to clear the ground for decision, not to reach conclusions, nor to prejudice the final settlement.

While Wilson was away, the experts continued to wrestle with the problem. Professor Lord had come to a tentative agreement with one of the British experts in assigning Danzig to Poland, and a larger group of British and American experts met at the Crillon on February 21 to canvass the grounds of that agreement. Bowman, Haskins, Johnson, Mezes, and Seymour met Akers-Douglas, Cornwall, Headlam-Morley, and Paton to consider possible alternatives to eliminate the danger of giving a purely German area to Poland, and they could find none that satisfied them.[20]

Two days later, Colonel House cabled Wilson about Clemenceau's insistent demands for wholesale settlement which boxed the compass of French policy. Entire terms of peace, not merely military terms, must be settled now, and they must include a Rhenish republic on the west, an independent Austria on the south to prevent its absorption by Germany, and in the east, the assignment of Danzig to Poland. As to Danzig, House added, "Our experts also believe this to be the best solution, and they are joined, I understand, in this belief by the British experts, but the British Government disagree on this point."[21] Wilson had already cabled House that he was not willing to have anything settled beyond the purely military terms, and warning the Colonel against any sort of commitment to official French policy with respect to the geographic boundaries of Germany.[22] But ultimately it was the resistance of Lloyd George which proved decisive in the Danzig question.

Lloyd George took his stand on the simple proposition "that we did not want any more Alsace-Lorraines in Europe, whether in the East or the West." On March 17, the day when military terms were finally settled, he carried on a preliminary skirmish with Clemenceau and Colonel House.

He first objected to Marshal Foch's scheme for incorporating the whole of East Prussia in Poland, and then attacked even the more modest proposal of awarding Danzig to Poland, because it isolated East Prussia completely. Colonel House said the American delegates were convinced that Danzig should go to Poland and he expected that finally the British delegates would also agree. He suggested that the problem of an East Prussian island could readily be solved by either internationalizing it or by converting it into a separate republic, and Clemenceau supported him in a highly characteristic remark which summed up centuries of French policy:

The more separate and independent republics were established in Germany, the better he would be pleased.[23]

The report of the Polish Commission was not yet before the Supreme Council, and the preliminary discussion of March 17 only served to indicate the attitudes which were likely to prevail when the report appeared. When it did appear, on March 19, it was of a nature to provoke one of the bitterest controversies of the entire Peace Conference. While establishing the Polish Corridor through Posen and West Prussia to the Baltic on the basically ethnographic principle that it was indisputably Polish in population, the report violated that principle in two vital areas—incorporating the admittedly German district of Danzig in Poland, as well as the equally German *Kreis* of Marienwerder. This latter area was a triangle of West Prussia, east of the Vistula river, formed by the Vistula on the west, the western boundary of East Prussia on the east, and by Danzig at the apex in the north. Through it ran two railroads from Danzig to Warsaw, one along the Vistula river to the west via the cities of Marienwerder, Bromberg, and Thorn, the other more directly via Rosenberg and Mlawa, close to the border of East Prussia.

180

The Commission said it was essential that Poland control both banks of the Vistula and both railroads. The Commission was uncertain about the character of Allenstein, the southern section of East Prussia itself, and proposed a plebiscite to determine its fate.[24]

Jules Cambon, former French Ambassador in Berlin and chief French member of the Polish Commission, undertook the defense of the Commission's recommendations in the Supreme Council meeting of March 19, and the meeting resolved itself into a bitter duel between Lloyd George and the French representatives, with President Wilson clearly on the fence. Lloyd George would not agree to the incorporation of purely German areas in Poland and flatly opposed the report on the two points of Danzig and Marienwerder, estimating that the report assigned to Poland no fewer than 2,132,000 Germans, of whom there were some 412,000 in Danzig alone. When economic and strategic arguments failed to convince Lloyd George, Cambon pointed out that the Commission's report was unanimous, and Tardieu said that his committee which had been set up to coördinate all recommendations from boundary commissions had unanimously approved the Polish report.

Lloyd George objected that the British delegates on these commissions had adopted the conclusions only very reluctantly and regarded them as a departure from the Fourteen Points. For himself, he would never agree to the creation of a *Germania Irredenta* which he feared as the seed of future war, and "felt bound to make this protest against what he considered to be a most dangerous proposal." [25]

Whatever Wilson's attitude had been before Lloyd George spoke, he was evidently impressed, saying "he had not reached a definite conclusion in his own mind" and hoped that discussion would bring out all elements of the problem. He admitted that the inclusion of so many Germans in the new state seemed to be a violation of one of his principles, but reminded the delegates that Germany herself had accepted the principle of a free and secure access to the sea. It was impossible to draw sharp ethnic lines in this part of Europe and there would continue to be racial minorities wherever the lines were drawn. The problem of Polish security was bound to be a serious one and the lines had best be drawn with due regard to that security. He was afraid of the extreme proposals of Lloyd George, but did share his anxiety about the recommendations of the report. When Lloyd George suggested that the report should be referred back to the Polish Commission with a view to readjustment of the boundaries of East Prussia, Wilson supported the proposal, while removing some of its sting, "that the Commission should be merely asked to reconsider its recommendations in the light of the discussion." [26]

The discussion had taken place in the Council of Ten, supposedly in the strictest secrecy, and naturally there had been no official communiqué of its deliberations. Yet French newspapers the next day were singularly well informed about Lloyd George's attitude as expressed in the meeting, and attacked it violently. As Lloyd George complained, these attacks "gave all the appearance of being concerted, inspired and intimidatory." [27] He reminded the Council, on the evening of March 21, that this kind of thing had happened before, in January, that the British had been to blame and that he had personally taken measures to prevent any repetition of the offense.[28] He demanded similar measures now and the effect of his insistence was to eliminate entirely the sessions of the Council of Ten and to substitute for that body as the official form of the Supreme Council, a Council of Four composed of Clemenceau, Wilson, Orlando, and himself.

Meantime the Polish Commission deliberated and adhered rigidly to its original proposals, still insisting that Poland's rail and water communications with the Baltic outweighed racial arguments in determining the fate of Danzig and Marienwerder.[29] It was impossible to reject outright the recommendations of a boundary commission unanimously adopted and twice considered and, in the Council meeting of March 22, Lloyd George was careful not to criticize the Commission. He still maintained his objection that the proposed boundaries would "have a deplorable effect on German public opinion" and warned the Allies against decisions which might drive the Germans to such desperation that no German Government would dare sign the treaty. At most, he was "inclined to accept provisionally the solutions proposed by the committee . . . with the clear understanding that the Supreme Council reserves the right of revision in considering the total effect of the proposals." When Wilson supported his reservations, the Council devised a formula with regard to the "receipt, discussion and reservation for final examination" of the recommendations of the Polish Commission in connection with other boundary decisions affecting Germany.[30]

The Polish question, like all other major issues of the German treaty in which France had primary concern—Rhineland, Saar, Reparation—entered upon a phase of complete deadlock. On March 28, the very day when Clemenceau accused Wilson of being pro-German because of his attitude on the Saar and Rhineland questions, Wilson had clearly made up his mind to support Lloyd George's stand on the Danzig question. Sidney Mezes, brother-in-law of Colonel House, titular head of the *Inquiry*, and American representative on the committee to coördinate the reports of all boundary commissions, ruefully reported to David Hunter Miller that Wilson had agreed to Lloyd George's proposition that Danzig was not to go to Poland. Neither was it to be joined to East Prussia. "It must be either free, or international, or independent." Meantime, Mezes was to work out the details with Sir Eyre Crowe of the British delegation and he was very anxious that Miller should join him. The latter at once suggested to Isaiah Bowman, actual executive chief of the *Inquiry,* and American representative on the Polish Commission, that he work on a map which was to rescue as much of the Polish Commission's report as was consistent with Wilson's commitment to Lloyd George.[31]

3 : *The Battle of Memoranda*

The last few days of March and the first week or ten days of April proved the most critical period of the Peace Conference. There was no meeting of the League of Nations Commission during that entire time. Wilson was confined to his bed with a severe attack of influenza from April 3 to April 8, and on the morning of April 7 cabled for the *George Washington* to come to Brest in anticipation of a possible break-up of the Conference. There were scarcely any negotiations of a serious sort, merely obstruction, delay, and polemics.

After the Supreme Council session of March 22, Lloyd George retired to Fontainebleau with several of his advisers to consider the whole problem of the kind of treaty which was likely to emerge from the hurly-burly of this period. The fruit of his deliberations was a statesmanlike document, entitled "Some Considerations for the Peace Conference before They Finally Draft Their Terms," dated March 25, 1919.[32]

In substance, it was an appeal to France for moderation of its traditional policy of disrupting and dismembering the German Reich, in the interest of a lasting peace and a European organization secure against Bolshevism. Specifically, it attacked French proposals in the Saar, the Rhineland, and in Poland, as unwarranted and dangerous violations of the principle of nationality likely to result in future wars. It played principally on the present danger of Bolshevism, reciting the news of Bela Kun in Hungary and the continued activities of the Spartacists in Germany, and predicting that the whole of eastern Europe would be swept into the orbit of Bolshevism.

The greatest danger that I see in the present situation is that Germany may throw in her lot with Bolshevism and place her resources, her brains, her vast organizing power at the disposal of the revolutionary fanatics whose dream it is to conquer the world for Bolshevism by force of arms.[33]

The sole weakness of this statesmanlike appeal lay in the fact that its author was not a statesman but a politician. It was only a day or so later that Lloyd George attempted to blackmail the American Delegation into a naval agreement by blocking the Monroe Doctrine amendment to the League Covenant, and within ten days, he abandoned his own principles entirely in the Reparation settlement which proved to be the worst feature of the Treaty of Versailles. Ultimately, Lloyd George could manage to be statesmanlike only where his conception of British interests and his own political commitments allowed—in other words, at other people's expense. Lloyd George was perfectly honest with himself, if not with others. On March 30, he said to Lord Riddell:

The truth is we have got our way . . . the German navy has been handed over, German merchant shipping has been handed over, and the German colonies given up. One of our chief trade competitors has been crippled and our Allies are about to become her biggest creditors. That is no small achievement. In addition we have destroyed the menace to our Indian possessions. Of course the French may say, in effect, "Now you have got all you want you are anxious to secure a speedy peace on terms that will satisfy the Germans and prevent them from declining to ratify the points which Great Britain has secured already!" That is not

185

true. Our aim is to secure a peace that will last, but from the French point of view there is a good deal to be said. That is one of our difficulties.[34]

And that is exactly what the French did say in their official reply of March 31, even after Clemenceau had toned down the truculence which Tardieu injected into the original draft. With excellent logic and perfect courtesy, the "General Observations on Mr. Lloyd George's Note of March 26th" demonstrated that a policy of appeasement could not be limited to Germany's European interests. Germany had been a World Power and "if it is necessary to appease her she should be offered colonial satisfaction, naval satisfaction, or satisfaction with regard to her commercial expansion." Lloyd George had taken no account of this aspect of the case. His note assumed that "maritime nations which have not known an invasion" would acquire "total and definitive guarantees" in the acquisition of Germany's navy, mercantile marine, colonies, and foreign markets; yet the note required sacrifices of the continental nations for whom he proposed "partial and temporary solutions."

The French reply reiterated the main points of their policy with respect to German boundaries, and concluded with the warning that if Lloyd George were really anxious to build a barrier against Bolshevism, he must give Poland, Bohemia, and France adequate territorial guarantees. Otherwise, the new states themselves would become a prey to Bolshevism and the only existing barrier between Germany and Bolshevik Russia would be broken down.[35]

The very flippancy of Lloyd George's rejoinder on April 1 betrayed the weakness of his position which he had already confessed to Lord Riddell. He recited the tangible advantages which were already guaranteed to France and bitterly remarked:

. . . if my proposals seem to M. Clemenceau to favour Britain, it is because I was, until I read his document, under the delusion that France also attached importance to colonies, to ships, to compensation, to disarmament, to Syria, and to a British guarantee to stand by France with all her strength if she were attacked. I regret my error, and shall be careful not to repeat it.

Moreover, in his original memorandum Lloyd George had offered to support French claims to a portion of Saar territory which had been part of France from 1792 to 1815 but, since "M. Clemenceau treats this suggestion as further proof of British selfishness," he promptly withdrew the offer.[36]

The bitter debate did not break, but intensified, the deadlock and, while the paper warfare was going on, Lloyd George and Clemenceau met face to face. The former repeated his objections to incorporating Danzig in Poland as equivalent to the creation of a new Alsace-Lorraine, and Clemenceau said, "If you don't give me what I want, I can't meet my people. I shall have to resign." Lloyd George told him that Wilson was supporting the British stand and that it was high time that he explained British and American views to the French press.[37]

By April 5, Wilson and Lloyd George were in agreement that the city and area of Danzig was to become a free city with full local autonomy under a League of Nations commissioner, connected with Poland by customs union and port facilities, and by Polish control of Danzig's foreign relations.[38] Though it is impossible to say precisely when Clemenceau yielded to Anglo-American pressure, there is no indication that any of the major controversies were settled before April 10,[39] and the Danzig settlement was probably even later than that. The American legal experts completed a draft of the Danzig articles on April 16, which must mean that by that time Clemenceau had accepted Anglo-American views in principle, and after technical alterations in the draft, the Supreme Council accepted it on April 22.[40]

The final arrangements were a profound modification of the Polish Commission's recommendations, and a very considerable check to the French policy of dismembering Germany. The Commission itself had recommended a plebiscite for the area of Allenstein in the southern section of East Prussia. Lloyd George, with Wilson's support, had now achieved a plebiscite for the region of Marienwerder as well, and though separating Danzig from the German Reich, had secured recognition of its racial character through arrangements for local autonomy in combination with all necessary guarantees for Poland's fundamental economic interests. Under the diplomatic conditions which prevailed at Paris, it is hard to see how more could have been accomplished. One commentator asserted that Clemenceau and the Poles were working to deprive East Prussia of Allenstein, Marienwerder, and Danzig in order to submerge the remnant in a Polish sea so that its complete absorption in the Polish state would be only a matter of time.[41] If that was their intent, Lloyd George and Wilson prevented it far more effectively than they did the so-called "Fourth and Final Partition of Poland" in September 1939.

The plebiscites of March 1920 eventually awarded the districts of Allenstein and Marienwerder to Germany, but German efforts to modify the Danzig arrangements were of no avail. The German Delegation said it "must reject the intended national oppression of Danzig and must demand that Danzig . . . remain with the German Empire," but they were informed that the separation was essential "for that free and secure access to the sea which Germany has promised to concede." [42]

German protests against the award of Upper Silesia to Poland were more effective because they were based on arguments so strong that they immediately convinced Lloyd George, and ultimately President Wilson, that there must be a plebiscite for this area as well. This province in the southeastern corner of the German Empire had not been part of the Polish state for four hundred years. Agricultural in the west, its eastern section had been industrially developed by German capital to the point where it provided 23 per cent of Germany's entire coal supply, 80 per cent of her zinc supply, and a large part of her iron production.[48] The Polish Commission having accepted Dmowski's assertion that the province was indisputably Polish in population, awarded it without more ado to Poland, and not even Lloyd George questioned the decision. He said later, "Which of us had thought of Upper Silesia until the reports of our experts had brought it to our notice?" [44] There is no sign that anyone paid any attention to the question even then.

The "German Observations" on the treaty late in May singled out the Upper Silesia settlement for its most vigorous attack on racial, historical, and economic grounds, warning the Allies that the award to Poland would lessen Germany's ability to pay Reparation and was certain to awaken an irredentist spirit.[45] This, with certain other German complaints, created consternation in the British delegation, partly because of the inherent justice of the German charges that the treaty violated the Fourteen Points, and also from fear that the German Government would refuse to sign the treaty.

Unfortunately, Lloyd George's behavior had been such as to convince Wilson that his present concern for justice was prompted more by fear than by righteousness. As Wilson bitterly complained to the entire American Delegation, it made him "sick and tired to have the same individual who had insisted on irrational and unjust provisions in the treaty now propose modifications just because he was in a "funk" about Germany's signing the treaty. Wilson agreed, however, to support modifications where he could be convinced that his principles had been violated, and it did not take long to convince him that Upper Silesia was a case in point.[46]

Again he had to contend with his own experts, chiefly Professor Lord, who to the very end resisted the proposal of a plebiscite, and once more House, despite his loss of influence with Wilson by this time, tended to take the French view of the case. As usual the French showed great reluctance to diminish Polish territory or to concede anything to Germany. They complained of Lloyd George's inveterate habit of being statesmanlike at other people's expense. All the modifications of the treaty which he proposed were at the expense of the continental countries, chiefly France, and "England proposed nothing about ships and colonies." [47] Clemenceau admitted that there could be desirable rectifications of frontier, but protested strongly against any serious weakening of Poland, which he regarded as a barrier to German expansion toward the east. Yet, in the end, the proposal of a plebiscite proved very difficult to resist.

On June 2, after consultation with the entire British Empire delegation, Lloyd George made his formal proposal and, on June 3, Wilson referred this, together with Lloyd George's other proposals, to a plenary session of the American Delegation. Wilson showed uncertainty in his own mind by the questions he put to Professor Lord, who resolutely insisted on the essentially Polish character of Upper Silesia:

The President: Creating a state out of Polish population in some places like Upper Silesia which never constituted a part of ancient Poland, isn't that right, Dr. Lord?

Dr. Lord: Not entirely, Mr. President. The German memoran-

190

dum is an extremely fallacious article in its historical data. It states repeatedly that Upper Silesia belonged to Germany for 750 years, which is not at all true. Upper Silesia was Polish from the beginning; was Polish for several centuries.

The President: You mean it was part of the Polish state, or only Polish in population?

Dr. Lord: Part of a Polish state, and it resulted in there being a Polish population. It passed from Poland to Bohemia sometime in 1500; from Bohemia it passed to Austria in 1600, and it passed to the Germans in 1700; so it belonged to the German state, to the Germans, about 200 years.

Mr. Lamont: It has not belonged to Poland for 400 years.[48]

Despite his insistence on the Polish character of the province, Professor Lord was flatly opposed to a plebiscite to test the accuracy of his assertion. He was bound to claim that a fair and free plebiscite would establish the Polish character of the area, but he denied the possibility of a really free vote under the social and economic conditions which then prevailed in Upper Silesia, and his analysis of those conditions was convincing. There was a tremendous concentration of landed estates in the hands of a few German families like the Hohenlohe and Von Pless, and the great industries of the region were controlled by German capital. He stated: "It means that the Polish population is economically, without a doubt, in great dependence upon German landowners and capitalists, and . . . it is extremely difficult for them to vote as they please without ruining their chances of a livelihood" [49]

Wilson showed the effect of Lord's argument that afternoon when he attended the session of the Supreme Council. When Lloyd George asserted the possibility of an accurate plebiscite if only German officials and troops were removed from Upper Silesia, Wilson was doubtful if even under those conditions a free vote could be taken, because Lord had informed him that the people were entirely dominated by a small group of German magnates. Lloyd George cited Reichstag election statistics of the pre-war period to prove that Polish deputies had been elected in the district, even a majority in 1907. He then appealed to Wilson's principle of self-determination, and asked, "Why plebiscites in Allenstein, Schleswig, Klagenfurt, but not Silesia?" Wilson only wanted to be sure that it was genuine self-determination and inquired what arrangements Lloyd George proposed to ensure a free vote. The latter suggested the removal of both German and Polish officials and the substitution of Allied police, but unwisely expressed his fear that "the refusal of a plebiscite will cause the renewal of war because Germany is greatly concerned about Silesia," which revived Wilson's suspicion that Lloyd George was actuated more by that fear than by a sense of justice. He said at once that he was less concerned about the German attitude than with ensuring that the treaty itself was just and sound.

Yet, even when Clemenceau reiterated Lord's argument about the impossibility of a free plebiscite, Wilson accepted the idea of a plebiscite in principle. He proposed that Germany be told that a plebiscite would be held under the strictest guarantees and safeguards to be laid down by an international commission. If Germany rejects the conditions, "there will be no plebiscite." [50] The following day, the Polish commission was instructed to prepare draft articles for the plebiscite.

It was the Polish premier, Paderewski, who clinched the argument. He was invited to present his views in the Supreme Council on June 5, and he admitted at the very outset that the western zone of Upper Silesia would probably vote German, as a result of the influence of the clergy, which supported that of the landowners. He confessed that there was very little racial consciousness among the Polish peasantry of the agricultural area in the west and, for this very reason, he opposed a plebiscite because, if Poland secured only the industrial area of the east, it would be too close to the German frontier to be secure. The treaty, as originally drafted, awarded the whole area to Poland, and this was a promise to Poland. A change now would compel Paderewski's resignation and the Polish people would lose faith in the Allies. Lloyd George, in an angry outburst, accused the Poles of being more imperialistic than the Great Powers in their persistent efforts to impose their rule on unwilling aliens. The case for a plebiscite was now even stronger.[51]

The Polish Commission was not ready to present its draft articles to the Supreme Council until June 11 and its members entered the meeting after a brief discussion between Lloyd George, Clemenceau, and Wilson. Clemenceau was still opposed, "but yielded to be in agreement with his colleagues," and even Wilson still had misgivings. The experts themselves were opposed in principle and agreed to formulate details only under direct orders from the Council.

When Clemenceau asked Lloyd George if he would like to hear the Commission, the latter replied, "This Commission is very partial to Poland. I do not wish to discuss Poland with it." Clemenceau reminded him that the Supreme Council had already agreed in principle on the plebiscite, despite his own opposition to the idea, and that it was essential to hear the Commission on the details of application. After the experts had explained the difficulties of ensuring a free vote and the precautions they had embodied in their articles, Wilson proposed the adoption of their provisions for a plebiscite to be held in one or two years, and Clemenceau, still doubting the wisdom of the decision, agreed to it.[52]

Colonel House recorded his disappointment at Wilson's decision: "I am afraid it cannot be honestly carried out."[53] Wilson's announcement of the decision to the Polish delegates on June 14 is significant for two reasons. It shows the

193

influence of Paderewski's admission on Wilson's own attitude, and it refutes later German charges that the treaty never envisaged the partition of Upper Silesia. Wilson reminded the Poles that Paderewski himself had distinguished between the industrial zone of the east and the agricultural zone of the west, predicting a certain Polish vote in the east while uncertain of the result in the west. For that very reason, the vote would be by communes and the fate of each individual commune determined by the local vote within it, which clearly provided for ultimate division of the area. Poland was assured of an adequate interval for the elimination of undue German influence, and the plebiscite would be conducted under the impartial guard of an Allied military force.[54]

The last promise was honored in the breach so far as Germany was concerned. Allied troops were present during the plebiscite in May 1921, but they were not impartial. The Polish free-booter, Korfanty, roamed the area with his irregular forces and the visible partisanship of the French troops for their Polish allies prevented any attempts to suppress them. Yet the total vote for Upper Silesia showed a three to two majority for Germany, and when the area was divided in accordance with local majorities, the western agricultural section allotted to Germany, the smaller but wealthier industrial east to Poland, the German Government charged a violation of the treaty. It is one of the many ironies of the Treaty of Versailles that its deliberate provision for dividing Upper Silesia was inserted by Lloyd George and Wilson as a defense of German interests against Polish rapacity.[55]

★ 8 ★

DISMEMBERMENT OF GERMANY—
II THE WEST

1 : *"Today We Have the Rhine"*

THE ARMISTICE TERMS of November 11, 1918, established Allied military occupation in the German Rhine provinces of the left bank and at four bridgeheads on the right bank, presumably as an interim measure to be abandoned when peace was declared. The English General Haig was opposed to such extensive occupation of German territory even as an armistice measure, on the theory that the Allies should occupy only those territories which they had agreed to free from German oppression—Belgium, Luxembourg, Alsace-Lorraine—but the Foch view prevailed when Clemenceau insisted that the French army must have *satisfaction d'honneur* for the long German occupation of French soil. Otherwise, said Clemenceau, he could not maintain himself in the Chamber of Deputies, and he would give his word of honor that France would withdraw *after peace conditions had been fulfilled.*[1]

To convert the temporary occupation of the Rhine frontier into a permanent military barrier against Germany became the abiding aim of the French Delegation at the Peace

Conference. The Rhineland policy was the very core and center of the French program of tangible military guarantees and to it they subordinated every other consideration. Clemenceau had confessed that the underlying purpose of Bourgeois' military amendments to the League Covenant was to provide additional argument and bargaining power for the achievement of the Rhineland program. The same consideration explains French policy toward the disarmament of Germany, the unwillingness to consider the military terms of the treaty apart from the territorial settlement, and the attempts to rush both sets of terms to completion during Wilson's absence. The most characteristic feature of French policy in that period was the persistent efforts of Foch and Tardieu to commit Lord Balfour and Colonel House to the French proposals in the Rhineland.

Those proposals contained two main elements, one political, the other military: political separation of the entire left bank of the Rhine from Germany and the establishment there of autonomous republics, or of a single republic; and Allied military occupation of the area of the left bank and of bridgeheads on the right bank for an indefinite period. Foch had even achieved a higher synthesis of the political and military elements of this program when he suggested that the male population of this purely German area be made liable to conscript service within the French military establishment, but that idea did not survive Foch's discouraging interview with Lloyd George in London on the evening of November 30, 1918, and subsequent editions of his memorandum omitted it.[2]

The historical and strategic arguments employed by Foch bear a striking similarity to those used by Von Moltke and Bismarck for Germany's seizure of Alsace-Lorraine in 1871. Control of the Alsace valley meant control of the Upper Rhine and access to the river Main which divides north from

196

south Germany, and this was the historic route of French invasion employed to keep Germany dismembered and helpless. Obviously, in order to promote national unity, a united Germany must be secure from this strategic threat and the south German states must be assured of a peaceful existence within the German Empire. So the creation of the German Empire was consecrated and fortified by the annexation of Alsace-Lorraine. France was now assured of the retrocession of Alsace-Lorraine, but German armies had twice, within a half-century, invaded France from the lower Rhine. France was now on the defensive, the victim of a permanent inferiority of man-power in the face of the German menace, and the sole guarantee of defense was the Rhine barrier from Alsace north to the Dutch border.[3]

There was no lack of sympathy for the French case in either the British or the American delegations and there was complete readiness to provide all essential guarantees for French security. Both Wilson and Lloyd George were willing to go to what they considered dangerous lengths in the disarmament of Germany, despite the curious apathy of the French on this particular subject. And, from the very beginning, they were willing to concede substantial guarantees to the French in the Rhineland. They proposed as an essential part of the military terms that the entire left bank of the Rhine and a 50-kilometre zone on the right bank be demilitarized, free of all fortifications, devoid of armed forces.[4]

At a later stage, Wilson and Lloyd George agreed, on behalf of their respective governments, to guarantee those provisions with military force if necessary and, although that guarantee never materialized, the Locarno treaties provided an even better substitute by binding the German Government, as well as the French, British, Belgian, and Italian governments, to maintain the demilitarized zone. When Hitler himself accepted Locarno as valid, and subsequently

197

denounced the pact, he provided the French and British with the soundest legal and moral case for action—and we now know that action would have been effective without a struggle. That the two governments declined to act—with consequences disastrous to themselves—is no criticism of the Rhineland provisions which they refused to enforce. Subsequent history has demonstrated, not disproved, the adequacy of those provisions for French security.

But Clemenceau, Tardieu, and Foch would be content with nothing less than the creation of a new Alsace-Lorraine, and Wilson and Lloyd George flatly opposed the French program in both its political and its military aspects. They would restrain German sovereignty in the Rhineland area from the exercise of military rights, but they would not eliminate that sovereignty entirely, nor would they permit France to establish her military domination there in place of the German.

Foch produced his second memorandum on January 10, 1919, at the very beginning of the Peace Conference. It abandoned the notion of conscripting German residents of the Rhineland for service with French armies, it eschewed all ideas of annexation, and it emphasized Wilson's League of Nations principle as the basis of the French program. In its new version, the French plan for dismembering Germany appeared as the only "sufficient base and particular force" for a thriving League of democratic states in the west. By granting the natural frontier of the Rhine to be held by the forces of the great coalition of democratic states, security would follow, neutrals and former enemies would join the League, and disarmament would be achieved. "Today we have the Rhine!" Stripped of League of Nations verbiage, the two essential features of French policy emerged in the insistence on separate republics in the Rhineland in customs

198

union with France, and indefinite military occupation of the area by Allied forces.[5]

Clemenceau well knew the opposition such proposals would encounter from both British and American delegations and took great pains to avoid rousing popular French sentiment about them. Throughout the Conference, he sent daily instructions to the Paris Press Bureau which amounted to official censorship, and the first Foch memorandum of November 27 had been suppressed entirely by this means.[6] He maintained the same official silence during the early stages of the Conference until Wilson left Paris on February 14, and during that period prepared the way for his later campaign by instructing Bourgeois to press the French military amendments in the League of Nations Commission, while he devoted his attention to preventing separate decision on military terms apart from the territorial settlement.

2 : Colonel House and Self-Determination

Colonel House seemed, at first, just as hostile to the French view as either Wilson or Lloyd George. He and Balfour discussed the problem at length shortly before Wilson's departure from Paris, and he charged that the French did not seem to realize that "to establish a Rhenish Republic against the will of the people was contrary to the principle of self-determination." While he and Balfour expressed great sympathy for French anxieties, they both felt that the only hope for France lay in a strong League of Nations and fair treatment for Germany and, with a touch of prophecy, House added: "If after the establishment of a League of Nations we are so stupid as to let Germany train and arm a large army and again become a menace to the world, we would deserve the fate of our folly."[7]

It was no accident that within a few days of Wilson's departure, the French shifted from obstruction and delay to hectic haste for immediate decision on all the major terms of peace—military, territorial, and financial. Lloyd George also left Paris, and his substitute, Balfour, was quite as anxious as Colonel House to speed up the work of the Conference in order to halt the rapid disintegration of Europe. They had Wilson's permission to settle the military terms in his absence, as well as to expedite the work of the expert commissions so that final reports would be ready for Wilson's decision when he returned. And the French worked with persistence and skill to determine that decision before his return.

Foch first tried the good offices of his English colleague, General French, who gave to Colonel House a new memorandum which Foch had prepared, and which the Colonel promptly cabled to President Wilson on February 19. Foch argued that at the moment Germany was so weak she would accept any terms which the Allies wished to impose, but since that condition might not last, he proposed immediate decision on the size of the German army, the precise delimitation of German frontiers, and the exact amount of German indemnity. The heart of the document appeared in the statement that "whatever may be the fate of the Rhenish provinces and whatever form of government for these provinces the Allies may decide in favor of, *under no circumstances will the German Empire extend beyond the Rhine.*" That, Foch insisted, "is essential for the security of France, and makes the settlement of the Western frontier a simple matter." [8] Wilson's reply, the following day, is so significant that it must be presented in full:

I have just read the memorandum given you by the Chief of the British General Staff of an interview with Marshal Foch. It seems to me like an attempt to use the good offices of the French [*sic*] to hurry us into an acquiescence in their plans with regard

200

to the Western bank of the Rhine. *Proposition for your consideration and in the light of which I see the matter, in no case accede.* I know I can trust you and our colleagues to withstand such a programme immovably, except of course I am willing to have the strictly military and naval terms promptly decided and presented to the Germans. I am not willing to have anything beyond the military and naval terms [settled] and believe that the Conference of Ten would be going very much beyond its powers to attempt anything of this sort. The determination of the geographic boundaries of Germany involves the fortunes and interests of the other peoples and we should not risk being hurried into a solution arrived at solely from the French official viewpoint. *I beg that you stand steady with regard to everything but the strictly military and naval terms until I return. Marshal Foch is acting in this matter I am sure under exterior guidance of the most unsafe kind.* Warm thanks for full information you are sending.[9]

The warning was plain and the deep anxiety underlying it apparent, yet whatever the Colonel may have reported to the French about Wilson's attitude, neither Clemenceau nor Tardieu abated their zeal. On February 23, House cabled an account of his conversation with the wounded Clemenceau on February 22. Clemenceau demanded a wholesale peace including the establishment of an independent Austria by forbidding its union with Germany, the award of Danzig to Poland, and the creation of a Rhenish republic:

He is insistent upon the creation of a Rhenish Republic. There will be about four million of Germans aggregated in this way. He desires that this Republic should be exempt from the payment of any indemnity; that they should have no armed force; that everything should be done to make them prosperous and contented so that they will not want to join the German Federation and if they have such a desire they will not be permitted to do so.[10]

Clemenceau's denial of the principle of self-determination where it worked to Germany's advantage in the Rhineland and in Austria was at least frank and outspoken. Tardieu saw

201

a better way of attaining French objectives by supporting the principle of self-determination, and he went to work immediately on both Balfour and Colonel House. The same day that the Colonel cabled Clemenceau's views to Wilson, he had a long talk with Tardieu in Vance McCormick's rooms, and Tardieu explained that France did not intend a permanent separation of the Rhenish provinces. After a period of five, ten, or some other number of years when the League of Nations was a going concern, there would be no objection to the provinces rejoining Germany if their population so decided.

Colonel House swallowed the bait at once, recording in his diary that Tardieu's suggestion relieved the problem "of one of its most objectionable features, since otherwise it would be quite contrary to the policy of self-determination," [11] and the next day he cabled Wilson that "The principle of self-determination would be in this way safeguarded." [12] Shortly after, he adopted as his own solution the proposition that "A buffer state should be created for five years and then the League of Nations should decide whether the buffer state should exercise self-determination or should continue for another five-year period." [13]

Tardieu was no less successful with Balfour. The latter wrote Colonel House on February 25, a letter which has never been quoted:

Since our conversations with Clemenceau and Tardieu I have had two long talks with the latter, and have received from him a written argument upon the subject. This is an able paper and not very long. I strongly recommend its perusal.

My general conclusion from all these sources of information is that while the French are still profoundly impressed by the dangers they and Belgium will run if the Rhine is not made the military frontier of Germany, they are ready to modify their schemes for neutralizing the left bank of the river so as to make them more tolerable to British and American opinion.

To this end they would be ready I think to abandon any plans for *the permanent dismemberment of Germany*. The administrative separation of the German provinces on the West from those on the East, and the occupation by Allied Forces of the Rhine bridges, would be regarded as a temporary measure, justified by military necessity, which would only last so long as Germany remained suspect among the peoples of the world and was not permitted to enter the League of Nations. If when this probationary period came to an end the German-speaking population of the left bank of the Rhine desired that their separation from the rest of Germany should be permanent, that would be another matter to be decided when the time came. For the moment the Associated Powers would only be concerned with securing from German aggression France, Belgium, and the Channel ports until the League had consolidated the civilized world into a peaceful organization of states.[14]

This document makes it entirely clear what Colonel House meant when he recorded in his diary on February 27 that, during a ride and walk with Balfour in the Bois de Boulogne, he and Balfour "practically came to an agreement as to what the United States and Great Britain would do" as to the Rhineland question.[15] While there is no evidence of any formal commitment to the French program, Tardieu had led both men pretty far in the direction of approving French projects "in principle" and as a temporary expedient, and, at least in the case of House, in the face of explicit warning against precisely that course from his chief.

Meantime, Colonel House had received direct from Tardieu the latter's memorandum [16] and cabled Wilson, on February 26, that he would send full particulars later when he had an opportunity to digest it. The Colonel recorded in his diary on March 2 that, after a long talk, he and Tardieu "got nearer together on the question of the Rhenish Republic."[17] On March 7, he cabled Wilson a report of his conference that morning with Lloyd George and Clemenceau. The nature of that report confirms the impression that House was in tentative agreement with Tardieu on the creation of a buffer state in the Rhineland for a limited period, and it caused Wilson renewed alarm:

> The left bank of the Rhine was discussed, but no tentative agreement was reached *because of Clemenceau's very unreasonable attitude. He wants the Rhenish Republics to be perpetually restrained from joining the German Federation. Tardieu tells me he will urge him to modify this view. . . .*[18]

It is clear from this account that in House's view the sole obstacle to agreement was Clemenceau's insistence that the separation of the Rhenish provinces from Germany must be *permanent* and that the Colonel was counting on Tardieu to persuade Clemenceau to be content with a *temporary* separation. Wilson's anxiety that Colonel House was letting him in for embarrassing commitments in defiance of express orders can easily be seen in the reply he sent on March 10 from the *George Washington* on the return trip to Paris:

> *Your cable of March 7th, 11 p.m. just deciphered. Am made a little uneasy by what you say of the left bank of the Rhine.* I hope you will not even provisionally consent to the separation of the Rhenish Provinces from Germany under any arrangement but will reserve the whole matter until my arrival.[19]

Lloyd George proved just as intransigent as Wilson and, however far their respective subordinates, Balfour and House, may have gone in approving French projects, Tardieu was able to make no further progress in the few days remaining before Wilson's return on March 14. The very day of Wilson's message, Clemenceau, Lloyd George, and House appointed a special committee to delineate the boundaries of Germany. The members were Tardieu; the Colonel's brother-in-law, Sidney Mezes; and Lloyd George's secretary, Philip Kerr (the late Lord Lothian, British Ambassador to the United States).[20]

Tardieu reiterated the substance of his earlier proposals—separate Rhenish republics for a period of fifteen to twenty years—then reduced his demand to a ten-year term, "later alluding to (though not accepting) a five-year term," and military occupation of the entire area by Allied troops. He offered to give up military occupation of bridgeheads on the right bank of the Rhine in return for rigid rights of military "inspection," an idea first advanced by Bourgeois to be incorporated in the League Covenant, and Tardieu argued its necessity because of the inadequacies of the Covenant in that respect. Mezes apparently said nothing during the two days of discussion on these proposals, March 11 and 12, and merely took notes on the acrimonious debate between Tardieu and Kerr. Kerr, evidently acting under instruction from Lloyd George, resisted every one of Tardieu's demands.[21] The heat of the discussion can be measured in Tardieu's words: "You say the British public does not understand this question. It is the duty of the British Government to make it understand. Neither did the British understand in 1914 the necessity of conscription. . . . To ask us to give up occupation is like asking England and the United States to sink their fleets. We refuse. We insist upon our demand."[22]

Lloyd George made it clear to Colonel House, during the second day of these conferences, March 12, that he would not tolerate French schemes in the Rhineland, while at the same time he suggested another means of providing France with the security she demanded. ". . . He would also be willing to say that in the event of an invasion, the British would come at once to the rescue, but he was not willing to maintain an army indefinitely at the Bridgeheads of the Rhine and to do all the other things the French desired which we both agree will eventually lead to another war."[23] This proposal of military alliance against the threat of German attack eventually gave an entirely new turn to the Rhineland negotiations, but for the moment there was nothing to do but stand fast until Wilson's return.

This same day Colonel House made ready to meet President Wilson at Brest, where the *George Washington* was due to dock early in the evening of March 13. The circumstances attending his preparations and the exact motives which prompted them are a matter of some mystery. Mrs. Woodrow Wilson has written that neither she nor the President expected to see the Colonel before they reached Paris.[24] What was the reason for his haste? Colonel House's own diary provides no clue,[25] but George Louis Beer's unpublished diary contains useful hints which Mrs. Wilson's memoirs corroborate. Beer records on March 12:

> . . . Dined with Shotwell and Headlam-Morley. Latter in favor of making Danzig a free city and giving Poles Baltic littoral in West Prussia. He seems to think that this solution is a *fait accompli,* i.e., that Poland will reach the Baltic and cut East Prussia off from the rest of Germany. *Colonel House is taking maps with all the proposed new boundaries of Germany to meet Wilson at Brest. If Wilson agrees I fear we shall have a vile settlement. Simonds said to me yesterday that all the things in which anyone was interested were now settled! If the Eastern and Western frontiers are settled on this basis, I am afraid of a fresh outbreak of war shortly.*[26]

Beer undoubtedly had an exaggerated notion about the extent to which matters had actually been settled in Wilson's absence and we know that the Polish boundaries were far from being settled at this time. Yet we do know Colonel House's views about Poland and his record on the Rhineland question had been so equivocal as to bring him two measured warnings from Wilson. Mrs. Wilson's account of what the President said to her about his conference with Colonel House aboard the *George Washington* late in the evening of March 13 confirms the impression that the Colonel had seriously compromised the President's position:

206

. . . House has given away everything I had won before we left Paris. He has compromised on every side, and so I shall have to start all over again and this time it will be harder, as he has given the impression that my delegates are not in sympathy with me. His own explanation of his compromises is that, with a hostile press in the United States expressing disapproval of the League of Nations as a part of the Treaty, he thought it best to yield some other points lest the Conference withdraw its approval altogether. So he has yielded until there is nothing left.[27]

Wilson went to work immediately with Lloyd George to retrieve the Rhineland negotiations from the unfortunate ambiguities which Colonel House and Balfour had permitted to envelop them.

3 : New Guarantees for Old

Lloyd George had suggested to House, on March 12, a way of meeting the French demand for physical guarantees of French security without permitting the dangerous plan of dismembering Germany. He proposed to offer France a British treaty of alliance against aggression. He conferred with Wilson when the latter arrived in Paris on March 14, before their joint interview with Clemenceau, and they evidently decided on an Anglo-American military guarantee of French security as the only way out of the critical impasse. When the Big Three met in the afternoon, Clemenceau encountered united opposition from the other two, but he fought for the full measure of the Rhenish program, asserting that he would not sign any treaty "which fails to give France the guarantees to which she has a right," the removal of Germany from the French frontier, and the permanent establishment of "military surveillance the length of the Rhine." To this, Wilson said:

There will be neither the establishment of an independent state on the left bank, nor occupation of the line of the Rhine, but America and England will sign with France a treaty by which they will engage themselves to support France with all their forces if Germany makes an unprovoked attack on France.

Lloyd George agreed on behalf of Great Britain, the British guarantee to become operative after American ratification of the treaty, and Clemenceau, apparently taken off guard for once, said he would like time "to reflect and consult." [28]

There followed a highly characteristic series of conferences of the French diplomatic general staff, appropriately held at the Ministry of War. In the course of three meetings on March 15 and 16, Clemenceau, Pichon, Loucheur, and Tardieu reconsidered their strategy in the light of the altered situation. They emerged in agreement that it was impossible to refuse the offer of an Anglo-American treaty of guarantee, and that some price must be paid for it by the reduction of French demands in the Rhineland. But they were equally agreed that the proffered treaty was not in itself a satisfactory substitute for the whole of the French program. They might give up the political demand for a separate Rhenish republic; they must still insist on military occupation.[29]

It was left to Tardieu, as usual, to formulate the French argument in a suitable memorandum and on March 17, he produced a masterpiece of precise logic and perfect organization in three main sections. The first restated his own argument for Rhineland guarantees which he had given to Balfour and Colonel House on February 25. Section two he called "Examination of the Suggestion Presented by the Allies," in which he skilfully used the Anglo-American offer as evidence that England and the United States recognized the necessity of physical guarantees. But, while France appreciated the offer as of great value, it was still essentially political, rather than physical, and must be given both precision and physical support.

This led him naturally to the third section, "Possible Bases of Agreement," which deftly applied the Anglo-American guarantee to military occupation of the Rhineland, combined with the favorite French plan for "inspection." For good measure, he suggested that France be permitted to annex the Saar valley up to the 1814 line and to occupy the rest of the coal basin in the valley as reparation for Germany's deliberate destruction of French coal mines at Lens and Valenciennes.[80] Since the Saar question entailed an entirely separate set of negotiations, it can be ignored here. There was sufficient substance in the Rhineland proposals to require the concentrated attention of both Lloyd George and Wilson.

4 : *Occupation, and Inspection Again*

From March 17, the date of Tardieu's memorandum and also of the adoption of the military terms, until March 28, the Peace Conference rapidly approached a crisis, and on March 28 Clemenceau broke up a conference with Wilson by calling him pro-German. Sessions of the League of Nations Commission which had witnessed renewed French amendments had to be suspended entirely from March 26 to April 10. The Polish question led to public recriminations between Lloyd George and the French and to the break-up of the Council of Ten. Nothing contributed more to the atmosphere of deadlock and crisis than the Rhineland and Saar questions and on both these questions Wilson had to fight on two fronts—against a general attitude among the American Delegation that he had gone too far, and against the French feeling that he had not conceded enough. Colonel House was not very helpful on either front, and Wilson's sole ally on the Rhineland question was Lloyd George.

The American Commissioners, Secretary Lansing, Henry White, and General Bliss, were shocked at Wilson's offer of a special treaty of alliance, which they considered "most prejudicial to the whole struction of the League of Nations" and a violation of the President's own principles.[31] When Colonel House first reported the project to the other commissioners on March 20, he seemed to favor it, but he quickly yielded to their view which they insisted that he bring to the President's attention. On March 20, House confessed to doubts about the United States Senate ratifying such an instrument, but argued that in specific terms it promised no more than the general terms of the League Covenant.[32] Since Clemenceau had no faith in the League of Nations, it might be necessary to grant him the special treaty. Yet, on March 27, after another meeting with the commissioners, House adopted their view and argued with Wilson that such a treaty "would be looked upon as a direct blow at the League." When he failed to shake Wilson from the promise he had already given Clemenceau, he again changed his tune and thoroughly commended Wilson's attitude.[33] That Wilson made a serious mistake in not taking all the commissioners into his confidence from the beginning on this problem is clear from Lansing's admission that, although the bitterest critic at the outset, he "later came to look upon it more seriously and to recognize there were some valid reasons for the proposal." [34]

Meantime, the French showed no sympathy for Wilson's difficulty within his own delegation and consistently urged occupation and inspection for the line of the Rhine as the necessary adjunct to the treaty of guarantee. At the same time Bourgeois was pressing familiar French amendments in the League of Nations Commission for the creation of an international general staff and a permanent commission of inspection. For a time, Clemenceau even proposed writing the specific terms of the Anglo-American guarantee into the text of the League Covenant itself.[35]

Clemenceau's efforts to use the good offices of Colonel House in persuading Wilson to grant these additional guarantees were a failure. He sent the Colonel "personally and confidentially" a copy of the Tardieu memorandum of March 17,[36] but by March 21, one of its most drastic proposals had been definitely rejected. It was not difficult to penetrate the disguise of a "Permanent Commission of Inspection," composed of English, American, and French representatives to supervise the demilitarized zone in the Rhineland, particularly since its reports of Germany's violation of any of the military terms of the treaty were to be followed by French military occupation of the bridgeheads of the right bank.[37] The American experts charged with drafting the treaty of guarantee eliminated this provision at once as equivalent to threadbare French proposals of an international general staff which had been rejected again and again in the League of Nations Commission.[38] They disapproved equally of the French plan of military occupation of the Rhineland for a thirty-year period, while quite willing that German military forces be kept 50 kilometres east of the Rhine. They held it fundamentally unsound to permit French troops on the west bank, while keeping German troops 50 kilometres away.[39]

The formula which Wilson and Lloyd George were willing to offer Clemenceau on March 28 was thus deficient in two vital respects from the French point of view and this, in connection with conflict over the Saar, caused a bitter quarrel on that day. The Anglo-American draft forbade German fortifications and armed forces in the Rhineland area to a depth of 50 kilometres on the east of the Rhine, and agreed that Germany's violation of these conditions was to be the occasion for Anglo-American military assistance to France.[40] There was no provision for military occupation of any part of the area by any Allied troops, much less for any commission of inspection. Moreover, the pledge was subject to the executive council of the League of Nations and was to continue only until the League itself was agreed to afford sufficient protection. In addition to his demands for occupation and inspection, Clemenceau insisted that the treaty guarantee remain in force until *all* three signatory powers were agreed that the League afforded sufficient protection, thus providing France with a permanent veto on its abrogation.[41]

On March 29, President Wilson sent for three of his experts and recounted the events of the day before:

> Gentlemen, I am in trouble. . . . The matter is this: the French want the whole left bank of the Rhine. I told M. Clemenceau that I could not consent to such a solution of the problem. He became very much excited. . . . [Clemenceau then demanded the Saar] . . . I do not know whether I shall see M. Clemenceau again. I do not know whether he will return to the meeting this afternoon. In fact, I do not know whether the Peace Conference will continue. M. Clemenceau called me a pro-German and abruptly left the room.[42]

5 : *Deadlock and Compromise*

From that day until about the second week in April, practically all negotiations were at a standstill. Wilson was seriously ill from April 3 to April 8 and, on the morning of April 7, dispatched the order to bring the *George Washington* to Brest. From all sides and from every commission came the same complaints of French obstruction and delay, and during the evenings of April 10 and 11, Bourgeois and Larnaude prolonged the sessions of the League of Nations Commission to register their objections to the Monroe Doctrine amendment as destructive of French security, not because they really objected but because it was "a good thing to bargain with."[43] It is now clear what they were bargaining for—French aims in the Rhineland.

During this period Colonel House sided strongly with the French on most of their demands, saying privately that President Wilson had made a great mistake in coming to Paris at all.[44] He yielded entirely to the French view on Reparation on April 5, during Wilson's illness, and consistently urged Wilson to yield to French demands in the Rhineland and Saar. The President's intimate friend, Ray Stannard Baker, bitterly remarked that "The Colonel would make peace quickly by giving the greedy ones all they want!" and Lloyd George complained directly to Colonel House, "You and I do not agree as well as the President and I agree." [45]

The French ultimately won considerable concessions to their demand for military occupation, and how much their success was due to obstructionist tactics, to an unremitting press campaign against Wilson, or to Colonel House's steady pressure on Wilson, it is impossible to say. All these factors operated in conjunction. It is possible that the French succeeded in making a definite bargain about the Monroe Doctrine amendment, permitting its adoption only after prior assurance that they might occupy the Rhineland, since only three days elapsed after the adoption of the amendment before they secured concessions in the Rhineland.

On April 14, Clemenceau came down in his demands from a thirty-year period of occupation to fifteen, even though he realized that he would have to fight Foch and other generals of the French army. "The President made a wry face over some of it," wrote House, "particularly the three five-year periods of occupation, but he agreed to it all. . . ." House went jubilantly to tell Clemenceau he was the "bearer of good news," and Clemenceau grasped both the Colonel's hands and embraced him.[46] When House then complained of French press attacks as endangering Franco-American relations, Clemenceau at once sent for his secretary and gave him orders for the French press. "The effect was magical. All the Parisian papers appeared on the morning of the 16th with the most enthusiastic praise of President Wilson." [47]

This description by Colonel House provides the basis for

Lloyd George's accusation that Wilson's consent to military occupation of the Rhineland was purchased by a French promise to stop press attacks upon him.[48]

Lloyd George held out alone against even the fifteen-year occupation until April 22 and then at last gave a grudging assent, "Very well, I accept." [49] Yet Clemenceau was still afraid of his generals, and he had one more card to play. Republican opposition to Wilson in the United States had become so notorious that Clemenceau had to censor the French press to keep the disturbing news from the French public.[50] There was still no reason why he should not use it to extract additional guarantees, and on April 25 he told Wilson he had no assurance that the Senate would ratify the guarantee treaty. Since France had sacrificed so much of her Rhineland program for the sake of that guarantee, what then became of French security? Wilson agreed that the difficulty was real, but it raised a "delicate question." By April 29, he had agreed that the date of evacuation might be delayed at the end of fifteen years if by that time guarantees against unprovoked aggression by Germany were not sufficient; in other words, if the guarantee treaty failed of adoption in the United States Senate.[51] Since the Reparation chapter of the Treaty of Versailles already provided for delay of evacuation, or for reoccupation as a means of enforcing Germany's financial obligations, Clemenceau was well armed to face his inevitable struggle with Marshal Foch.[52]

6 : *The Conscience of Marshal Foch*

A diplomat has to negotiate, but a general may indulge the luxury of hard-and-fast principles, and Marshal Foch held inexorably to the full measure of Rhineland guarantees. On March 31, at the very height of crisis, he produced his third memorandum to the text; "All alternatives to the Rhine as a frontier are insufficient," [53] and throughout the period of compromise, during the last two weeks in April, he remained incorrigible.

By mid-April, the chief delegates were sufficiently near agreement on all important questions affecting Germany to decide on an invitation to German representatives to present themselves at Paris later in the month. In default of regular diplomatic channels of communication, Marshal Foch was to transmit the formal convocation to Germany through his subordinate, General Nudant, President of the Armistice Commission. This he flatly declined to do on April 17, and the following day the *Matin* published an article inspired by Foch and proofread by one of his own officers, attacking the conditions of peace for their failure to provide France with adequate guarantees of security in the Rhineland. Clemenceau was able to prevent reproduction in the French press of an interview to the same effect which appeared simultaneously in the *Daily Mail*, but echoes of Foch's attack reverberated in the lobbies of the French parliament, and Senator Paul Doumer—later President of the French Republic—supported by thirty-eight of his colleages, proposed a formal resolution requiring that the Peace Treaty incorporate all "the military guarantees recommended by the Inter-Allied High Command" i.e., by Marshal Foch. The intervention of the French Foreign Minister Pichon prevented a repudiation of Clemenceau's commitments to President Wilson and Lloyd George,[54] but Marshal Foch remained to be dealt with.

Lloyd George and Wilson told Clemenceau that they had willingly placed their armies under the supreme command of the Marshal, for whom they had the "highest admiration and the deepest gratitude," but he had now become an obstacle to the decision of governments, and that they could not tolerate. Clemenceau personally intervened, himself dispatched the necessary order to General Nudant, and took Marshal Foch to task. The latter at first denied all knowledge of the press articles until confronted with the name of his own staff officer who had corrected proof. Foch was then silent and Clemenceau said, "Come, you are sorry for all that, aren't you?" to which the Marshal replied, "I regret it with all my heart." When Clemenceau then warned him that he was letting himself be used by reactionary French papers and politicians, Foch said, "All right, I will call off my dogs of war." On April 20, Clemenceau reported to Wilson and Lloyd George that all was well and that the Marshal was sorry.[55]

But Foch had an inflexible conscience that would not let himself or others alone. The President of France, Poincaré, was not merely as ardent a militarist as Foch but a president who did not hesitate to overstep the bounds of political neutrality imposed on the presidency by French constitutional law. There was a slight atmosphere of intrigue about Poincaré's notification to Clemenceau that the Marshal would like to be heard in a special meeting of the French Cabinet, presided over by Poincaré. Clemenceau, nevertheless, consented to such a meeting, to be held on April 25. Foch brought General Weygand, who distributed the Foch memoranda of January 10 and March 31 to the ministers present, but at the outset Clemenceau asserted his constitutional rights against both General Weygand and Poincaré. He informed the generals that they might speak as freely as they liked, but warned them that the decision rested with the Council of Ministers. Then turning to Poincaré, he said:

The Council of Ministers will deliberate alone. I shall withdraw if discussion should be opened with participation by persons on whom the Constitution has not conferred the right to deliberate with the government and who are present only in consultative capacity.

216

Foch had his say and was apparently disappointed in his hope that Poincaré and certain of the ministers on whom he had counted would rally to his support. When Foch and some others had retired, Clemenceau dominated the session with an eloquent speech about his difficult negotiations with Lloyd George and Wilson. He stressed the value of the Anglo-American treaty of guarantee, and particularly of the rights of military occupation which he had won. He concluded his speech with a direct and moving appeal to Poincaré which revealed the very essence of French policy:

M. le Président, you are much younger than I. In fifteen years I shall be no longer. In fifteen years the Germans will not have executed all the clauses of the treaty, and in fifteen years if you do me the honor to come to my tomb, you may say to me, I am convinced, "We are on the Rhine, and we stay there." [56]

Unanimous approval of the Cabinet greeted Clemenceau's words, yet it is a curious commentary on the prediction they contained that France voluntarily relinquished military occupation in the Rhineland after only ten years, five years less than the treaty allowed.

Marshal Foch had one final opportunity to protest against Clemenceau's sacrifice of French security. He rose in the plenary session of May 6, which was to register merely formal approval of treaty terms, in order to proclaim the complete inadequacy of the Rhineland provisions. The fifteen-year military occupation he described as worthless in terms both of the area to be occupied and of the time limit for occupation. He must have the Rhine passage—the bridgeheads of the right bank—at least until all indemnities were paid, not less than thirty years. Clemenceau confronted him in a fury and asked why he chose to make such a scene, and the Marshal calmly replied that it was to give his conscience ease.

When the heads of governments met that evening in

Pichon's room to consider the Foch demands, they quickly agreed that he had not made a case for reconsideration. Lloyd George's colleague, Bonar Law, remarked that if a British general had behaved like Foch, he would lose his post in five minutes, to which Clemenceau replied, "You know my opinion. No matter how much I regret the attitude of the Marshal, we cannot forget that he led our soldiers to victory." [57]

7 : Federalism for Germany and Separatism in the Rhineland

The final failure of French policy to achieve an actual dismemberment of Germany's Rhine provinces through treaty provisions coincided with efforts to disrupt the German state in other ways. Most of these efforts were an attempt to use the federal structure of the German state as a disintegrating principle, and there were actual plans at the time of the armistice to decentralize Germany into the loosest form of confederation, composed of from six to eight separate states. This was undoubtedly the meaning of the French advocacy of "Federalism" in Germany as an essential part of their Peace Conference program late in November 1918,[58] and when that plan was quietly ignored, French delegates sought other less direct means of achieving the same end.

During the period when the Allied blockade of Germany still continued, Pichon proposed, on March 27, that the Allies send food direct to Bavaria in order "to diminish Prussian influence," and Secretary Lansing promptly replied that here was a fundamental question of policy. "Did we want to separate Bavaria from the rest of Germany?" The Supreme Economic Council blocked that effort by means of its food contracts with the central government of Germany,[59] but in one form or another, the French delegation continued its efforts. Clemenceau remarked concerning the status of East Prussia, "The more separate and independent republics were established in Germany the better he would be pleased." [60]

One method for achieving that result was for the French Delegation to insist on separate negotiations with each of the federal states of Germany while refusing to deal with any representatives who claimed to speak on behalf of the central government of Germany. Such a course had been advocated in the reactionary press at the time of the armistice,[61] but there was no opportunity to try this device until German representatives presented their credentials early in May 1919. There was all the more reason to attempt it then, because the effort to create a separate Rhenish republic had failed. Immediately after the Cabinet Council of April 25 had supported Clemenceau against Foch on this issue, Jules Cambon, who had attended the meeting, wrote Pichon that France should continue its efforts to detach the Rhineland from Prussia and should recognize the federal states of Germany as independent.[62] He had an opportunity shortly to try his hand as French member of the "Commission of Verification" appointed to examine the credentials of the German delegation.

On May 2 Cambon gave a learned disquisition on German constitutional law to prove that some of the federal states of Germany had retained their sovereign rights in the sphere of foreign relations. Consequently, representatives who presented credentials solely in the name of the German Reich could not legally speak on behalf of these federal states, and France must insist that such states ratify the treaty individually. The argument was highly artificial and rested largely on the special prerogatives accorded to Bavaria in the German Empire. Bavaria, Württemberg, and Baden had

219

separately signed the preliminaries of the peace, as allies of Prussia, at Versailles in February, 1871, but not the Treaty of Frankfort in May of the same year. The federal constitution of that year gave to Bavaria the presidency of the imperial Commission on Foreign Affairs, and a separate treaty of the same period permitted Bavaria to retain the right of "active legation" as a member of the Empire. Bavaria had maintained a legation in Paris, as in Vienna and St. Petersburg, up to 1914, but all this was a very thin wedge for the French thesis and, when it came to juristic arguments, Secretary Lansing was a match for Jules Cambon. Lansing assured Cambon that, in any case, it was useless to present a proposal that the United States was bound to oppose, and Henry White, as the official American representative on the Commission, merely agreed that the whole matter be referred to the drafting committee and thereafter to the Supreme Council.[63]

The report of that committee killed the project and it never got to the Supreme Council. On May 4, it cited the provisions of the new Weimar Republic as evidence that the "full powers presented by the German plenipotentiaries under the signature of the President are of a nature to confer the capacity to negotiate and sign on behalf of the German Reich." Cambon made an effort to get the question out of the unfriendly Commission and before the Supreme Council where Clemenceau could fight for the French proposal, but Henry White insisted that the Commission was competent to settle the matter and that there was no need to bother the Supreme Council, which was occupied with other matters. Cambon made one final attempt to get the Commission to notify the Supreme Council of the larger "political question which it had felt beyond its competence to examine," but when other members supported White he had to record that the Commission "has by majority decided for validation

220

pure and simple of the full powers of the German delegation." [64]

French diplomats had failed all along the line in the campaign for the disintegration of Germany, and it was time for the generals to take matters into their own hands. Anyone who had noted Foch's ringing phrase, "Today we have the Rhine!" and had followed the Marshal's consistent policy of sabotage could have predicted how he would use the actual physical presence of French troops in the Rhineland. Marshal Foch was in close touch with General Mangin, who commanded troops in the French zone of occupation and, by the end of April, mysterious reports of an independence movement in the Rhineland began to reach Paris.

It later developed that General Mangin had been advising political agitators in the area since the middle of April, about the time that Wilson and Clemenceau compromised on a fifteen-year period of occupation. By May 22, French military intrigues came into the open because they required the coöperation of both British and American troops who controlled other zones of occupation in the Rhineland, and on that date General Mangin sent staff officers to negotiate with his British and American colleagues. He asked General Liggett to give free entry into the American zone of occupation to some fifty deputies who had been active on behalf of a separate Rhenish republic in the French zone. Liggett very properly declined the request and telephoned at once to General Pershing, who immediately brought the matter to President Wilson's attention.

A general uprising had been scheduled for May 24, but Clemenceau's loyal response to Wilson's appeal undermined the whole movement and betrayed its artificial character. Clemenceau sent an undersecretary to investigate and report on Mangin's activities. On the basis of the report he sent the General strict orders to observe complete neutrality in all political matters, and he sent to President Wilson copies of both the report and of his order to Mangin. A Rhenish republic was actually proclaimed on June 1 at Aix, Maintz, Speyer, and at Wiesbaden, but it deceived no one and died a natural death without the artificial respiration of French support.[65]

When on June 3 Wilson met the whole American Delegation, he told them that the separatist movement was not genuine and when Colonel House said the recently proclaimed republic was an imposture, the President said, "Yes, I know it is." [66] Some days later, June 9, General Mangin admitted to the British military expert, Colonel Repington, that the Rhineland Republic was his own creation. When the Colonel told Harold Nicolson, the latter pronounced the epitaph on the whole movement, "But how silly!" [67]

It was worse than silly, because it provided Lloyd George with just the argument he needed against a prolonged period of occupation. He had always contended that continued foreign occupation of German soil was certain to provoke incidents leading ultimately to renewed warfare, and he struggled fiercely for the first ten days of June to cut the fifteen-year period to two. Wilson had given his promise and supported Clemenceau, upholding the original provisions for occupation.[68]

Clemenceau at least proved loyal to his bargain by personally renouncing French plans to dismember the Rhineland and by officially restraining French military efforts to sabotage his agreement. He paid for his loyalty with his political life and, in 1922, the former President of the Republic, Poincaré, succeeded to the premiership with a freer hand to pursue the policies he could not achieve while Clemenceau held office. His seizure of the Ruhr valley on the right bank of the Rhine in 1923 stimulated anew the artificial separatist activity in the French zones of military occupation. No other single action contributed as much to both political and economic chaos in post-war Europe. In the instinctive urge to dismember Germany, the official elements of France tend to perpetuate the Bourbon tradition of forgetting nothing and learning nothing.

DISMEMBERMENT OF GERMANY—
III THE SAAR VALLEY

---

1 : *"Clear Violation of the President's Principles"*

THE SAAR BASIN is part of the general Rhineland area just north of the Lorraine border, touching the Grand Duchy of Luxembourg on the west, but to the French mind it was distinguished from the rest of the Rhineland by two special characteristics. Strategically, it was desirable, like the whole district of which it was a part, but historically, about half of it had once been French territory, and economically, it was one of the richest industrial regions in Europe. Before the first World War, its coal mines had produced 17,000,000 tons annually, 8 per cent of the total output of the German Empire. Since invading German armies had deliberately destroyed the delicate machinery in the principal French mines at Lens and Valenciennes during the war, the French had a reasonable claim to recompense from the Saar area, and their claim could be further buttressed by the historic argument that France had the right to regain territory she had possessed from 1793 to 1815.

Annexation of the territory she had been permitted to retain by the preliminary peace of 1814, known as the "frontier of 1814," but wrested from her at Vienna in 1815, would transfer about 250 square miles to France with a population of 355,000 people and about two-thirds of the coal in the entire basin, while extension of French control over the remainder of the mining and industrial region would double this area.[1] The French were content to claim direct annexation of Saar territory up to the 1814 line with economic control of the remainder. France had been promised restitution of Alsace-Lorraine by President Wilson's Fourteen Points; why not the Saar as well? "We are entitled to the same reparation and the same restitution," said Franklin Bouillon on behalf of the Commission of Foreign Affairs in the Chamber of Deputies on December 29, 1918, and only the two Socialist members of the Commission opposed the demand.[2]

In this case, as in the Rhineland, French aims ran counter to the principle of nationality. Whatever the character of the Saar in 1815, by 1919 it was overwhelmingly German, despite the claims of Clemenceau to the contrary. When Walter Lippmann and Frank Cobb drafted their commentary on the Fourteen Points at the end of October, 1918, they seemed to be in no doubt about it:

The status of Alsace-Lorraine was settled by the official statement issued a few days ago. It is to be restored completely to French sovereignty.

Attention is called to the strong current of French opinion which claims "the boundaries of 1814" rather than of 1871. The territory claimed is the Valley of the Saar with its coal fields. No claim on grounds of nationality can be established, but the argument leans on the possibility of taking this territory in lieu of indemnity. It would seem to be a clear violation of the President's proposal.[3]

It soon seemed otherwise to the American experts and to Colonel House, and the British experts were equally impressed by French arguments. All the early reports of British and American experts in January and February agreed as to the German character of the district, but yielded to the French argument that only annexation could provide adequate guarantees that France would get the Saar coal to which she was entitled as reparation. Both British and American reports conceded considerably more than the 1814 line.[4] It was the story of Danzig all over again, the same complicated problem, the same stress on economic arrangements to the disregard of the principle of nationality. Colonel House, who yielded so readily to the experts' arguments on Danzig and to the French arguments on the Rhineland, was not likely to resist the same sort of reasoning when applied by the same people to the Saar question. Shortly after Wilson's return to Paris, he recorded his acceptance of the American experts' view that

in the basin of the Saar a proposal to reëstablish the frontier of 1814, with possible enlargements so as to include secure possession of the adjacent coal fields, may be entertained, irrespective of strategic considerations, as a suitable compensation (with due allowance on the German war indemnity) for the destruction of the French coal mines of Lens and Valenciennes.[5]

2 : *Battle of the Saar—Self-Determination*

It was only when Clemenceau began to lose his battle for the Rhineland that the French Delegation officially put forward their claims to the Saar. During Wilson's absence from Paris, they had expended most of their energy in trying to trap Colonel House into a commitment to a separate Rhenish republic, and they had all but succeeded in spite of Wilson's repeated warnings. Wilson's return turned the tide and, on March 14, he and Lloyd George offered Clemenceau an Anglo-American treaty of alliance as a substitute for the whole of the French Rhineland program. Though he held out inexorably for rights of military occupation, Clemenceau had to yield the political projects which would have placed the whole Rhineland virtually under French control and would have thereby ensured French domination of the Saar. Consequently, when Tardieu on March 17 drafted his general proposals for solution of the whole Rhineland problem, he included the Saar demands as a separate item. Great Britain and the United States were invited to "recognize the French frontier of 1814, and by way of reparation, the right of occupation without annexation of that part of the Saar coal basin not included in this frontier." [6]

The Saar, from that moment, became the subject of separate negotiations, and Tardieu dignified it by a special series of memoranda, because this was the problem which American delegates apparently "least understood." First came the historical argument, neatly blended with the principle of self-determination. The fortress of Saarlouis had been built by Louis XIV and the inhabitants of that city still retained strong French sentiments, according to Tardieu, while the larger part of the Saar region became French between 1792 and 1795, and its seizure at Prussia's behest in 1815 had been strongly condemned by both Metternich and the English as a violation of the wishes of the population. If the population now was largely German, that was the result of "systematic colonization of country conquered by force," which was no excuse for, but an aggravation of, the original offense. Hence, by the principle of "Restitution," France was entitled to the 1814 frontier. On the principle of "Reparation," France must have guarantees for the coal produce of the entire area, and this meant ownership of the mines even outside the 1814 district and a special political régime to permit their exploitation.[7] Tardieu and Loucheur were summoned to the Council of Four to present these views on the morning of that historic day of crisis, March 28.

It is curious that Lloyd George, who fought so strenuously to prevent the transfer of Danzig Germans to Poland, and who joined Wilson in resolute opposition to the separation of Rhineland provinces from Germany, should have been so apathetic about the Saar question. To be sure, he supported Wilson's refusal to permit French annexation of the 1814 area, but he was quite willing to concede ownership of the mines to France, to sever the entire area from Germany, and to permit a political régime which would make it a French protectorate. Similar French projects for the whole Rhineland he had described as the creation of a new "Alsace-Lorraine," yet Tardieu and Loucheur noted at once that Lloyd George did not attach first-rate importance to the Saar question and that their real difficulty would be Wilson, whose "quizzical smile" foreshadowed objections.[8] If Lloyd George led the fight on the Polish Commission report and shared equally with Wilson the honors of the Rhineland battle, it was Wilson alone who fought the French to a standstill on the Saar question.

There was a bitter quarrel between Clemenceau and Wilson, which has been toned down in some of the accounts of this memorable meeting.[9] Wilson first attacked the historic basis for French claims to "restitution" of the 1814 frontier by remarking that one hundred years was a long time ago, and Clemenceau agreed savagely that one hundred years was perhaps a long time in the history of a new country like the United States.[10] When Clemenceau made the preposterous claim that there were 150,000 Frenchmen in the Saar, Wilson then accused him of a deliberate misstatement.[11] Clemenceau countered by accusing Wilson of pro-German sentiments, and the latter inquired, "Then if France does not get what she wishes, she will refuse to act with us? In that event do you wish me to return home?" Clemenceau replied, "I do not wish you to go home, but I intend to do so myself," and abruptly left the President's rooms.[12]

The French board of strategy met that afternoon at the War Office. Clemenceau, Loucheur, and Tardieu agreed that claims to the 1814 line would have to be abandoned in the face of united Anglo-American opposition, but Lloyd George's willingness to grant ownership of the mines to be operated under an autonomous political régime suggested a new strategy to be employed. Wilson himself had acknowledged the justice of the French claim to Saar coal as reparation, while refusing to concede actual ownership of the mines, much less any special political system which would disturb German sovereignty.

Clearly, the historical argument had not worked with Wilson, but the economic argument was a good entering wedge. It must be demonstrated to Wilson that the right to Saar coal necessitated outright ownership of the mines, and that effective operation of the mines required a special political régime to prevent German interference. Finally, the President's own principle of self-determination could be used against him by insisting that whatever French inhabitants there might be in the Saar should have the opportunity to elect French citizenship. Tardieu insisted, "If the Allies believe there are too many Germans in the Saar to permit an immediate reunion with France, France asserts there are too many French to permit continued Prussian domination." [13]

The new Tardieu memorandum which was ready the next day embodied these three elements, but the provisions for "self-determination" were the most ingenious. We have already seen how skilfully Tardieu used that principle to justify the separation of the Rhineland from Germany, but in this instance, he manipulated it in a way that would have ensured a disguised annexation of the Saar to France. He con-

229

ceded at the outset that the majority of the population was German, and although that was due to one hundred years of "germanizing," France was prepared to recognize the fact by giving up all claims to annexation. But there must be an arrangement which would recognize, partially at least, France's "unquestionable claim on a country consecrated French by the will of the inhabitants." The area was to be placed under the protection of the League of Nations, which would grant to France a double mandate. All German and Prussian officials were to be removed, and France was to have full political control of the local administration, including the nomination of mayors and deputy mayors. France was likewise to enjoy rights of military occupation.

Under these two guarantees, the inhabitants of the Saar were to exercise rights of self-determination. Individuals might adopt French citizenship any time during a fifteen-year period and when a majority of citizens of any administrative section had so voted, that area was to be annexed to France after the League of Nations had accepted the decision. At the end of fifteen years, the inhabitants who had not already voted were to be given the opportunity to do so, and *"no demand for reunion with Germany is to be considered before that time."* Tardieu revealed the whole purpose of his scheme in this last provision, which he explained as necessary to undermine the Prussian influence of the past one hundred years, even though he did not phrase it precisely in that way. What he said was that "Prussia had one hundred years in which to consolidate the work of violence" and that he fixed a term of fifteen years "with a view to allowing events to shape themselves and the population to decide justly and freely as to their sovereignty." [14] We know how General Mangin allowed "events to shape themselves" in the Rhineland at a later date, yet Tardieu could write solemnly that this was no breach of self-determination.

It was clear that Wilson would never yield to such logic, despite persistent efforts of the experts and Colonel House to make him modify his position. The Colonel deplored Wilson's obstinacy and, after the row on March 28, he had told Lansing that the President had made a mistake in coming to Paris.[15] On the same day, he "asked the President to bring his position on the French boundary proposition into harmony with the British," warning him against an isolated stand which might justify the charge that the American Delegation was unreasonable. According to the Colonel, Wilson promised to modify his attitude.[16]

On March 29, Clemenceau sent Tardieu to Colonel House, who commissioned Professor Charles Homer Haskins of Harvard to work out a solution with Tardieu. Though House described the basis on which they were to work as an attempt to assure France of unhampered control of coal mines without transferring large German populations to French sovereignty,[17] Haskins wrote Wilson the following day, supporting French arguments for annexation of the 1814 frontier and for the establishment of at least enough French political control in the remainder of the Saar to ensure French operation of the coal mines.[18]

It was all of no use. Wilson, completely isolated within his own delegation, refused all the French political demands. There was to be no tampering with German sovereignty in a German district, no special political régime for any part of the Saar valley. He said to three of his experts that he was "willing to give France any indemnity in kind to which she is entitled. I have no right to hand over to her, people who do not want to go to her, or to give them a special government, even if it is better for them, if they do not want it."[19] He would not even grant outright ownership of the coal mines. There was nothing for the French to do but abandon their schemes for annexation, open or disguised, and to ham-

231

mer away at the one opening the President had given them. He had offered them the coal and, after a meeting on March 30, Tardieu went away to prepare a new memorandum about that.[20]

3 : *Battle of the Saar—Special Political Régime*

On March 31, Tardieu produced a new memorandum which asked only for French ownership of the mines and a special political régime to prevent German interference with their operation. Wilson finally conceded the first point while resolutely refusing the second. Ownership of the mines necessarily implied adequate economic facilities for their exploitation, and Wilson had to agree that an expert commission, composed of Haskins, Tardieu, and Headlam-Morley, should draft the articles to guarantee the necessary freedom from German taxation, full mobility of labor, and proper means of rail and water transport. Since these economic guarantees seemed to impinge upon the legal and political sphere, it was only reasonable that the commission should be authorized at least to inquire into any special political and administrative arrangements which might be required to give full effect to the economic articles.[21] Without consenting in advance to extinction of German sovereignty, since he had announced he would never consent to that, Wilson had widened the opening to French strategy.

The commission did not report for several days, but there was not much doubt about what they would recommend. Haskins had only recently urged the French case for annexation of the 1814 frontier and a special political régime for the rest of the Saar. On April 1, after talking with Clemenceau, Haskins sent Colonel House a proposal that France receive a mandate from the League of Nations to occupy and administer the entire Saar valley for fifteen years, at

232

the end of which there should be a plebiscite.[22] At the same time, Colonel House, having asked the present editor of the London *Times*, Wickham Steed, to persuade Clemenceau to come closer to Wilson, undertook to handle Wilson himself. Neither of these efforts was very successful.

When Steed suggested to Clemenceau that he talk to Wilson, he replied, "Talk to Wilson! How can I talk to a fellow who thinks himself the first man in two thousand years to know anything about peace on earth?"[23] House scarcely fared better, and wrote in his diary on April 2, "The President tried to get me to admit that the solution of our experts . . . was inconsistent with the Fourteen Points. I replied that there were many who thought otherwise."[24] The next day the President took to his bed for a week.

The special commission on the Saar, with the indispensable assistance of French engineers, on April 6 made its report, composed chiefly of detailed economic articles to provide for French operation of the mines. The economic articles were prefaced with the statement:

The undersigned are agreed in thinking that if the following articles, of which the substance appears to be necessary from an economic and social point of view, must be applied without the establishment of a special administrative and political régime, difficulties will inevitably arise.[25]

They did not presume to suggest what the precise character of that régime should be, as outside their terms of reference. That problem could safely be left to the fertile brain of Tardieu.

This period saw the height of French obstruction in every phase of the Peace Conference negotiations. On the morning of April 7, Wilson dispatched the order to the *George Washington* from his sick-room, and the following morning the Supreme Council met without him, to consider the commission's report on the Saar. The case for a special régime having been established, Lloyd George proposed an independent state—of the sort that he had opposed for the Rhineland as a whole—united by customs union with France. The French were disposed to accept such an arrangement as a substitute for their own proposal of French occupation and administration of the Saar under mandate from the League of Nations. Both schemes violated Wilson's principle that German sovereignty must not be disturbed and, consequently, Colonel House could only describe these plans as "very interesting and worthy of close examination," intimating that they might be considered, without definitely accepting either of them. Nevertheless, Tardieu felt that real progress had been made.[26]

When Wilson came to the Supreme Council session that afternoon, he opposed both the proposals which had been made in the morning session. He had read the report of the special commission and realized that he must offer something in the nature of a special political régime. He still insisted that there be no interference with German sovereignty, and he therefore adopted the suggestion of David Hunter Miller in proposing a mixed commission of arbitration to settle all disputes between the French operators of the mines and the local German authorities, throwing in for good measure the offer of a plebiscite at the end of fifteen years. Clemenceau rejected that proposal as quite inadequate, and the deadlock continued.[27]

That evening, the French board of strategy sat again till past midnight at the War Office. Clemenceau, Tardieu, and Loucheur agreed not to yield, and Tardieu that same evening drafted a very able and cogent reply to Wilson. He accepted Wilson's offer of a plebiscite and used it to demonstrate the inadequacy of Wilson's other proposals, pointing out that to leave German officials in undisturbed control of the area for fifteen years was to predetermine the result of the plebiscite. But the most skilful part of the note was the attack on the proposal of an arbitration commission as a device for settling disputes and conflicts, not for preventing them. This he described as a veritable government by litigation, and such a reign of perpetual lawsuits was entirely unacceptable.[28]

Wilson could no longer escape the consequences of his concession of ownership of the coal mines and French logic had led him straight to the necessity of eliminating German sovereignty in the Saar for fifteen years. He would still fight, however, to prevent French sovereignty from filling the vacuum.

4 : *The League Commission*

President Wilson still resisted French proposals on the morning of April 9, while Lloyd George continued to support them as he had done from the beginning, but in the afternoon, Wilson proposed that a neutral administrative commission, appointed by the League of Nations, exercise all sovereign rights in the Saar valley for fifteen years. Tardieu wanted to be sure that German sovereignty would be totally suspended during that period and that the proposed League Commission would exercise the fullest rights of government. Wilson gave the desired assurance on both points and the French accepted this solution in principle, the details to be worked out by the special commission, which went right to work at 5 P.M. and concluded its task at 3 A.M. Its articles were approved by the Supreme Council later that morning, April 10, and after certain minor changes were finally adopted on April 13.[29]

The emphasis of the Saar articles lay in the neutral character of the governing commission. The League of Nations Council was to appoint five members, including one French

235

citizen, one local Saar resident—not a Frenchman, and three other members who were to be neither French nor German. In general the League Council was to supervise closely the administration of its Saar Commission. It was fully expected that an American, Professor Haskins, would be appointed chairman by the League Council, but rejection of the Treaty of Versailles by the United States Senate prevented that appointment, and a Frenchman, M. Rault, became chairman in his place. During the critical period culminating in French occupation of the Ruhr valley and in renewed separatist activity through the Rhineland, the Saar Commission displayed French bias, though not nearly so much as a purely French administration would have done, and during the ensuing period of Locarno, the League Council effectively exerted its authority to extinguish the pro-French character of the administration. A Canadian became chairman of the Commission in 1926, and by 1927, garrisons of French troops had been practically eliminated. From that date until the plebiscite in 1935, the Commission achieved an enviable record of efficiency and impartiality in its administration, and the actual conduct of the plebiscite by a special League commission is rightly regarded as a model of international administration.[30]

The result of the plebiscite, more than 99 per cent German, has inevitably again raised questions about the justice and wisdom of the original extinction of German sovereignty in such an overwhelmingly German district. But, granting the justice of French claims to the coal as reparation—which few will deny—it is hard to see how a sounder solution for this problem, complicated in both principle and practice, could have been devised.

Wilson's opposition to tampering with German sovereignty was laudable, but it was incompatible with rights to reparation which he was one of the first to acknowledge. The all-important issue was to prevent the French Government from achieving extensive political control under the guise of merely extracting coal to which they were entitled, and Wilson's isolated opposition succeeded in that major task. It has been suggested, with some cynicism, that Wilson too easily succumbed to Haskins' argument that the Saar articles would give the League of Nations "something very real and important to do" and consolidate its position in the world.[81] It was a valid argument, and the administration of the Saar stands out as one of the most effective accomplishments of the League.

The Saar question was a special case to be distinguished from the status of the Rhineland area as a whole. It was one thing to apply League of Nations administration to a small district, compactly organized as an economic unit, to guarantee its coal produce to France. The economic and technical argument did not apply to the Rhineland, and, granted that Colonel House seemed to be consistent in advocating similar arrangements for both the Rhineland and the Saar, President Wilson showed proper discrimination in treating them differently.

★ 10 ★

GERMAN INDEMNITIES

1 : *Justice and Common Sense*

Not one of President Wilson's principles had been more clearly defined than the one which was to determine what Germany must pay the Allies, and not one was more definitely violated by the settlement at Paris. Negatively, Wilson had said there were to be no "punitive damages" and positively, he had declared that Germany must repair the destruction she had wrought in occupied areas. The Allies proposed that Germany should make compensation for all damage to civilians and their property and both President Wilson and the German Government accepted that definition. That ruled out the traditional right of the victor to exact "indemnity" to cover the "cost of the war," since the cost of the war could be measured solely in terms of governmental expenditure on armies and their equipment. The Pre-Armistice Agreement admitted only the category of civilian damage.[1] This was the concept of "Reparation" as opposed to "Indemnity."

The moral and legal case for exacting only Reparation from Germany was strengthened by the irrefutable economic argument that any attempt to collect more would plunge Germany and the rest of the world into economic and finan-

238

cial chaos. No one saw more clearly than Lloyd George that a nation can sustain international payments on a large scale only by the export of goods, and he realized, therefore, that in the long run Great Britain could collect large sums from Germany only at the expense of Britain's export trade. Economic self-interest seemed to dictate a just and reasonable settlement.

Unfortunately, neither the French nor the British public was in a mood to be concerned about justice or to be impressed by the arguments of economists. Both nations felt entitled to recover the entire cost of the war which had been imposed upon them, and Lloyd George had no intention of risking his political life for the sake either of his pledges or of financial common sense. In his Bristol speech, December, 1918, he said: ". . . as far as justice is concerned, we have an absolute right to demand the whole cost of the war from Germany. The second point is that we proposed to demand the whole cost of the war." [2] He went on to warn his listeners that it might not be practically possible to collect, and that it would be unwise to attempt full collection if it would injure British trade to do so. His listeners certainly got the impression that Lloyd George had promised to collect the full cost of the war, and his colleague, Bonar Law, raised questions as to the wisdom and honesty of the course he had chosen. He said that President Wilson could legitimately complain that this position violated the Fourteen Points as well as the dictates of common sense. If it turned out, as it probably would on examination, that German capacity for payment would barely cover Reparation, why raise the question of principle now? ". . . It was foolish to quarrel about indemnities." Lloyd George's reply was debonair but not convincing:

. . . unless President Wilson was prepared to pool the whole cost of the war, and for the United States to take its share of the whole, he was not in a position to reject our claims for indemnity.

239

As regards the figure claimed for Reparations, he did not believe that that sum could be obtained.[3]

At least Lloyd George could be counted upon to work practically for a sensible solution, as far as his fear of public opinion would let him, but the French were much less concerned about any practical solution. They wanted all the money that could practically be got, but they were not likely to be scared into relinquishment of exorbitant claims by the specter of Germany's financial and economic ruin. If it was an abiding aim of French policy to dismember Germany and to disrupt her internal political organization, impossible financial demands might serve that purpose, even though they defeated their ostensible object of collecting money for reconstruction. John Foster Dulles, who was in the thick of the fight at Paris concludes:

> It is my personal belief that both the British and French reparation delegates were actuated by an honest desire to collect from Germany, although the French Government may have felt that an overestimate of the economic and financial possibilities would not involve serious consequences for France, since there would then be compensating political advantages.[4]

In any case, the French Delegation openly advocated "integral reparation"—full war costs—with none of the qualifications or misgivings which appeared in Lloyd George's program, and the French Finance Minister, Klotz, inserted an apparently harmless phrase in the Armistice terms on November 2, 1918, to offset the Pre-Armistice Agreement on Reparation and to provide the basis for a French claim to full war costs. Clemenceau insisted that the Armistice make mention of "Reparation for damages," and Klotz suggested the prudent phrase to be added to Article 19 of the Armistice Convention dealing with interim financial demands upon Germany: "With the reservation that any subsequent concessions and claims by the Allies and the United States remain un-affected, the following financial conditions are imposed:"—. Colonel House quite rightly held that the Pre-Armistice Agreement, not the terms of the Armistice Convention, would govern the final terms of peace, and made no objection to the Klotz proposal.[5] The next day—still a month before his own fatal commitments to the British electorate—Lloyd George opposed putting anything into the armistice terms which would lead Germany "to suppose that we want a war indemnity."[6]

2 : The Battle of Words—"War Costs" and "Reparation"

Yet, when the Peace Conference finally got under way, it was Lloyd George who proposed, on January 22, 1919, that an expert commission be appointed to study "reparation and indemnity." Wilson objected to the world "indemnity"—which was struck out—and a commission was appointed to study what the enemy countries ought to pay, what they were capable of paying, and how they were to make payment; ultimately, what guarantees were to be taken to ensure payment.[7] If the American members of the commission assumed that the matter of principle had been settled and that they could confine their attention to working out the practical details of its application, they were much mistaken.

John Foster Dulles, the legal adviser of the American members, bore the brunt of defending the American position against the unanimous demand for war costs on the part of all the delegates of the other states. The battle of principle and of words continued throughout the month of February, with Dulles holding resolutely to the terms of the Pre-Armistice contract precluding war costs against the ingenious arguments of Premier Hughes and Minister Klotz for evading the contract. Klotz tried to argue that the Armistice Convention itself was the true contract governing the terms of peace, and that his own reservation in that Convention with regard to future claims of the Allies now justified the demand for war costs. Dulles simply replied that the Armistice had been negotiated only *after* general terms of peace had been accepted in the Pre-Armistice Agreement; that it was essentially a military instrument of an interim character which could not possibly modify the agreements made by the responsible heads of governments.

Hughes was more difficult, because more intransigent. He argued from the principle of abstract justice that the Allies had the right to recover war costs. He argued that Belgium's right to war costs, arising from the admittedly illegal character of German violation of Belgian neutrality, was logically extended to those powers which had come to the rescue of Belgium. He argued that war costs were a legitimate category of civilian damage, because it is the civilians who pay the taxes and, therefore, the costs of the war. And finally, he shook his finger at the American delegates and said: "Some people in this war have not been so near the fire as we British have and, therefore, being unburned, they have a cold, detached view of the situation." [8]

Under these circumstances, Dulles' irrefutable logic was but little help. The feeling of moral justification for the exaction of war costs was real, and Dulles was disposed to make some concession to the sentiment, provided the Allies would forgo the actual demand. He therefore proposed a formula which would require Germany to admit a moral and theoretical responsibility for the entire cost of the war, while accepting an actual liability for only civilian damage, and this ultimately became the basis for the so-called "War Guilt" clause of the final treaty. But more effective for the immediate future was his demonstration to the French delegates that their proportion of the total German payment would

242

be greater if war costs were excluded, because France had much the biggest bill for civilian damage. The "play of percentages" eventually decided the French to abandon their clamor for war costs but not soon enough to resolve the debate within the commission.[9] Meantime, a message from Wilson had stiffened American resistance.

On February 11, Vance McCormick reported to the American Commissioners, White, Bliss, and Lansing, about the serious difficulties the American delegates were encountering within the commission on reparation. He wanted instruction and he personally favored a strong fight on the basis of the President's principles as "the first real test in the application of the accepted armistice terms. . . ." Lansing thought that adherence to the Fourteen Points was certainly the wisest course, since Germany had accepted them, but he feared that to press the American view too strongly might incur the animosity of England and France. He suggested, therefore, that the American representatives merely present their own claims, state the interpretation on which they were based and "let the different nations fight out the division between themselves."

Lansing's suggestion appears to have been the decision of the Commissioners, despite McCormick's objections. They certainly advised the American delegates not to press their views too strongly on the other delegates.[10] Yet Dulles continued his firm stand on the Pre-Armistice Agreement during the following week, and McCormick again appeared before the Commissioners, on February 18, to report on the struggle. This time the Commissioners agreed that a full report should be made to Wilson by cable, so that they might have his instructions before his return to Paris on March 14.[11]

Wilson's reply was categorical:

I feel that we are bound in honor to decline to agree to the inclusion of war costs in the reparation demanded. The time to think of this was before the conditions of peace were communicated to the enemy originally. We should dissent and dissent publicly, if necessary, not on the ground of the intrinsic injustice of it but on the ground that it is clearly inconsistent with what we deliberately led the enemy to expect and cannot now honorably alter simply because we have the power.[12]

Colonel House was in complete agreement with the President's position and informed him by cable that if the Allies still insisted on war costs, the American delegates should announce their withdrawal from any arrangement which violated the Pre-Armistice Agreement. He thought such an intimation would cause the Allies to "reconsider their position."[13] The American delegates continued their resistance and the commission, deadlocked on the matter of fundamental principle, referred the whole question to the Supreme Council. The Supreme Council, on March 1, in the absence of both Wilson and Lloyd George, agreed to postpone the whole matter until their arrival.[14]

Clemenceau and Lloyd George yielded even before Wilson returned. The French had been convinced by the "play of percentages" that war costs were against their own interests, and Lloyd George was indifferent to principle, so long as he could satisfy his public with large sums. The Council decision of March 10 was apparently a resounding victory for the American Delegation, since both Lloyd George and Clemenceau declared their acceptance of the principle of Reparation, as opposed to Indemnity or war costs. Yet the very terms of their surrender showed that the American victory was largely verbal. Both said they wished large sums to satisfy public opinion. They were quite willing that these sums should be called "Reparation."[15] The French had shown a similar concern with substance rather than with form in their projects for a permanent grand alliance against Germany, which they had no objection to christening a "League of Nations" to please President Wilson. That, they said, would hurt no one. In the same way, the French and British could be counted upon to devise categories of civilian damage which would actually violate the Pre-Armistice Agreement, without doing so literally or verbally.

It remained for the American Delegation to translate their victory of principle and words into concrete reality by devising practical means of limiting Germany's liability to a reasonable interpretation of civilian damage and to a sensible calculation of what Germany could actually afford to pay. The battle of Reparation had only just begun with the definition of the terms upon which it was to be fought out.

3 : German Capacity—The Fixed Sum

In every phase of the work of the Commission and of its sub-committees, the American delegates worked for a definite sum of money which Germany could afford to pay, to be written into the treaty to represent Germany's reparation debt. They worked, in one sub-committee, for an evaluation of civilian damages which would accord with the Pre-Armistice Agreement and would be paid by Germany, without disaster to herself and the rest of the world. In another sub-committee, and outside, they worked for a reasonable estimate of German financial capacity to match the evaluation of damages for which she was liable.

At every point throughout the month of March they encountered the same difficulty—the Lloyd George and Clemenceau commitments to public opinion in their respective countries. Not only did the French and British peoples expect to recover the entire cost of the war; they had earlier been told it was possible. Both Lloyd George and Clemenceau knew better, but they were still determined to collect the largest sums obtainable, and there were both British and French delegates who indulged in the most optimistic calculations as to what Germany could afford to pay. French figures ran as high as $200,000,000,000, while the British "heavenly twins," Lords Cunliffe and Sumner, justified their nickname by the astronomical calculation of $120,000,000,000. Lloyd George himself had once characterized such figures as a "wild and fantastic chimera," but he dared not risk a public debate with the *twins* in view of his own election pledges. The outside limit of the American estimates was $30,000,000,000 and the gap was too wide to be bridged.[16]

Shortly before Wilson's return, Clemenceau, Lloyd George, and Colonel House appointed a special expert committee of reasonable men to see if they could break the deadlock. Mr. Norman Davis, President Wilson's chief financial adviser, met with Sir Edwin S. Montagu, the former British Treasury official and then Secretary of State for India, and with Clemenceau's Minister of Reconstruction, Loucheur. Montagu, like John Maynard Keynes, had a lively sense of economic realities, and was no problem, but Loucheur, though open to reason, was terrified at the political results of his own intelligence. Davis had constantly to ask him to put aside political considerations and to confine his attention to factual economic analysis. On this basis, the three experts reached agreement. They calculated that Germany's total liability for civilian damage probably ran to $30,000,000,000; that Germany could probably pay half that amount in gold within thirty years through liquidation of her foreign properties and by crediting to her the value of her merchant marine and of her properties in ceded territories; and that Germany could probably pay the other half if the Allies were willing to receive it in German currency and they themselves take the responsibility for converting that currency into their own values. Loucheur agreed to this economic analysis of the limitations of German capacity, but warned Davis that if quoted to this effect, he would be forced publicly to deny it.[17]

The committee was summoned to meet Lloyd George, Clemenceau, and Wilson the day after the latter's return to Paris, March 15, and Norman Davis, on account of the nervousness of his colleagues, agreed to act as spokesman. Lloyd George did not like the report. He admitted that it was probably correct, but said it would be very difficult to get the British public to accept the conclusions of the report, especially because Cunliffe and Sumner still held to their astronomical calculations of German capacity for payment.

At the conclusion of the meeting, Lloyd George took Davis aside with Clemenceau, and said to the latter: "There is nothing for us to do but simply tell our people the facts, and that we cannot collect anything like what we had anticipated." Clemenceau reluctantly agreed, and Davis got the impression that there was a tacit understanding that the experts might proceed to work out the details of a settlement along the lines of the report.[18]

Three days later, March 18, the experts were summoned again to the Supreme Council but on this occasion, in the absence of Montagu, Lord Sumner and Keynes took his place. The Americans were startled to hear Sumner advocate sums nearly double the figure of the earlier report which they thought had been accepted as a reasonable estimate. Davis attacked the Sumner figures and Keynes supported Davis but when President Wilson said he thought agreement had been reached in the previous meeting, Lloyd George replied that it was not his understanding.[19] From this time, Davis had to deal with both Lord Sumner and Lord Cunliffe in the expert committee, nor was it much help that Lloyd George promised both Lamont and Davis that he would agree to the earlier American figure provided they "could get Lords Sumner and Cunliffe to agree to this amount, which he would like to have them do for his own protection and justification." [20] There was not the slightest chance of the "heavenly twins" agreeing to such a figure and Lloyd George did not dare lay himself open to their attack by accepting it himself.

All the expert committee could do was to turn in a set of widely variant figures representing the calculations of the American, French, and British experts, respectively.[21] By this time, March 25, as the affairs of the Peace Conference were rapidly approaching a crisis, Lloyd George and Clemenceau had made up their minds that it was unwise to fix a figure in the treaty and, by March 28, the day of actual quarrel between Clemenceau and Wilson, the Supreme Council abandoned the effort.[22]

4 : German Capacity—The Time Limit and Reparation Commission

An alternative method for achieving the American objectives had already appeared. Davis said that "you had either to fix . . . a limitation of years or a maximum of money to be paid." [23] A limitation of years had been assumed from the beginning, in the attempts to calculate a fixed maximum sum, and there was a general disposition to conclude German payments within a generation, from twenty-five to thirty-five years at most. The time limit of thirty years appeared in the expert report which Davis presented before the Supreme Council on March 15, and at the same time, Davis argued the necessity of a Reparation Commission with full discretion "to modify, suspend, extend, and possibly even to cancel, payments that may accrue over a long period of years" (within a thirty-year limit).[24]

His proposals would have provided a double check to keep the reparation settlement within German capacity for payment, first in the original estimate of a maximum sum which Germany could afford to pay within the period stipulated; second, in the powers granted to the Reparation Commission to modify, suspend, extend or even cancel the payments due. When for political reasons Lloyd George and Clemenceau blocked the calculation of a fixed sum to be inserted in the treaty, there was still the possibility of using the Reparation Commission to enforce a time limit on German payments to protect Germany from unreasonable demands. It was a sensible way of dealing with the immediate impasse and it had the great political advantage of offering Lloyd George an escape from his commitments to the English electorate. It was a concrete embodiment of his own earlier plan of laying the whole problem in the lap of an expert commission to deal with on sound financial lines, remote from public excitement and political influences. Naturally, the French delegation would object, but if Lloyd George supported the Americans, sanity might yet prevail.

No one was surprised when the French Finance Minister Klotz opposed the American program. On March 28, the very day of acute crisis over French demands in the Rhineland and the Saar which provoked Clemenceau to accuse Wilson of pro-German sympathy, Klotz seized on the American project of a Reparation Commission and distorted it to serve French purposes. By all means, let there be a Reparation Commission to act as an adding machine in calculating Germany's total bill of damages, and even give it discretion in determining the size of German annuities and the period of years during which these annuities were to be paid.[25] Obviously, the bill of German damages was to be calculated without respect to German capacity for payment simply by adding the claims for damage under specified categories, and the bill must be paid in full, no matter how long that might take. The Reparation Commission would have no authority to reduce the figure of Germany's debt, but solely to prolong the period during which it was to be paid.

The conflict between American and French conceptions of the powers of the Reparation Commission was direct and fundamental, and the issue thus drawn provided one of the chief elements in the general crisis over French demands during the next week or ten days. Its outcome depended on Lloyd George's ultimate position and on American powers of resistance.

5 : "I Don't Give a Damn for Logic"

Lloyd George had said he wanted the largest possible sums, to satisfy English public opinion and his own election pledges. He was willing that these sums be called "Reparation." What was more natural than to devise new and ingenious categories of civilian damage to be "repaired," particularly because, on a strict interpretation of civilian damage, the French share of German payment would far exceed the English share? The English would receive only 20 per cent, the French more than 50 per cent.[26] During the height of the crisis over the powers of the Reparation Commission, Lloyd George injected his demand that pensions and separation allowances be accepted as a category of civilian damage for which Germany must be held liable under the Pre-Armistice Agreement.

Pensions to wounded soldiers and payments to families and relatives dependent on former civilians called up for military service are clearly a government expense incident to the prosecution of war. These expenditures are, therefore, an item of war cost, not of civilian damage, and they cannot be made to fall under any reasonable interpretation of the Pre-Armistice Agreement. The decision to adhere to that agreement and to exclude war costs from the categories of Allied claims likewise excluded demands for pensions and separation allowances. Such demands were not only a violation of the letter of the Pre-Armistice Agreement; they were a much more important violation of its spirit. The very essence of that spirit was that there were to be no "punitive damages," no excessive demands beyond German capacity to meet them, and these new categories would double the German bill.

But Lloyd George had rhetorical devices with which to overcome such cold logic. He could sentimentalize the argument by appeal to humanitarian sentiment, and he had colleagues who were adept in the art. The argument in its simplest terms was that the discharged soldier was originally a civilian, forced to become a soldier by German aggression, suffering injury from that fact, and returning disabled to civilian life. Here, then, was a clear case of injury to a civilian, a sound argument solely on the assumption that he could receive no compensation except by charging it to the German Government; but the Allied governments had already accepted this charge as an essential cost of the war.

When Lord Sumner wrote a lengthy memorandum to prove Lloyd George's case, President Wilson threw it out almost contemptuously as "very legalistic" [27] but when Lloyd George persuaded the liberal Jan Smuts from South Africa —whom Wilson greatly admired—to try his hand at virtually the same argument, the President was persuaded. On April 1, the American experts assured him that none of the legal advisers of the American Delegation would agree that pensions could be properly included as a category of civilian damage under the wording of the Pre-Armistice Agreement; that all logic was against it. Wilson replied, rather petulantly, "Logic! Logic! I don't give a damn for logic. I am going to include pensions!" [28]

Although many of the American experts were bitterly disappointed because they felt that the President had laid himself open to criticism for abandoning his principles, most of

251

them did not take this surrender tragically. It was certainly a violation of the letter of the Pre-Armistice Agreement, but both President Wilson and the experts were sure that they still had adequate means of enforcing the spirit of the agreement. If a Reparation Commission were to calculate the total bill of damages on the basis of their estimate of what Germany could afford to pay in thirty years, if it then lay within their discretion as to what Germany must pay in any single year, and finally, if they had authority to conclude Germany's payments at the end of thirty years, or thirty-five at most, no matter how much or how little Germany had actually paid in that time, then categories of damage meant very little. Total German payments would have been kept within the limits of German financial capacity, and the legal categories of damage written in the treaty would merely have affected the distribution of the money among Germany's creditors.[29]

It could even be argued that conceding pensions and separation allowances might be the most effective way of tying Lloyd George to the American program. It increased the British percentage of German payments, and thereby increased the British stake in German solvency—a stake already sufficiently large to argue the wisdom of that course. The French, to their own financial disadvantage, had supported the pensions proposal since early March,[30] either because of its humanitarian appeal to their own electorate, or because they approved of the biggest possible German debt in order to weaken Germany politically and to justify continued military occupation of the Rhineland.[31] At a time of complete French recklessness and irresponsibility, vital British interests dictated the closest collaboration with the American Delegation. While the concession on pensions might purchase British support, it made that support more than ever essential to the American Delegation, since the concession itself had exactly doubled the American stake in the outcome. If the French conception of the Reparation Commission were to prevail, pensions would double the bill and the Commission would be under mandate to collect it, no matter how long it might take.

Just as the American victory in excluding war costs was largely verbal, so the defeat on pensions would be a simple matter of words, if the American conception of a Reparation Commission could be made to prevail. The major battle was still to be joined.

6 : *"War Guilt"*

Verbal and theoretical issues continued to obscure the real issues of the Reparation question in early April. While both Lloyd George and Clemenceau had been brought to recognize that there were practical limitations on what Germany could afford to pay, as well as legal limitations on their right to exact payment under the terms of the Pre-Armistice Agreement, they still labored under fatal commitments to their respective publics. Not even the pensions decision could bridge the gap between their promise to Germany to require only civilian damage and their promise to their own people to collect war costs. Both delegates insisted that the treaty assert at least the moral right of the Allies to recover the cost of the war forced upon them by Germany.

Lloyd George said: "We must in some way justify the action of the British and French governments which find themselves obliged to accept less than full war costs. We must make it thoroughly clear that, if we do not exact it, it is not because it would be unjust to claim it, but because it would be impossible to obtain it." [32] Lloyd George was under special pressure at this time, April 2, because of accusations in the House of Commons that he had abandoned his election pledges.

The American Delegation had no objection to a theoretical statement of Germany's responsibility for all the costs of a war which they, in common with all the Allies, believed was entirely the result of German aggression. Indeed, Dulles had proposed some such formula as early as February 21 as a means of satisfying Allied sentiment without conceding the actual demand for full payment of war costs.[33] That the question was chiefly a technical one of drafting is clear from the minutes of the Council of Four meeting on April 5:

> *Mr. Lloyd George:* We must say that the Allies assert their claim and that Germany recognizes her obligation for all the cost of the war.
> *Mr. House:* This would be contrary to the terms of the armistice and the note you addressed to the American Government. The text must be drafted so as not to constitute a violation of our engagements.
> *Mr. Davis:* It can be said that Germany is morally responsible for the war and all the consequences thereof, and legally that she is responsible in accordance with the formula adopted for damage to property and persons.
> *Mr. Clemenceau:* This is a question of drafting. I think we can reach an accord.[34]

The experts had no difficulty in reaching accord on the drafting of the proposed article by April 7, and as finally adopted, Article 231 of the Treaty of Versailles read:

> The Allied and Associated Governments affirm and Germany accepts the responsibility of Germany and her allies for causing all the loss and damage to which the Allied and Associated Governments and their nationals have been subjected as a consequence of the war imposed upon them by the aggression of Germany and her allies.[35]

The financial consequences of the article were precisely nothing, since Article 232 confined Germany's actual financial liability to civilian damage, in language taken over bodily from the Pre-Armistice Agreement. But the political consequences were far-reaching. The moral overtones in the lan-

254

guage of Article 231 encouraged popular condemnation of the article as the "War Guilt Clause," and subsequent German governments—none more successfully than Hitler's—made political capital of the cliché. Liberal opinion throughout the world was quick to respond in sympathy to German and "revisionist" demonstrations that Germany had not been uniquely responsible for the World War, and to the undiscriminating propaganda against the entire Treaty of Versailles as resting on the untenable basis of German "guilt." Probably no single item of the Treaty of Versailles has been so useful to Hitler in destroying the morale of his democratic opponents before attacking them.[36]

7 : *"This Is a Complete Departure from the Principles upon Which We Have Been Working for Three Months"*

But neither "War Guilt" nor pensions would have much material or moral effect if the American Delegation held firmly to their program for a Reparation Commission to enforce the time-limit on German payments. In that case, German capacity not Allied claims would govern the settlement; and even Article 231 would be reduced to empty rhetoric. During the early days of April, the American experts worked at drafts to embody their program, with encouraging signs of support from their British colleagues.

It was a hopeful indication that Lloyd George had designated Montagu to represent him in the experts committee, since both Keynes and Montagu agreed with the American view of the problem, while those "heavenly twins," Cunliffe and Sumner, invariably created difficulties. The American delegates could easily gauge Lloyd George's attitude by his choice of financial experts at any particular moment, but they had learned by experience that the British experts were as subject to sudden change without notice as Lloyd George's own policy.[37] At least, they had Montagu to deal with in three successive meetings, April 1, 2 and 3, and they made the most of it.

The Anglo-American draft which emerged from these conferences placed the reparation settlement squarely on the basis of capacity rather than claims, in two ways. The original British draft had required Germany to pay Allied claims "at whatever cost to themselves," and the Americans persuaded Montagu to substitute a phrase limiting Germany's payments "to the extent to their utmost capacity." But, more important, the Anglo-American draft fixed a time-limit of thirty years, established a Reparation Commission to calculate Allied claims under the agreed categories; to estimate what Germany could afford to pay on these claims within the period of thirty years; to modify the manner and date of payments within that period, and even to extend payments, in part, beyond that period, though presumably to not more than thirty-five years at the outside.[38]

The French, as was to be expected, resisted both the principle and the details of such a program. Klotz and Loucheur attacked the time-limit of thirty years, first suggesting it be raised to forty years, then proposing that it be abandoned completely. Their purpose appears most clearly in the comment, "The French contend that the Commission should be required to secure complete payment. . . ." [39] This was the Klotz proposal of March 28 that the Commission function as adding-machine and bill-collector, and it made Allied claims, rather than German capacity, the criterion of settlement.

The crucial day of decision was April 5, when deadlock and crisis over the whole series of French demands was at its height. President Wilson had taken to his bed with a severe attack of influenza on the afternoon of April 3, and Colonel House represented him in the Council of Four. On April 2, members of the House of Commons attacked Lloyd George for abandonment of his election pledges, and Bonar Law communicated with Lloyd George from London that evening to warn him of the rising discontent.[40] It was not difficult to predict that Lloyd George would again sacrifice the American program rather than his own political life, and Colonel House was scarcely the man to fight single-handed against an Anglo-French united front.

Clemenceau opened the attack on the Anglo-American draft by flatly refusing to confer on the Reparation Commission "the power of fixing Germany's capacity for payment." The Commission must add the total figures of German indebtness under the various categories of claims, and collect the entire bill. He was willing that the Commission attempt to collect in thirty years, but "if this is demonstrated to be impossible, the Commission will have the right to postpone beyond thirty years." Klotz suggested that Germany be required to pay the total, even if that took fifty years. In determining the actual period of time required for payment, the Commission might take account of German capacity, but not otherwise. Only the Allied Governments would have the right to reduce the figure of German indebtedness.[41]

Colonel House said, quite simply, "It seems to me that Mr. Clemenceau's conclusion is very close to the American proposal." Loucheur seemed surprised at the remark and undertook, rather painstakingly, to point out to Colonel House the very considerable differences. Norman Davis somewhat heatedly said:

This is a complete departure from the principles upon which we have been working for three months. We have been working on the theory that Germany must pay all that she can for thirty years or thirty-five at most. Beyond this date the interest charges are so heavy that payment of principal becomes impossible.

With respect to capacity, we have made studies and those of the

257

American delegation are between twenty-five and thirty-five billion dollars. These figures were reached without consideration of the amount due. Finally we decided that it was better not to attempt to fix any figure, but in working on this new basis we tend to abandon our principle that Germany should pay measured by her capacity.[42]

Norman Davis's protest was too late to save the American program which Colonel House had deserted. Lloyd George came to the support of his French colleagues and the Council of Four directed the experts committee to redraft the reparation clauses to embody the French conception of the Reparation Commission. Significantly, it was Klotz's draft of these articles which was to be incorporated in the settlement.[43]

In this way the American Delegation submitted to a reparation settlement which violated both the letter and the spirit of the Pre-Armistice Agreement. The violation of the letter of the agreement which President Wilson had committed in conceding pensions as a category of civilian claim could be justified only if German capacity and not Allied claims were to provide the basis of settlement, but the French proposal, which Colonel House had characterized as very close to the American program, substituted claims for capacity, and the pensions claim doubled the bill of damage. It made the earlier American victory in excluding war costs largely a matter of words.

Colonel House went in and out of the President's sick-room at intervals to keep him informed of the progress of negotiations,[44] and the next day President Wilson tentatively approved the surrender.[45] The Colonel evidently felt fully qualified to settle the main lines of the reparation settlement in Wilson's absence, and a few days later, when the French were still making difficulties over the details of authority and of personnel in the actual construction of a Reparation Commission, House wrote that he spared President Wilson all he could by making important decisions himself, knowing that Wilson would sustain him.[46] The same day he recorded, with satisfaction, that in a meeting with the Allied premiers, "The President yielded more than I thought he would, but not more, I think, than the occasion required."[47] The Colonel, on his own admission, had settled the essentials of the reparation question in the meetings of Saturday, April 5, through Monday, April 7,[48] and from that time, President Wilson was committed to the settlement beyond any possibility of withdrawal. The mystery of why Colonel House felt free to assume such authority has been solved by his own statement to George Sylvester Vierack:

. . . outside of myself there was no one who could or would speak with any degree of authority—not that I had the actual authority, but I assumed it, feeling certain that, as in the past, Wilson would confirm my decisions. I knew then, as I had known before, that I took my fortunes into my hands every time I did this, but I was never lacking in courage of this kind, and it was essential that I should act promptly and decisively if the work was to be efficiently done. . . .[49]

Certainly the American experts were disposed to blame House for the surrender. Two days before making it, he had told Lamont and Davis that "it was more important to bring about peace quickly than it was to haggle over details," that he "would rather see an immediate peace and the world brought to order . . . than . . . a better peace and delay," [50] and when the treaty was complete, Norman Davis expressed disgust at the compromises, for which he blamed House.[51]

Yet, if Colonel House continued to trade on President Wilson's confidence in him, it is hard to blame anyone but President Wilson for permitting it. The President had been disturbed at Colonel House's earlier disposition to compromise on the Rhineland problem and evidently felt that the Colonel had weakened the entire American position during

259

the month of his own absence from Paris.[52] Many of the American experts and all the other Commissioners—White, Bliss, Lansing—were by this time distrustful of Colonel House's influence, and the Commissioners were appalled that the Colonel should represent Wilson in the Council of Four.[53] By April 10, rumors of estrangement between Wilson and House began to circulate among representatives of the American press and, while probably unfounded, they were significant straws in the wind.[54] It was unlikely that President Wilson's confidence in Colonel House would survive another episode like that of the reparation decision. Both in period of time and in its character, the struggle with Italian representatives over Fiume proved a decisive episode in destroying that confidence. There was, however, a sequel to the reparation story, and that must be related first.

8 : *"That Makes Me Very Tired"*

"Mr. Lloyd George kicked over the traces," said Thomas W. Lamont on June 3, 1919, "but now he has come back to the fold." [55] Lloyd George was worried about the German complaints against the Treaty and now proposed revision, for fear that Germany would not sign. The French complained that, as usual, Lloyd George was being statesmanlike at their expense by suggesting a plebiscite for Upper Silesia, reduction of the period of occupation in the Rhineland from fifteen years to two, immediate admission of Germany to the League of Nations, and reconsideration of the reparation settlement. The French were willing to discuss Silesia and agreed reluctantly to the plebiscite when Wilson supported Lloyd George. If Lloyd George would drop his wider demands for revision and agree to proportionate British sacrifices, there was a chance that France would consent to modify the reparation sections of the treaty. For the moment it looked as if Lloyd George would do his part.[56]

Wilson discussed Lloyd George's proposals very fully with all the members of his delegation on June 3. There was an understandable atmosphere of skepticism at the meeting about the sincerity of Lloyd George's intentions. Lamont and Davis discussed his earlier tactics, the former saying, "If it had not been for the British *'heavenly twins'* we could have got together with Loucheur months ago"; the latter commenting on Lloyd George's habit of changing the British personnel of the financial commissions to represent his personal shifts in policy.[57] President Wilson was particularly bitter, and, since his words have been quoted out of their proper context, they require extensive quotation:

Well, I don't want to seem to be unreasonable, but my feeling is this: that we ought not, with the object of getting it signed, make changes in the treaty, if we think it embodies what we were contending for; that the time to consider all these questions was when we were writing the treaty, and *it makes me a little tired for people to come and say now that they are afraid the Germans won't sign, and their fear is based upon things that they insisted upon at the time of the writing of the treaty; that makes me very sick.*

And that is the thing that happened. These people that overrode our judgment and wrote things into the treaty that are now the stumbling blocks, are now falling over themselves to remove the stumbling blocks. Now, if they ought not to have been there, I say, remove them, but I say do not remove them merely for the sake of having the treaty signed. . . .

Here is a British group made up of every kind of British opinion, from Winston Churchill to Fisher. From the unreasonable to be reasonable, all the way around, they are all unanimous, if you please, in their funk. *Now that makes me very tired. . . .*[58]

Wilson had asked that his remarks about the British Delegation remain confidential, but inevitably they were repeated and garbled. It is as characteristic of the atmosphere of Paris,

261

as of the misrepresentation which beset human affairs generally, that the British expert Harold Nicolson, should receive only the most distorted version.

. . . The extinction of my worship of Wilson occurred when a member of his delegation informed me how the President had reacted to the endeavours of Lloyd George to render the Treaty more just and reasonable. Mr. Wilson informed his staff that these endeavours had "left him tired." I was appalled by this revelation.[59]

Verbal accuracy in the use of the word "tired" scarcely conveyed the real meaning of Wilson's remarks. Moreover, he was the first to recognize that the reparation chapter should never have been written into the treaty. Both he and the American experts canvassed the matter thoroughly and agreed on renewed efforts to get a reasonable fixed sum to represent German liability written into the treaty.[60] Baruch and Lamont went to see Lloyd George, and President Wilson again urged the fixed sum in the Council of Four. It was no use. "The crazy echoes of the General Election" still rang in Lloyd George's ears and he could not agree to the fixed sum.[61] His own financial expert, John Maynard Keynes, deserted him at this period in June, and went home to write that scathing indictment of the Peace Conference, *The Economic Consequences of the Peace.*

This episode in June at the eleventh hour is sufficient commentary on the claim of some of the American experts to have retrieved the substance of the American program by technical provisions governing the issue of German Government bonds. The treaty had set the maximum of these bonds at sixty milliard marks and the maximum could not be increased except by unanimous consent of the members of the Reparation Commission. Accordingly, David Hunter Miller and Norman Davis have argued that the American member of the Commission had veto power which could effectively have kept demands on Germany within this limit—regardless of the total of the German debt—and thereby, indirectly, would have achieved the benefits of the fixed sum. Actually, there was no evidence for assuming that Germany could not be called upon to pay her acknowledged, or imposed, debt in other ways than by paying interest on an issue of German bonds. If any such limitation had been accomplished, it is surprising that nothing should have been said about it on June 3, when Norman Davis himself was as eager as the other experts and Wilson to get a fixed sum written into the treaty. All those other experts regarded the settlement as a defeat for the American program,[62] at the time and ever after.

It is correct to argue that American participation in the whole Versailles settlement, including membership in the Reparation Commission, would have done much to mitigate in practice the rigors of the financial provisions of the treaty. Put in another way, this is to argue that the reparation settlement on paper was so thoroughly at variance with the dictates of common sense, let alone Pre-Armistice pledges, that only American participation in the settlement could have prevented the crises which inevitably occurred from the attempts to enforce it. American defection from the entire Versailles settlement brought into sharp relief the inherent folly of the reparation clauses.[63]

★ 11 ★

PRESIDENT WILSON AND
COLONEL HOUSE

1 : *The Jackal Tradition of Italian Politics*

THE FINAL RIFT between President Wilson and Colonel House was fully as much a result of the methods employed by the Colonel in negotiation as it was the substance of proposals that he was prepared to support. In precisely the same way, the Italian Delegation at Paris may be said to have fatally compromised the actual substance of their proposals by the methods they adopted to achieve them. When Colonel House not merely supported Italian claims and condoned their methods, but appeared also to ignore the opposition of President Wilson and of the American experts to both claims and methods, he finally impaired the confidence Wilson had bestowed upon him.

The traditions of Italian national policy, like those of any other national state, are much more the result of geography and physical circumstances than they are of any peculiar biology or special racial character, or even of the special nature of the political and social régime which governs the country. Just as French national policy has shown a remarkable continuity through centuries under a bewildering variety of political systems, so Italian policy, over a much briefer span of years, has developed a similar consistency which has carried over from the parliamentary order to the Fascist Italy of Mussolini, without essential change of character but with rather an intensification of degree. Mussolini has merely crystallized and clarified Italian traditions without changing them. The liberal and constructive policy of Count Sforza as Foreign Minister in the early post-war period is the exception which proves the rule. Not the least of the weapons which Mussolini used to discredit Sforza's régime was the charge that it had betrayed Italian interests.

The basic physical fact which has shaped these traditions is that Italy, as the weakest of the Great Powers, cannot play a dominant rôle in the power politics of the European continent. Instead she must play on the rivalries of others, constantly shifting to keep the balance even in order to enhance her own bargaining power or, if the balance becomes hopelessly upset, to be on the side of the biggest battalions. In the lawless jungle of power politics, others may play the rôle of lions and tigers, but for Italy it is safer and more productive to be a jackal, to let others kill the prey before venturing to attack the carcass. It was the German Chancellor Bismarck who first characterized Italian policy as a jackal policy:

> Insatiable Italy, with furtive glance, roves restlessly hither and thither, instinctively drawn on by the odor of corruption and calamity—always ready to attack anybody from the rear and make off with a bit of plunder. It is outrageous that these Italians, still unsatisfied, should continue to make preparations and to conspire in every direction. On the one hand, the Irredenta, and on the other, machinations in Albania, Montenegro, and the Balkan territories. . . .[1]

Bismarck had his uses for even a jackal, and Chancellor Hitler is not more squeamish, but Mussolini's delay in declaration of war until German armies had killed his French prey has done nothing to abate the reputation which Bismarck originally fixed on Italian policy.

Italian policy during the first World War and at the Peace Conference was subject to the same interpretation. Alone among the Great Powers in Europe, Italy entered that war as the result of a deliberate bargain. Neutral at the outset, Italy negotiated actively with both sides to obtain the maximum price for intervention, and naturally obtained it from the Entente Powers, who could afford to be generous at the expense of Italy's erstwhile ally, Austria-Hungary. Yet both the British and the French felt that the Italians had driven an unjustifiably hard bargain; and the physical weakness which Italy displayed in the disaster of Caporetto in 1917 put a strain on the resources of Britain and France and did not dispose them to take a more generous view of the bargain they had made for Italian assistance. Britain and France hardly entered the Conference with clean hands, yet the Italian delegation entered the Peace Conference under a cloud of suspicion and contempt which their own demands and, above all, their own methods merely intensified. Whatever the merits of their demands—and there was real disagreement about them—there was almost universal condemnation of Italian unreliability, Italian intransigence, Italian importunity. Harold Nicolson has written, "We recognized in the methods rather than in the purposes of the Italian delegation all that was most odious in the old diplomacy." [2]

2 : *Fiume*

The Italian demands were extensive enough. They comprised all that had been promised in the Treaty of London of 1915, and more, too. There was already fundamental conflict between Italian claims under the Treaty of London and Wilson's clearly enunciated principle, "A readjustment

266

of the frontiers of Italy should be effected along clearly recognizable lines of nationality." [3] The Treaty of London was a purely strategic line, incorporating within Italy about 200,000 Austrian Germans of the Trentino up to the Brenner Pass in the Alps, and some 500,000 South Slavs of the Dalmatian shore of the eastern Adriatic.[4] Not content with the degree of strategic control which that line gave them in the entire Adriatic area, Italian delegates now proposed extension of the line to include the town and harbor of Fiume which the Treaty of London had specifically awarded to the Austrian province of Croatia, now part of the new Yugoslav kingdom.

The claim on grounds of nationality which the Italians adduced was spurious, since to identify the town of Fiume as Italian was to separate the town from its adjoining Slavic suburb of Susâk and to isolate it entirely from its surrounding Slavic sea.[5] The harbor was, moreover, the only possible economic outlet in the Adriatic area for the new Yugoslav kingdom of the Serbs, Croats, and Slovenes. The real argument underlying the Italian claim was the strategic one that Italy, and Italy alone, must be in a position to dominate the Adriatic. Barzilai, who formulated Italian claims, said frankly, "It will be very difficult for us to keep up the commerce of Trieste unless we control Fiume and are able to divert its trade to Trieste," [6] and Sonnino, the Italian Foreign Minister, wrote Colonel House that the unforeseen collapse of Austria-Hungary created new problems of security for Italy in the Adriatic which made possession of Fiume essential.[7] Orlando, the Italian Premier, frankly regarded the new Yugoslav state as an enemy:

If in consequence of the breakup of the Austro-Hungarian Empire, new states had been formed, some of which desired to join Serbia, that meant that the Conference no longer had to deal with the Kingdom of Serbia, but with a new state consisting partly of the old kingdom of Serbia and partly of other territories which belonged to an enemy state. . . . Certainly the recognition of the new state would not constitute an amiable act toward Italy. . . . Furthermore he regarded the Croats and Slovenes, that is to say, the people whose frontiers were in question, as his enemies.[8]

Such an attitude removed the Italian case entirely from the category of British, French, and even Japanese imperialist policy. The British Government had accepted the Mandates principle, while asking exceptions only in the case of their own self-governing Dominions, which were themselves brought to recognize a degree of mandatory responsibility. The French program for dismembering Germany had at least the excuse that France had been twice invaded and overrun by German armies within fifty years, and the 1940 débâcle will convince many that their program was justified. They abandoned the major part of their program in the face of Anglo-American objections.

The Japanese, while just as cynical in their demands as the Italians, at least did not ask for more than the letter of their bond, and even glossed that over by arrangements with China which they could represent as generous and renunciatory. The Italians, who had not been menaced by the war, had chosen to enter it for a price which they now declared to be inadequate, on the extraordinary plea that they had not foreseen the completeness of their enemy's collapse, which had produced a new danger in the Adriatic!

Moreover, they pretended not to rest their claims on the Treaty of London at all, since fulfillment of the letter of that treaty would have assigned Fiume to Yugoslavia. They simply claimed all that the treaty assigned them, *plus* Fiume, using a variety of arguments ranging from strategic necessity, economic requirements, and historical title to appeals to Wilsonian principles of nationality.[9] If the Italians would have renounced Fiume and frankly resorted to the Treaty of London as the basis of their claim, they could have been assured of French and British diplomatic support and Wilson would have had to yield. While denying any commitments to support the Treaty of London where it ran counter to his Fourteen Points, Wilson admitted that Italy had not been clearly committed to the Fourteen Points in making peace with Austria.[10] Yet, by demanding Fiume over and above the Treaty of London, the Italians impaired the validity of all their demands under that treaty which violated the Fourteen Points, and they challenged the American Delegation to battle in the open field without benefit of fortifications. The Italian issue was the most clear-cut of any presented to the Americans in Paris.

3 : The American Delegation—A Split Personality

The main group of territorial and economic experts and President Wilson began early to view Italian aspirations in the Adriatic with considerable suspicion. President Wilson made one bad slip at the outset, which both he and the experts bitterly regretted as implying recognition of the Treaty of London. Late in December 1918, before the experts had prepared that careful study and report on Italian claims as a whole which appeared on January 21, 1919, he conceded to Italy the Brenner Pass in the Alps as the northern frontier, thereby including some 200,000 Austrian Germans within Italy. The experts later advocated a more southerly line, adequate for defense and more in accord with ethnic principle, but Wilson had already settled the question on the basis of Walter Lippmann's (and Frank Cobb's) semiofficial commentary on the Fourteen Points, which frankly justified the strategic line of the Brenner.[11]

The January report of the experts denied Italian claims to Fiume and to the Dalmatian coast, south of the Istrian peninsula, while making all reasonable concessions to Italian eco-

269

nomic and strategic requirements, even at the expense of some violation of ethnic principle. It has recently been characterized as ". . . a sane and fair-minded analysis of local situations."

As to the physical and ethnographic facts which lay behind them (the recommendations), there could not be much dispute. The American Report took into account—first ethnographical, then economic and strategic considerations, and struck a moderate compromise between them. . . . On the basis of the Fourteen Points, it is difficult to criticize the proposed American settlement. . . .[12]

Yet, then and since, the American experts were criticized for narrow and unrealistic preoccupation with details of settlement, with rigidity, and with failure to take the large view; and President Wilson has shared in the indictment for supporting his experts. President Wilson and his experts did display the weaknesses as well as the strength of the academic temperament, in their grappling with the problems of the Peace Conference. Their strength lay in the thorough and disinterested study they devoted to complicated affairs and the entire honesty and courage with which they supported the conclusions they arrived at. Their weakness derived from the same source as their strength—unwillingness to compromise on the principles they believed in—which occasionally led them to confuse details of settlement with eternal principles. The experts responsible for the January 1919 report were men drawn entirely from academic life: W. E. Lunt, Chief of the Italian Division; Charles Seymour, Chief of the Austro-Hungarian Division; Clive Day, Chief of the Balkan Division; Douglas Johnson, Chief of the Division of Boundary Geography and specialist on the Adriatic problem. With these men, the economist, Allyn A. Young, associated himself in the later recommendations, and all of them worked under the executive direction of Isaiah Bowman, also a man of academic experience, and since 1915, Director of the American Geographical Society of New York. These men held, through thick and thin, to their original recommendations of the January report.

Such views did not commend themselves to a variety of members of the American Delegation whom Lansing has loosely described as the "House Group,"[13] composed of the Colonel himself; his brother-in-law, Sidney E. Mezes (the titular head of the American expert group); his son-in-law, Gordon Auchincloss, and Auchincloss' law partner, David Hunter Miller, both of whom served in the capacity of legal advisers to the American delegation. On the Italian issue, these men were joined by the colonial expert, George Louis Beer, and for a short time by James T. Shotwell, the only purely academic member of this group.

They were impressed by the necessity of dealing with things as they found them. They felt that Italy, as a Great Power, was entitled to be treated with the consideration due that station. Miller and Beer said, again and again, that culturally the Italians were a superior people, the Slavs an inferior people, that it was better to subject the Slavs of Dalmatia to Italian rule than to permit Yugoslav domination of any Italians in that area.[14] Both men were in frequent contact with members of the Italian Delegation, who became acquainted with their views during the critical month of March. Miller was a close friend of Count Macchi di Cellere, the Italian Ambassador to Washington, and Beer was in close touch with Piacentini in the discussion of colonial problems, and while both Miller and Beer made it clear to their Italian colleagues that they had no direct responsibility for Adriatic questions, the Italian delegates were not slow to detect the divergence of philosophy within the American Delegation and to profit from it. Mezes was even more encouraging and, as titular head of the expert group, could be regarded by the Italians as speaking with the authority of that group. Colonel House himself was alarmed at Mezes' generosity. He reported to Miller that an agreement had been reached on certain Greek claims "by Mezes giving away, which was one way of reaching agreement," and caustically added that every time his brother-in-law dined with the Italians "he was willing to give them another island." [15]

Yet Colonel House also was willing to go as far as any member of this group in satisfying Italian claims, since the two things he most desired were maximum support for the League of Nations and a speedy peace. The Italian Premier, Orlando, unlike his French colleagues in the League of Nations Commission, had given steady support to the American proposals for the League of Nations Covenant. If French obstruction in the League Commission was to be rewarded by tangible concessions to French security in the Rhineland, why should Orlando's welcome support go unrewarded by denial of concessions to Italian security in the Adriatic? If the United States made concessions to one nation which violated the Fourteen Points, why uphold the Fourteen Points rigidly against another nation? There was some sympathy in American circles with Sonnino's sardonic remark that Wilson, having lost his virtue by his concessions to Great Britain and France at an early stage of the Conference, was belatedly attempting to re-establish his virginity at Italy's expense.[16] They felt that this course might alienate Italy from the Western World and wreck the League of Nations from the start.

Above all, there was Colonel House's anxiety to make peace quickly. He had said early in April—apropos of French claims—that he would rather make peace quickly than haggle over details and, referring to Italian claims, he later said to one of the experts, "You may know what is right, but you can't always get it. And you want to get the next best thing. True statesmanship is a series of wise compromises." [17] This attitude of the "House Group" constituted a claim to superior political wisdom and realism which had little tolerance for the rigid adherence of Wilson and the experts to the "American line," or the "Wilson line," in the Adriatic. Colonel House repeatedly attempted to persuade President Wilson to modify his attitude and, as previously mentioned, privately expressed his conviction that Wilson had made a great mistake in coming to Paris.[18]

Beer regarded Wilson as "sophomoric"[19] and frequently recorded his contempt for the experts who viewed questions so narrowly. His contempt was increased by the refusal of two experts to attend a luncheon he had arranged in order to bring the Americans and Italians together,[20] whereas the experts in question really declined because the division in American ranks was already sufficiently advertised among the Italians, without its being further demonstrated at a formal luncheon.[21] To make the misunderstanding complete, the experts not only denied the "realism" of the House Group, but claimed a monopoly of realism for their own proposals, which were designed to check Italy's habitual Balkan intrigues by assigning to Yugoslavia the port of Fiume, wanted by Italy primarily as a base for intervention in Balkan politics.[22] By the middle of April, when consideration of Italian claims could no longer be postponed, the tension between experts and others in the American delegation had reached considerable proportions.

4 : "Who Are the Experts?"

The real conflict originally lay between the experts and Mezes, their titular chief. On March 16, Mezes sent Colonel House a letter with recommendations "totally at variance with those of the Inquiry; they read rather like quotations from the Italian Memorandum of Claims."[23] The four chiefs of divisions concerned—Lunt, Day, Seymour, Johnson—promptly countered with a reminder that every one of their memoranda had recommended that Fiume and Dalmatia should go to Yugoslavia, adding, "We are still unanimously of that opinion. . . ." [24] Johnson followed up with a special letter to reinforce this view, containing the statement that both French and British delegates were supporting the American position and, to make perfectly certain that Mezes' views should not be regarded as their own, the four chiefs of division (and the economist, Allyn A. Young), addressed themselves directly to Wilson on April 4,[25] at the very height of the controversy over French claims. Wilson accepted the views of the experts and his firm stand upon them in his interview with Orlando on April 14 [26]—the very day that his final concession of a fifteen-year period of military occupation in the Rhineland settled the last of his major conflicts with France—led to complete deadlock with the Italians.

At one point, Wilson indicated to his experts the possibility of compromise. He was willing to fight for the "American line," but it might seem best to make Fiume an independent port.[27] On April 15, Orlando called on House in his discouragement, and the latter consoled him with the thought that apparently insoluble difficulties with the French had yielded to compromise and that there was no need to despair about Italian claims; Fiume was the chief hurdle.[28] The next day, Auchincloss directed Miller to prepare a memorandum, on lines indicated by Colonel House, for the solution of the Fiume question. Miller called at the Colonel's office to work up a preliminary draft, and later worked the scheme out in greater detail with Douglas Johnson and with Warrin.[29] The scheme combined nominal Italian sovereignty, Yugoslav port control, and League of Nations administration of local affairs.[30]

Now Johnson was the only member of the expert group

274

called upon to participate, and he did so reluctantly, on the basis of assumptions furnished to him by Colonel House, via Miller. Johnson stated his objections to Miller at the time,[31] and when he learned later that Mezes was representing him to President Wilson as favoring the proposal,[32] he wrote letters to both Miller and Mezes denouncing the plan as "fundamentally unjust" and "in practice unworkable." [33]

Meantime, Auchincloss tried to get support for the plan from the other American Commissioners: White, Bliss and Lansing. On April 17, he approached Lansing, who told him that he was "sick of these impossible compromises," and Auchincloss went back to report to House.[34] White and Bliss evidently took the same stand, since Auchincloss told someone on the same day that Mezes and Miller disagreed with the Commissioners. Moreover, Lansing's diary shows that Auchincloss represented Mezes and Miller as "experts" on the Fiume question, and Lansing's comment on such tactics was extremely bitter.[35]

The real experts heard that Mezes and Miller were being described as "experts" in support of proposals which they completely repudiated, and this was a repetition of the situation which had provoked their protest to President Wilson on April 4. It revived their distrust of Mezes and their fear that his views would be taken for theirs. The five men who had signed the earlier letter suggested to Bowman that they at once draft another appeal directly to the President. The letter was drafted on April 17, signed by all six—Bowman, Lunt, Day, Johnson, Seymour, Young—and dispatched directly to the President, at exactly one minute past midnight, together with a copy addressed to Mezes. By 10 A.M. of that same day, April 18, Wilson's reply was on Bowman's desk, offering complete support to his experts' view.[36]

When the Commissioners met that day, Colonel House asked the others for their opinion on a certain memorandum with regard to Fiume which he had sent them the day before. Lansing records: "I repeated my utter opposition to all these compromises, White and Bliss said the same, *and so did House*," [37] whereas the official minutes of the meeting merely say:

The Commissioners discussed at some length the whole question of principle involved in the settlement of Fiume and finally came to a decision as to what, in their opinion, the ultimate disposition of this city with its immediate hinterland should be.[38]

One of the Commissioners told a member of the expert group that, on the same day, House had put his compromise proposal to President Wilson, alleging that it was supported *by the experts*. Wilson, presumably having had the letter signed by the six experts, asked who "the experts" were, and House replied by naming Mezes, Miller, Beer and Shotwell.[39] President Wilson sent a confidential agent to General Bliss to inquire further into the matter, and Bliss promptly sent for one of the six, who was asked the direct question, "Who are the experts?" [40] The reply which went to Wilson evidently convinced him that an unfortunate ambiguity had confused the real issues, and Colonel House, for his part, abandoned this particular effort at compromise. He wrote despairingly at the end of this difficult day:

The President and I discussed the question of Fiume, and I urged him to settle it one way or the other. I have about come to the conclusion that, since we cannot please the Italians by compromise, we might as well do what seems best in the judgment of our experts, and that is to give it directly to the Yugoslavs, safeguarding the rights of all those contributory to the port. This solution appealed to the President. I urged him to take it up with Lloyd George and Clemenceau and commit them in order to present a united front.[41]

276

It looks as if the events of the day put a strain upon the relations between House and Wilson. House continued to see Wilson at intervals during April, May, and the early part of June, and to advise him on the hopelessly tangled Italian problem. For a period during the middle part of May, he even took charge again of negotiations with the Italians, but it was under fairly rigid restrictions which hampered the freedom of action he thought essential for a settlement. The most marked symptom of the altered character of his relations with President Wilson was the fact that when he did see him it was more frequently than not in the company of the other Commissioners—a complete reversal of Wilson's earlier habit of conferring with House alone. Whereas the other Commissioners had complained, during the end of March and early in April, that Wilson reserved his confidence for House alone,[42] it was now the Colonel's turn to complain about the difficulty of his access to Wilson alone.

All the Commissioners met with Wilson, on April 19, to discuss the line he should take with the Italians. When told of the Italian Delegation's threat to leave Paris unless they got what they wanted in Fiume and Dalmatia, Wilson said he would never assent to those demands. After he left, the Commissioners then agreed to recommend putting the entire question on ice by establishing an International Commission to exercise sovereignty over the areas in question, and to determine their final disposition only after a year, at the same time making it clear that the Italians would never get the areas under any circumstances.[43] It was a purely face-saving device, though baited with some territorial concessions at other points. It was flatly rejected by Orlando the next day.[44]

Accordingly, when Wilson met the Commissioners on Monday, April 21, it was to consider the form of statement he proposed to make public as an appeal to the Italian people. Lansing recorded that there was no compromise in it; that he, Bliss, and White strongly approved, while Colonel House said very little.[45] When Wilson asked as to whether he should publish the statement immediately, or wait until a break had actually occurred, House urged him to consult with Lloyd George and Clemenceau and be guided by their advice.[46] There is nothing to indicate that House saw Wilson the next day, though he may have seen him the day following, for his diary records that, on the morning of April 23, he advised Wilson to put out his statement, but only after conferring with the other premiers. Later in the day, after the President had given out the statement, Mrs. Wilson telephoned messages from the President and inquired of House how the statement had been taken.[47] House reported that Wilson was too tired to come to the telephone himself. At the end of the next day, House went to see Wilson, who was closeted with Clemenceau. He talked with Mrs. Wilson instead, giving her messages for the President, and returned to the Crillon to record his fear that the "President will isolate himself when there is no need of his doing so. . . ." [48]

The same evening, Orlando left Paris for Rome and the next day, Friday, April 25, Lansing reported that Colonel House complained to him that he had not seen Wilson for four days, that all he knew came from Sir William Wiseman, and that he was much disturbed.[49] Lansing's record is probably an exaggeration, since it is likely that House had seen Wilson as recently as two days earlier, but it is unlikely that Lansing concocted this episode out of his imagination for entry in his diary. The Colonel's own diary mentions Wiseman as one of the "go-betweens" at this time.[50] House certainly saw Wilson on April 26 at a meeting with the other Commissioners to discuss Japanese claims in Shantung.[51] And

278

again on April 28 at the plenary session of the Peace Conference to adopt the final form of the League of Nations Covenant. In fact, after that meeting Lloyd George took House aside to complain that Wilson was being unfair to the Japanese and to ask House to "get the President in a more amenable state of mind." [52] It is a significant detail that Colonel House undertook the task by letter and not personal interview, since his diary for April 29 says only, "See my three letters to the President today and one of his to me. . . ." [53] On May 3, House saw Wilson, but at a meeting of the Commissioners again to consider the inevitable Italian crisis, and the Colonel utilized the occasion in unsuccessful efforts to "stir him from his inflexible position." [54]

On May 5, the President called on House at the Crillon to report a decision taken by the Big Three Clemenceau, Lloyd George, and Wilson himself—to omit the name of Italy entirely from both the German treaty and the Covenant of the League. House remarked that the Three had exceeded their powers in deciding what only a plenary session of the Conference had any right to decide, and he succeeded in securing a reversal of the decision. [55] However right he may have been on this matter, it can hardly have improved his relations with Wilson, to whom he evidently spoke with considerable frankness. Moreover, on May 7, without consulting anyone, the Big Three apparently completed distribution of the first set of mandates, in complete disregard of Italy's colonial claims under the Treaty of London, in order to punish her representatives for their defection from the Conference.

The Colonial expert, George Louis Beer, returned from London to Paris, on May 9, to learn that the matter was settled, and "Evidently House knew nothing of this. Certainly Mezes did not." [56] It is clear from the record that House had not been consulted confidentially by Wilson on any matters of importance since the crisis within the American Delegation over the compromise Fiume proposals, on Good Friday, April 18.

6 : *House and the Experts*

There is a conflict of evidence about the effect of the Fiume crisis on the relations between Colonel House and the experts. It is sufficiently clear that many of them felt bitterly about him, and, on May 5, "Bliss spoke of the great irritation of the experts at House." [57] About two weeks later, Norman Davis blamed the Colonel for the compromises in the treaty. [58] Yet, not only is House's own diary completely free from references to the letter of protest signed by the six experts and from allusions to its consequences, but he later maintained relations of complete cordiality with many of these men. Moreover, when one of the six later put questions to him about the episode, he seemed to have no clear recollection about it.[59] But against the Colonel's silence must be set considerable positive evidence that, at the time, he resented their action and even took steps to retaliate.

He never knew that one of the six had been consulted by General Bliss in the presence of a confidential agent of President Wilson, but he cannot have been unaware of the change in Wilson's attitude toward him which immediately followed the letter of protest signed by the six experts. He may well have attributed the whole difficulty to that fact. It is certain that in all honesty he would have regarded the experts' protest as unrealistic and childish, and there is no doubt that he deeply deplored the rigidity of attitude which it induced in Wilson. On much more than purely personal grounds he would have had every reason to object to an action which, in his view, had wrecked a promising negotiation and brought about the worst crisis of the entire Peace Conference. Something might yet be salvaged, if negotiations could be brought back to a proper basis, but that could scarcely happen unless the six experts were relegated to their proper sphere. Broad considerations of policy would reinforce whatever personal motives the Colonel might have for an attempt to achieve that result.

George Louis Beer had established close relations with Colonel House during the Fiume negotiations and was in a position to know the Colonel's mind. He had reason to believe that the letter of protest was, in part, directed against himself for intervening in Adriatic questions which were not in the immediate sphere of his responsibility. His own explanation of the letter emphasizes that notion very strongly, and colors his account with a tinge of emotion which requires that caution be used against taking his version too literally. The substance of that record appears in his diary for April 29:

Learned inside history of letters signed by six—Young, Bowman, Lunt, Johnson, Day, and Seymour—about Fiume which determined the President and led to his public statement causing Italy to withdraw from the Conference. Mezes and House were working in favor of a compromise and both were furious at the letter. He (sic) weakened House with the President and weakened Mezes with House. House, I understand, resents the conduct of the six and considers it disloyal. All six are to go home on or about May 15, while Shotwell, Hornbeck, I and the rest are to be asked to stay—So be it! . . .[60]

One is struck by the definiteness of the statement that the six are to go home—as if it were a matter already decided. Ten days later, May 9, Beer was summoned back to Paris from his journey to England to attend to colonial matters. It was Mezes who sent for him and, on his return, he discovered that a distribution of mandates had already occurred, apparently without either House or Mezes knowing anything about it. He noted in his diary on May 9:

281

While I was away, Mezes wrote to the President, evidently at House's instruction, that most of the men on the Inquiry could go home. The three Commissioners who are opposed to House—Lansing, White, Bliss—recommended that they stay and the President upheld them. Thus here and in the Fiume case House has been overruled. The feud is evidently a bitter one. The protesting Commissioners are working together and want to keep their record clear for later explanation at home. . . .[61]

This was not gossip. Beer was in close touch with Mezes, and wrote from a viewpoint that was sympathetic toward both House and Mezes. This entry in his diary, taken in conjunction with that of April 29 dealing with essentially the same matter, would constitute strong positive evidence concerning Colonel House's attitude and intentions and when it is confirmed independently by two different members of the expert group who were opposed to the House group, it becomes conclusive. These other two men cited respectively as their informants the Commissioners Henry White and Robert Lansing, and each stated that his informant was indignant at House's proposal to send the experts home.[62] Finally, when Dr. Bowman, for personal and family reasons, applied to the Commissioners for leave to go home about May 15, the Commissioners were extremely reluctant to have him go, lest his departure look like a victory for House's proposal. The relevant extracts from the official minutes of their meeting of May 7 read:

. . . At the same time they expressed regret on seeing that Dr. Bowman intended to leave Paris on May 15th, and General Bliss offered on behalf of the Commissioners to speak to Dr. Bowman and ascertain whether it would not be possible for him to remain longer.[63]

Against this positive evidence, Colonel House's own silence can hardly prevail, althought it is perhaps easier to explain his later silence than to account for his failure to allude to these matters, day by day, in his diary. There is implicit in these events a deep personal humiliation for Colonel House that he had every human right to conceal, and he would be entitled to perpetuate that privacy did it not conflict with the rights of others. But the effect of the concealment has been to cloud President Wilson's reputation with imputations of pettiness in his personal relations with House, and both men can be judged fairly only in the light of the full record and not with such parts of it as will serve each man's reputation best. As men who willingly assumed vast public responsibilities, their personal relations form an essential part of the story of how they discharged those responsibilities. They are, therefore, the legitimate concern of the historian.

7 : *Fiume for the Last Time*

President Wilson's public appeal of April 23 to the Italians was a resounding failure and, although he made it only after the fullest consultation with all the American Commissioners Plenipotentiary, it must be recorded as one of the worst mistakes he made in Paris. On the other hand, the Italian defiance of Wilson was a boomerang. In their absence from Paris, the Big Three completed the German treaty and proceeded with settlements which ignored Italian claims. Orlando and Sonnino returned to Paris on May 6.

About May 12, Colonel House resumed the initiative in the Italian negotiations, with Wilson's assent, but not with the free hand he considered necessary to achieve a settlement. Thomas Nelson Page, the American Ambassador to Italy, had arrived in Paris to explain that "nothing can save Italy but giving her Fiume." [64] Page wrote two notes to President Wilson and House telephoned in the effort to have Wilson receive Page, but still there was no disposition to see

283

him. On May 11, House warned Wilson by telephone that Page might resign immediately if subjected to such treatment, and Wilson replied that it made little difference whether Page resigned now or later.[65] The following day, Wilson called at the Crillon, where he discussed the Italian situation with Henry White and Colonel House. House felt that, for the first time, Wilson realized the seriousness of the situation, and he became more hopeful.[66] It is evident that House secured Wilson's permission to try again.[67]

During the confusion of the next few days, it became apparent that the restrictions surrounding the permission robbed it of any real value to Colonel House. David Hunter Miller was to act as his agent in dealing direct with Orlando, but had to explain to him that, whereas Colonel House promised definitely to support any arrangement they could agree upon, President Wilson had promised only to consider it. Miller warned Orlando that he had no authority to commit the President, and remarked jokingly, "I have not full powers from President Wilson, but I have full powers from Colonel House."[68] Although Orlando replied, *"C'est beaucoup,"* it turned out to be not enough.

The stumbling block was not merely Wilson's own intransigence, but the Yugoslav resistance, which had been encouraged by the official American attitude. The Yugoslavs were not likely to yield now to compromise proposals unless required to do so by American coercion. Wilson would never permit that, and when he was asked if he would accept a direct Italo-Yugoslav deal, he agreed, provided that it were *"freely reached."*[69]

Colonel House played an entirely honorable rôle and a very exacting one in this affair. He kept President Wilson fully informed of what he was doing at each stage and when Wilson expressed alarm that Orlando might regard House's proposals as coming officially from the President, House ". . .

284

calmed his mind about this. . . ." [70] He kept within the letter of his instructions.

The final effort failed for want of authority to coerce the Yugoslavs. The Colonel arranged a three-room conference at the Crillon on the afternoon and evening of May 16, from five o'clock until nine, putting the pro-Yugoslav Frazier and Johnson, in one room with Trumbitch; the pro-Italian Miller and Beer in another room with Orlando, while directing the conference from a room between, and going from one room to another. [71] The points of difference were narrowed considerably, but not eliminated. Miller, Beer, and House felt that the Italians had been conciliatory, the Yugoslavs recalcitrant. They, therefore, proposed to reach an Italo-American agreement which the Yugoslavs should be required to accept. As Beer put it, the "plan now is to get President Wilson to agree to the Italian plan and to put it into effect, no matter what the Yugoslavs think." [72] The President would not permit that. Before the elaborate conference, he had seen Colonel House to thank him for his efforts, "but showed no inclination to be conciliatory to the Italians." [73] The next morning, Colonel House, in conference with Miller, Beer, Orlando, and di Cellere, telephoned President Wilson for authority to proceed on the basis of Italian concessions and the request was denied. [74]

From then to the end it was the same story: Wilson's refusal to accept Italian concessions and to force the Yugoslavs to do likewise. Colonel House felt that he could have got agreement at that time if Wilson would only grant him authority to coerce the Yugolavs, [75] and Beer was in despair that Wilson and Johnson had made a "fetish" of their particular line in the Adriatic. [76] Beer even suggested trying to work through Lloyd George's secretary, Philip Kerr, to get Lloyd George to use his influence with Wilson, [77] and Lloyd George himself tells a circumstantial story of a private meeting with House and Clemenceau, arranged by House for the sake of ending the nerve-racking dispute—a meeting interrupted by Wilson with every evidence of suspicion.[78] The Fiume dispute was never settled at Paris.

8 : *The Aftermath*

It is certain that Colonel House saw President Wilson from time to time during the latter part of May and early June, but, again, it was usually in the company of the other Commissioners. After the crucial conference of May 16, House did not see Wilson until May 20, in conference with the other Commissioners; he saw him alone at Wilson's own quarters to discuss Italian matters, on May 25. He telephoned him and went up to see him again about Italy, on May 28. On May 29 and 31 and June 2, President Wilson met all the Commissioners at the Crillon and on June 3 he met the entire American Delegation—experts and all—to discuss Lloyd George's proposals for revising the German treaty. The following day, he and Colonel House were in communication by telephone. On June 8, House had an interview with Clemenceau and later saw Wilson to report the substance of the interview. On June 11, he recorded, "My interview with the President was in the nature of a farewell." House was leaving shortly for England.[79]

In the light of this chronology, it is impossible to take literally the entry in Lansing's diary for June 10:

White, Bliss, and House in my office discussing the present situation. House complained bitterly that he has not been able to get to the President since he was here in my office and that he could not find out about what was going on since Sir William Wiseman left.[80]

Yet, in three weeks, House had seen Wilson alone only about three times, according to the evidence of his own diary, although about half a dozen times in the company of the other Commissioners. This is not evidence of a complete break in personal relations; but it does prove extinction of the unusually close tie of personal intimacy which had bound the two men prior to the Fiume crisis of April 18. Moreover, Wilson's attitude toward Colonel House at this period is indicated by Admiral Cary Grayson's remarks that the Colonel's disposition to compromise had caused much of the difficulty at the Peace Conference.[81] Grayson, as the President's physician and intimate of his household, would presumably know the President's views. However, House and Wilson met once more, face to face, on June 28, just before the President's departure for home, and the Colonel's record of that meeting hints at the divergence between them:

My last conversation with the President yesterday was not reassuring. I urged him to meet the Senate in a conciliatory spirit; if he treated them with the same consideration he had used with his foreign colleagues here, all would be well. In reply he said, "House, I have found one can never get anything in this life that is worth while without fighting for it." I combated this, and reminded him that Anglo-Saxon civilization was built up on compromise. . . .[82]

Colonel House never saw President Wilson again. During August rumors of a break became current and on August 29, Wilson cabled House that he was "deeply disturbed by malicious story about break between us," and advised "silent contempt" as the proper way to treat the story. However Colonel House himself may have regarded the message, Henry White, knowing the background of events in Paris, said, "Of course, his wording is tactful. But what he really meant is this: 'The story is true, and I do not wish you to deny it.'"[83] Later, White delivered his own verdict on the rôle of Colonel House at Paris. On November 8, 1919, he wrote Lansing:

287

. . . I was not aware until recently of the extent to which intrigue went on "upstairs" during the earlier months of the Conference, with a view to preventing any of the views of our experts, which happened to be contrary to those held there, from reaching the President. Still less had I any idea of the attempts made to get some of the experts to change their views and adopt those advocated in the small upper chamber previously mentioned.

Since your departure I have realized more and more how grievously misled the Italians and others were by the tendency to compromise and by the assurances of friendship and sympathy, of a general nature at least, if not actually with their particular views, expressed during their interviews upstairs; and there is no question in my mind that the Fiume and other questions would have been settled while the President was still here, if they had been left in your hands, or kept in the President's, and had not been hampered by a feeling upstairs that no decision should be attempted, much less reached, which would in any way be likely to cause jeopardy to the adoption of the Covenant of the League of Nations. . . .[84]

With all allowance for exaggeration, Henry White has called attention to an important factor in American diplomacy at the Paris Peace Conference.

★ 12 ★

RETROSPECT AND PROSPECT

---

1 : *Who Were the Realists?*

THE INTELLECTUAL NIHILISM of the twenty years since Versailles has destroyed faith in the Wilsonian program at Paris. By misrepresenting the character of the treaty, the motives that inspired it, above all by denial of any genuine American stake in European settlement, it has provided the strongest moral force by which Hitler "softens" his victims before striking them down with physical force. The disillusioned liberal has been the unwitting ally of the cynical advocate of physical force as the only conceivable basis for world politics.

In such an atmosphere, any constructive effort like Wilson's is bound to appear silly and unrealistic. The romantic liberal must see the immediate realization of his hopes or turn on the author of his hopes with charges of betrayal, and those who have thoroughly cynical reasons for opposing a new order will welcome the charges. The statesman who labors for the best constructive results obtainable in a chaotic world starts under the terrible handicap of a war on two fronts: against cynical opposition, and equally against his sentimental and perfectionist supporters. At Paris the situa-

289

tion was complicated by the fact that the American Delegation contained not merely representatives of the Simon-pure liberal school, but advocates of the opposition itself, not in any cynical sense, but because they were so profoundly impressed with political realities as they existed that instinctively they thought in terms of compromise beyond the limits of any real necessity.

In this welter of conflicting viewpoints it has recently become fashionable to eschew all standards of judgment and to resort to the methods of social psychology in describing the mêlée. The result has the pleasingly remote, detached, and scientific atmosphere of a study in anthropology. It becomes a study in abstraction and determinism, and involves no issues or principles with which any reader need concern himself. It is both the realistic and the scientific method applied to the writing of history, and it reinforces the intellectual nihilism of the disillusioned liberal.

Is it really scientific in taking account of all the data within the particular field of its concern? The only thing this method leaves out is the set of standards and principles which men themselves accepted as the basis upon which they agreed to work, and thereby accepted as the standards by which they might legitimately be judged. The only element which gives coherence and significance to the study of the Paris Peace Conference is the set of principles with reference to which it acted, the degree to which it embodied them in the treaties, the extent to which it departed from them, and the reasons—personal and political—for the result. No account which ignores or prejudges that frame of reference can claim to be scientific.

To assume at the outset that the Fourteen Points were unreal and impractical, incapable of being translated into concrete terms of peace, ignores the simple fact that they constituted a legal contract between the Allied and Associated

Powers and Germany to govern the terms of peace. It is just as unrealistic to impugn the intelligence and integrity of the Peace Commissioners who took the contract seriously in the first place as to denounce them all indiscriminately as hypocrites who systematically violated principles in which they never believed, or as fools who could not recognize the violation of a principle when they committed it. The contract was there as the basis of all their efforts. It was a reasonably ascertainable contract, the details of application admittedly difficult, but by no means so impossible as many writers have alleged. It is quite as possible to distinguish between the degrees of good faith and intelligence brought to the task by the different national delegations at Paris, as it is possible to distinguish the degrees of intelligence and good faith within the personnel of any one of these delegations. Such treatment must, obviously, take account of the real political pressures upon men by national tradition and public opinion. To ignore the necessity of reasonable compromise in political affairs is just as fatal to realism as to assume that, all politics being of the essence of compromise, there are no rules at all and no standards of judgment but those of immediate political success.

It is an extraordinary fact that as yet there has been no balanced interpretation of Peace Conference diplomacy to take the measure of all the factors involved. When a penetrating critic like Harold Nicolson undertakes to recall the discussion to a firm basis of reality by emphasizing the fundamental conflict of principle, he does so only to go off the deep end of romantic-liberal disillusionment, and produces a spiritual autobiography of his loss of faith in Wilson. In his reaction against the prophets and dreamers of the world, he embraces the realists who at least know the rules of the balance of power in Europe—for example, Eyre Crowe of the

British Foreign Office and Colonel House, "the best diplomatic brain America has yet produced."

The issue of realism at Paris is mainly the question of the short-term as against the long-range view. The pressures of national demands, made effective and menacing through diplomatic strategy in the League of Nations Commission, made immediate and pressing by the danger of delay in pacifying a turbulent and disintegrating Europe, necessitated a degree of compromise. The realists of the American Delegation lost their perspective under such pressure and were ready to throw away all their cargo in the scramble for the lifeboats. The cargo consisted of the Fourteen Points, the substance of the Pre-Armistice Agreement, the contract with Germany. Colonel House felt that if the boat were lightened sufficiently, it would still carry the League of Nations, but Harold Nicolson's description of a general *sauve qui peut* attitude in the later phases of the Peace Conference applies well to elements within the American delegation. In this atmosphere, one concession was an argument for the next.

Mezes could not see why the American delegation should "stand up so much straighter" on the Fiume question against the Italians than in other questions involving other Powers; Colonel House advocated extreme concession to the Japanese on the ground that, although clearly a violation of principle, it was no worse than many other concessions which had already been made. There was little attempt to discriminate between detail and principle, between the relative merits of national demands, between the varying degrees of diplomatic strength which supported the demands. Above all, there was no thought save for the immediate future—make peace quickly and start the League of Nations. The realism of these men consisted in an abdication of sheer nerve and intelligence.

Naturally, President Wilson looked stiff and unrealistic

292

when viewed through the eyes of such men, at the very time when William Bullitt was resigning from the American Delegation in protest at Wilson's sacrifice of principle, and others were grumbling that the treaty was thoroughly bad. To the former group he seemed rigid and uncompromising, to the latter weak and uncertain in his stand on principle. A careful study of the record reveals an extraordinary consistency in Wilson's fight for his program under overwhelming difficulties, as well as a high degree of political intelligence in translating the abstract principle of his program into concrete details of application.

The President's understanding of the real issues involved in the Saar case was superior to that of his own experts, and that was the only issue where he stood completely alone against everyone in Paris. In the Polish case, he was convinced by the arguments of Lloyd George as to the long-term results of a settlement based on the Polish Commission's report and loyally supported Lloyd George's efforts to modify that settlement in the face of the Polish sympathies of the American experts. He withstood steadfastly Colonel House's pressure to compromise on the Colonial question, the Rhineland, the Saar, the Adriatic. His worst defeats were the Reparation settlement and Shantung; the first occurred while Wilson was ill, when Colonel House abandoned the American program; the second, because of an impregnable political and diplomatic position held by the Japanese.

Throughout the conference Wilson maintained his stand on principle as the only safe guide in a welter of conflicting interests, as the sole safeguard against laying foundations for future conflict. That was the meaning of his attempt to force an admission from Colonel House that the pro-French proposals of the American experts for the Saar valley were a violation of the Fourteen Points. The record for the crucial April period is eloquent testimony to the President's perspective and force, and Fiume is the final symbol. In the nature of the case, Wilson's rôle—aside from the arduous work in the League of Nations Commission—had to be negative rather than constructive, to concern itself with prevention rather than cure. Consequently the failure of his curative and constructive work, as the result primarily of American refusal to ratify the treaty and enter the League of Nations, has obscured the real nature of his achievement at Paris. It is so much easier to record failures than to carry through the laborious task of assessing a man's work by careful measurement of what he prevented, as well as by study of positive achievements.

Perhaps the most general criticism President Wilson has encountered, at the time and since, has been on the score of his decision to attend the Peace Conference in person. The decision itself was attributed to excessive vanity, and the effect has generally been described as the degradation of the remote and lofty, almost godlike arbiter to a bloody and battered contestant in the European prize ring. The assumption is that Wilson in Washington could have retained his detachment with an ultimate power of decision while delegating the rough-and-tumble of negotiation to Colonel House in Paris. It is interesting that Secretary Lansing and Colonel House, who agreed upon practically nothing else, should have consistently concurred on the unwisdom of the President's coming to Paris. Independently, they tried in advance to prevent it; subsequently, they communed over the misfortune of the event. Yet, in view of Lansing's attitude toward Colonel House, it is difficult to imagine his acquiescing in the Colonel's primacy in Paris. It is possible that each man in the assurance of his own superior wisdom felt confident of exercising greater influence in Wilson's absence.

The present book affords the most positive answer on this

point. The record clearly shows that on every major question but that of Reparation, the Treaty of Versailles would have been a worse treaty had Wilson remained in Washington. With all his mistakes, he emerges as the only man of real stature at Paris.

His fight for ratification—when he returned to the United States—is another story and another Wilson. The strain of his intensive speaking campaign on behalf of ratification super-added to the long strain of the struggle in Paris, brought a physical collapse. After the stroke of paralysis, in October 1919, he became readier prey to the tactics of the Senate Irreconcilables, whose game was so to amend and denature the League Covenant that the author himself would reject his own handiwork. At the very moment when French and British officials indicated their willingness to accept the de-naturing amendments for the sake of continued American collaboration in Europe, Wilson gave the fateful order of rejection:

I shall consent to nothing. The Senate must take its own medicine.

2 : *Versailles to Hitler*

The treaty was essentially a compromise between Anglo-American and French conceptions of a stable international order. On the one hand, immediate French concern for military security was taken care of by the limitation of German armaments, demilitarization of the Rhineland area and Allied military occupation for a fifteen-year period, and—finally—an Anglo-American treaty of military guarantee. These were certainly adequate guarantees, granted the full weight of English and American resources to support them, and there could be every hope that they would enlist France in the cause of an effective League of Nations. They repre-

295

sented the minimum price which English and American negotiators had to pay for French abandonment of their traditional policy of entirely dismembering Germany. They were a realistic concession to French needs without violating the Fourteen Points in any important particular. Above all, they were regarded as essentially interim measures to provide the necessary breathing spell for the consolidation of the League. Military occupation of German soil would end in fifteen years, at the very moment when residents of the Saar valley might vote to return to German sovereignty; German disarmament was to be the prelude to general disarmament; and the Anglo-American treaty of military guarantee was to cease when the League itself was thought strong enough to provide general security.

The Reparation settlement was the chief stumbling block, partly because of impossible financial demands, even more because it combined an egregious breach of faith with an impolitic accusation of moral turpitude. In both financial and political results it proved disastrous. Yet, even here, American participation in the settlement could be counted upon to exert a moderating influence, while the English were certain to recover their sanity on a subject so close to their own interest, and would try to undo the harm they had done by their original collaboration with the French to defeat the American program. The Reparation issue emphasized more than any other the necessity of continuing Anglo-American coöperation to make effective Anglo-American conceptions of a world order.

It is vitally important to distinguish between the treaty as a written constitution and as a policy in action. Students of constitutional law have long since learned to distinguish between the intentions of founding fathers, as expressed in the verbal niceties of a constitutional document on the one hand, and the practical application of organic law to a con-

296

stantly changing society on the other hand. Students of international politics, more particularly students of international law, have on the whole been less discriminating. The history of the Treaty of Versailles would have been very different if the United States had ratified it, since the treaty itself was largely shaped on the assumption that it would have behind it both the authority of the United States and the impartial influence of the United States as a constantly moderating influence in its enforcement.

The defection of the United States destroyed the Anglo-American preponderance which alone could have stabilized Europe. It impaired the authority and prestige of the League at its birth and it precipitated an Anglo-French duel which reduced Europe to the chaos from which Hitler emerged to produce new chaos which he has christened the "New Europe." Practically and immediately, it destroyed the Anglo-American treaty of military guarantee which was to have been one of the main props of French security, and it removed every prospect of material American support for all the other guarantees of French security. The French had very reluctantly yielded their extreme program for the dismemberment of Germany in return for guarantees which were now made to appear worthless. Here was complete confirmation of the French military logic which had always been skeptical of Anglo-American sentimentalism, professions of faith, and reliance on the voluntary principle. Clemenceau did not long survive, politically, his concessions to Anglo-American blandishments, and a reactionary nationalist like Poincaré, who had intrigued in 1919 to prevent those concessions, was more than likely to revive traditional French military projects in a dangerous form.

English sentiment was already developing the guilt-complex about the whole Treaty of Versailles which, among other factors, paralyzed English foreign policy from Versailles to

Munich. It would be interesting to speculate as to how much that guilt-complex was the result of the brilliant writing of John Maynard Keynes. Devastatingly accurate and prophetic in its analysis of the economic aspects of the treaty, his *The Economic Consequences of the Peace* included the whole treaty in one sweeping condemnation as a "Carthaginian Peace," and his caricatures of the leading negotiators at Paris immediately fixed stereotypes which still affect much of the writing about the Paris Peace Conference. At the very time that the United States Government repudiated the Versailles settlement legally, the English people did so morally, and the French Government saw all the guarantees of the settlement doubly impaired. *Perfide Albion* became the popular text for French commentary on European affairs in the early post-war years.

The weak and necessarily opportunist German Republic, itself the artificial creation of President Wilson's pre-armistice notes, was quick to observe the divergence and to capitalize on the opportunity offered for evasion. The French naturally attributed their difficulties with Germany to English bad faith, and the more England displayed sympathy for Germany, the more the French tended to resort to reactionary, violent, and military measures of very doubtful legality under the terms of the treaty. The greater the ruthlessness of French efforts to enforce the treaty on an evasive Germany, the more sympathy was available for Germany in England, and in the United States.

No one of the three Powers involved in this contest was strong enough to make its will and its policy prevail to break the vicious circle of conflict. English sympathy was sufficient to encourage German resistance, but official British policy was not strong enough to prevent the retaliatory measures taken by the French Government. France, single-handed, was strong enough to impose punitive and destructive measures on Germany, but not sufficiently strong to effect a lasting settlement, while Germany was strong enough to resist complete capitulation only at the cost of measures ultimately destructive of German economy and political stability.

Reparation demands were the focal point of the struggle and they proved the nemesis for Lloyd George's behavior at the Peace Conference. Here, the French had a strong legal case based on provisions which the English themselves had helped to write into the treaty over the objections of the American Delegation. English enlightenment came too late to alter the treaty legally and, consequently, British exhortations to the French for greater reasonableness looked like characteristic betrayal and a breach of contract. French leaders felt that both Great Britain and the United States had betrayed the Versailles provisions for French security and felt entitled to use undoubted legal rights to reparation as the means of gaining security in their own way.

Poincaré secured a verdict from the Reparation Commission—over the protest of the British representative—that Germany was in default on her reparation payments and, in conjunction with Belgium, ordered a military occupation of the industrial nerve center of Germany in the Ruhr valley on the right bank of the Rhine. Law Officers of the British Crown vainly pronounced the action illegal under the terms of the treaty; the British Government could do nothing to prevent it. Although Poincaré justified the occupation as legitimate application of treaty sanctions merely to secure the economic resources to which France was legally entitled—"Productive Guarantees" was the phrase he used—the occupation soon became the cover for familiar French military intrigue to dismember Germany. Again the entire Rhineland area seethed with "Separatist" activity of the sort which Clemenceau had stopped in 1919 as the result of President Wilson's protests.

French action was a failure in both its economic and its political aspects. It encountered the passive resistance of the German workers in the Ruhr and could not capitalize on its physical control of German resources, while the Separatist movement as a purely artificial creation of French generals could not survive the spotlight of publicity which the English Government was able to throw upon it as the result of investigations by their Munich consul, Mr. Clive. Meantime, the costs of occupation in connection with the collapse of German economy had reacted violently on the French financial structure. The reactionary nationalist Poincaré fell from office and was replaced by Herriot, internationalist by party doctrine and by conviction, at the same time that Ramsay MacDonald became the first Labor Prime Minister of Great Britain. The Anglo-French duel was temporarily at an end. Was it too late?

Germany, too, had produced a realistic and moderate leader in Stresemann, who would coöperate with his French and British colleagues to stabilize Europe, provided economic resources could be found to heal the financial and psychological wounds of both the war and the peace. Today it can be seen that the German wounds were fatal. Although in an immediate sense they were self-inflicted and warrant the technical verdict of suicide, neither psychiatrist nor historian can be content with a coroner's verdict and would want to know something of the circumstances which drove the victim to desperation. The weak German Republic fell heir to a currency already inflated by the strain of war economy and reparation liabilities, which could be bolstered only by drastic taxation, and the incidence of that taxation would affect those elements of the population most hostile to the republic and most bitter against the peace treaty.

The German Government was between the upper and nether millstones of impossible reparation demands and the intransigence of the only people within Germany who could afford to make any effort to pay them. Under the circumstances, it employed the printing presses to create money which gave immediate relief to both government and industry from their bonded debt, by decreasing the value of the currency with which they paid it. Such a course inevitably led to default on reparation payments, but in any case that was probably inevitable in the long run, and in view of the British attitude there was a reasonably good chance that default would escape punishment.

It is likely that one object of the French occupation of the Ruhr valley was to break the resistance of the large industrialists by seizure of the citadel of their strength. In that object, as in all others, French policy was a failure. It was not the Ruhr industry, but the already hard-pressed German Government, which bore the cost of subsidizing the German workers of the Ruhr in passive resistance to French exploitation. In default of taxes on industry to support the cost, the Government once more had recourse to the printing presses. To cheat the French, it destroyed the value of the German mark and, with it, the economic position of the most stable element in German politics—the German middle class. While the large industrialist was being freed of the remainder of his bonded debt, it was at the expense of his creditors, the investors, and of all people who lived on fixed income or salary.

The balance of political power almost inevitably shifted from the impoverished middle groups—which were potentially the most loyal supporters of the German Republic—toward the industrialist element whose Republican sentiments were, at best, lukewarm. Nor was it merely that a formerly important class had lost both its economic and its political position. It did not, thereby, become negligible, passive, impotent. It developed a positive hostility to the institutions which had betrayed them. It became a productive

301

recruiting ground for Hitler's Nazi movement. The very foundations for republican and democratic institutions in Germany were thus permanently impaired as a consequence of the Reparation Settlement, American defection from the whole Peace Settlement, and the Anglo-French duel culminating in the occupation of the Ruhr.

Stresemann was the only German leader with sufficient realism and force to secure support from his erstwhile colleagues among the industrialist group, in his efforts to stabilize the Republic and to institute a policy of genuine collaboration with Great Britain and France in stabilizing Europe. The era of Locarno suffused the international scene with an unreal glow which hid the fatal lesions in the European body politic. The two essentials for a genuine stabilization were lacking. The deep fissures in the economic foundations of Europe had been merely papered over with American loans, and, as Stresemann complained shortly before his death, the political concessions which British and French leaders were willing to offer him had always been too little and too late to popularize his régime and his policy within Germany; too late to win German youth for the cause of peace.

With the world-wide economic collapse, Germans increasingly accepted Hitler's thesis that the victors of 1919 would yield only to force and never to reason, and the policy of "appeasement" adopted by Britain and France fortified their faith. Voluntary appeasement of Stresemann's, Germany— the Germany of the Weimar Republic—could have been largely confined to the economic sphere and could have won German support to the other major provisions of the Treaty of Versailles.

Only too late did British and French leaders observe that Hitler was less concerned about rectification of the "injustices" of the *Diktat* of Versailles than with the conquest

302

of Europe. The muddle and confusion in liberal and democratic communities about the real character of Versailles contributed to the stupidity of Allied policy from Versailles to Armageddon.

3 : *National Traditions*

The voice of Vichy is certainly not the voice of France. Traditions of national policy developed in periods of freedom can be apparently extinguished by conquest, but they are likely to reappear with the freedom of action to exercise them. Poland disappeared from the map of Europe for a century and a half, but its rebirth as a military state in 1919 reproduced familiar patterns of national policy, such as alliance with France. Those patterns lie buried deep in the logic of geographical position and historical development. "The fourth and final partition of Poland" by Hitler and Stalin in 1939 was equally, as this characterization implies, a reassertion of traditional German and Russian policy. It would not be difficult to forecast the main outlines of Polish foreign policy if, by any chance, Poland rises again from her "final" burial.

Before the French military collapse in June of 1940, there was renewed talk of the dismemberment of Germany and of the seizure of the Rhine frontier. It was plausible to argue that the rise of Hitler and the outbreak of war twenty years after Versailles proved the justification of French proposals at Versailles, but the really significant factor in the revival of traditional French policy was the amount of sympathy it evoked from British liberal opinion. To cite only one instance, there is the recantation of the late Robert Dell, for years correspondent of the *Manchester Guardian* in Geneva, who wrote in *The Nation*, December 23, 1939:

One thing is certain. The French will not, if they can help it, tolerate the menace of a united Germany on their frontier any longer. They have put up with it for nearly seventy years and they have had enough of it. If the Allies have the victory, the French will probably insist on the break-up of the German Empire into its constituent parts and on the reduction of Prussia to its original dimensions. They will certainly insist on what they asked for in 1919, namely, the separation of the Rhineland from Germany and its conversion into an autonomous and neutral state with its bridgeheads garrisoned by the French army. *I was opposed to the French demand in 1919, but experience has taught me that the French were right.* They abandoned that demand in return for guarantees by England and the United States, which were not implemented. The French felt, quite rightly, that they had been badly let down, and they are determined not to be let down again. When the German sheep were split up into little flocks with inoffensive little Führers, they were harmless. When the sheep became united in a single flock with a single bellwether, they became *Moutons enragés*. Germany is a pathological case and needs pathological treatment. I do not say that the German people will never change, but it will take a long time to bring them to sanity and civilization.

This may have been only a straw in the wind, but taken in conjunction with other symptoms, it may indicate a real revolution in British habits of thought. Russians, Germans, Frenchmen, and Italians still seem to be acting in ways consistent with the traditions developed by their national governments in response to geographical and physical conditions. Hitler's treatment of his victims is the logical application of the Von Clausewitz philosophy of war and the extension of Ludendorff's specific plans for German hegemony in Europe. A victorious Hitler is likely to treat his Italian ally with the same contempt and the same parsimony which Italians charged against their allies of 1919.

Official and unofficial England has recently been talking and acting differently from the England of 1919, or even the England of the Napoleonic era. Six months before war

304

broke out in 1939, Great Britain officially adopted conscription and shortly thereafter undertook a military guarantee for the preservation of one of the central European states. This was the sort of policy which France had been vainly urging the English to adopt at Versailles and for the twenty years thereafter. The French had argued that the problem of peace was *integral,* whole and indivisible, but the British had persisted until the eleventh hour in their traditional assumptions based on insularity, detachment, relative isolation from European affairs. Britain would defend Belgium and France from attack and invasion, the time-honored principle of limited liability applied to the Channel coasts directly opposite the English shore, but there would be no conscription and no further guarantees of a stable European order.

The revolution of British policy was a belated response to a fundamental change in geographical situation wrought by the technology of modern warfare. The English Channel may yet prove an effective defense line, and naval power the ultimate deciding factor in the second World War, but neither the Channel nor naval power can provide the impregnable barrier they once did to afford the English their traditional luxury of spiritual isolation from continental affairs. The impact of the Hitler régime has embedded England firmly in continental Europe, and may well have inaugurated new traditions of policy more in line with those practiced for centuries by France.

Under these circumstances a new Versailles would probably dismember Germany politically and territorially. It required a united Anglo-American front to prevent France from achieving that result in 1919. Speculation in 1941 about the ultimate outcome of the wars is idle, but there is adequate data for forecasting the contours of Europe that would emerge from a British victory over Hitler. Officially, the British have said little about their war aims; unofficially, they have talked a great deal about a federated Europe. "Federation" as an ideal for an economically stable and a politically coöperating world is the counterpart of the League of Nations in the public discussions of English and American groups from 1915 to 1919, and, like its counterpart in those preliminary stages, remains equally vague. Yet its aim is clearly constructive, its intent is to weld together in indissoluble bonds the separate national sovereignties of Europe. How can such a program be reconciled with the apparently destructive schemes France has advocated for the "Federalization" of Germany?—schemes which the British themselves now seem to regard with more favor than in 1919. The British are certain to show as much concern with the immediate problem of destroying the military menace of a united Germany as the French did in 1919. It is difficult to see how that can be combined with a constructive program for a federal Europe.

One British liberal has suggested how it can be done. Robert Dell, formerly of the *Manchester Guardian,* has insisted on the federalization, the dismemberment, of the German Reich, its disintegration into the separate federal entities of which it was composed. That was what the French had proposed in 1919 and what Versailles failed to do. In that respect the treaty was too lenient politically. Yet Dell would break down only to rebuild. If the Treaty of Versailles was too lenient politically, it was too severe economically in the Reparation Settlement. This time everything possible "must be done to foster the economic life of the German states," and that leads straight to the construction of a European federation:

. . . The matter would be immensely simplified by a European federation of which all the German states would be members. In any case a European customs union is essential, for we cannot

306

permit the German states to have a customs union of their own. We must get rid of all the tariff barriers that are ruining the economic life of Europe. A European federation would be particularly to the advantage of the small countries, for it would make the continued existence and autonomy of even the smallest country possible. Without federation, the very small European countries can hardly survive. . . .

Here is a possible synthesis of the necessarily destructive work that must be done and the constructive work that must now be accomplished to avert new chaos. It fits well the historical forces and the historical lessons of the twenty years since Versailles. It requires the opportunity provided by British victory to be tried at all, and it demands a leadership of realism and vision to attempt it and to make it productive. Destruction is always easier than construction, and a new Versailles might conceivably make the original Versailles seem the embodiment of wisdom and justice.

4 : *"Union Now"—or Never?*

Have the twenty years since Versailles wrought any change in the American tradition of isolation? American rejection of the Versailles settlement emphasized the tradition by repudiating the Wilsonian policy for American participation in a new world order. By a curious logic the inevitable European chaos which resulted from American isolation has been used as a further foundation for isolationist argument. Scholars and publicists, with all the wisdom of hindsight, discovered that American participation in the World War in 1917 had been an unwarranted departure from sound historical tradition, and legislators in Congress guaranteed the United States from future errors by an elaborate series of neutrality laws. The complete distortion of the rôle of the United States in the first World War and at Versailles crystallized a powerful isolationist sentiment which threatens to paralyze American foreign policy in the present increasingly critical world situation.

A year and a half of the new World War has dissipated much of that sentiment by creating an actual sense of danger to American interests, even within the American hemisphere. Under the impact of the danger, American habits of thought have undergone nearly as much transformation as did British habits in the year between Munich and the outbreak of war. The actual third-term candidacy of President Roosevelt and his reëlection mean, more than anything else, maximum aid to the powers fighting Fascist aggression as the best insurance of American security.

Both the administration and the popular majority which supports it *hope* that sufficient aid to Britain will stop Hitler without active American participation in the war, and they doubtless *intend* that American aid shall stop short of actual war. But does the decision actually lie in their hands? It is clear already that Hitler regards American aid to Britain as an important factor in British resistance to Nazi conquest, and it is likely to become more so. He has already tried to frighten the American Government into abandonment of its policy by the indirect threat of an alliance with Japan. The Japanese menace in the Pacific was supposed to paralyze American aid to Britain. It failed to do so, but if Hitler becomes sufficiently desperate he may resort to more direct methods, which can only mean war. That would be merely a repetition of 1917, when the Imperial German Government declared unrestricted submarine warfare in an effort to stop American supplies from reaching Britain. True, American ships do not now enter the war zone, but it is conceivable that Hitler may attempt interference with American supplies near the embarkation points in American harbors.

In other ways the present period of 1941 presents analogies

308

with pre-1917. In 1915 leading American publicists, like ex-President William Howard Taft, Abbott Lawrence Lowell of Harvard University, and Hamilton Holt, formed an unofficial association to consider and promote international institutions for the establishment of a new world order after the war. "The League to Enforce Peace," in collaboration with comparable British associations, developed plans subsequently incorporated in the League of Nations Covenant. The American League to Enforce Peace and the British League of Nations societies committed their respective governments to their principles, and these governments took the work of the unofficial societies as their starting point in the elaboration of the League Covenant. The principles of Clarence Streit, formerly Geneva correspondent of the *New York Times* and close observer of League sessions, bear much the same relation to the issues of war and peace as did those of the League to Enforce Peace in the earlier period. Popularized in the pamphlet *Union Now,* they are appealing to exactly the same group of publicists who were so influential last time.

The views advocated in *Union Now* are a drastic advance from the principles of the League of Nations. They diagnose the failure of the League as the perpetuation of the principle of national sovereignty, an unrealistic reliance upon the principle of voluntary coöperation. Nothing will do now but a complete abandonment of those principles. If we are to save Democracy from Nazi annihilation, we must at once pool the resources of the remaining democratic states. Economic, military, naval, and popular resources are to be merged and traditional barriers of national sovereignty swept away, leaving a federal structure to ensure a modicum of political autonomy in local affairs as the only relic of the formerly sacrosanct principle of unfettered sovereignty. The most immediate and the most necessary application of this drastic remedy lies in the complete fusion of the United States and the British Empire. But the prescription for the immediate crisis is also the design for the future order. Once victorious over the powers of fascist aggression—and who could deny the victory of such united force—the new democratic "United State" would incorporate within its structure the remainder of the democratic civilized world.

Are such ideas to be subjected to the same ridicule which greeted the League to Enforce Peace? Certainly something came of those earlier efforts to achieve a new world order, an actual world organization which in some respects did its work well. Nor was it necessarily foredoomed to failure in its essential purpose of consolidating world peace. The chief criticism to be made of *Union Now* is its impatient rejection of all the wreckage of the past.

A discriminating study of the history of the League would suggest the value of beginning precisely where the League left off. The institutions and the principles of the Covenant of the League are sound groundwork on which to build. If the name League of Nations has unfortunate connotations, the name can be changed. No matter what you call *Union Now*, its central idea of scrapping the national sovereignty of the United States is much further beyond any conceivable development of American opinion than was the idea of the League of Nations in 1917.

It would require two major developments to bring *Union Now* into the realm of political reality and these developments would have to coincide. First, the United States would have to enter the war wholly, and, second, there would have to be the prospect of an imminent British collapse so overwhelming as to threaten our very existence. Such was the combination of circumstances which impelled Great Britain to offer complete union to France in June 1940. France was in a state of complete collapse and Britain faced the prospect of immediate German invasion with no likelihood of being able to resist. The offer came too late to prevent virtual French surrender, though a large minority in the French cabinet wished to accept the offer and fight on. It is difficult to foresee any circumstances in the immediate future which would bring American opinion to support a similar offer to Britain on behalf of the United States.

Britain can undoubtedly federalize western and central Europe in the event of victory, both by smashing German unity and by incorporating the fragments in a general federal structure for Europe. The United States will not have much to say on either point, short of an actual participation in the present war and an expressed willingness to share the burden of maintaining the post-war settlement. American participation in the responsibilities of the settlement—if it occurs at all —is much more likely to occur under the type of voluntary pledge contained in the League of Nations Covenant than in the form of *Union Now*—or later.

NOTES

CHAPTER I

1. John W. Wheeler-Bennett, *The Forgotten Peace, Brest-Litovsk, March, 1918*, New York, 1939.

2. *Official German Documents Relating to the World War*, New York, 1923, II, Nos. 78-90, 1059-1073.

3. John Maynard Keynes, *The Economic Consequences of the Peace*, New York, 1920, 27-55.

4. Harold Nicolson, *Peacemaking 1919*, Boston and New York, 1933, 37.

5. David Lloyd George, *The Truth about the Treaties*, two volumes, London, 1938. The American edition is *Memoirs of the Peace Conference*, New Haven, 1939. All references are to the American edition except where otherwise specified.

6. Lloyd George, I, 88.

7. *The Edward M. House Collection*, Yale University Library, New Haven, Conn., Minutes of the Meetings of the Council of Foreign Ministers.

8. R. W. Seton-Watson, *Britain and the Dictators*, London, 1938, 314.

9. Ray Stannard Baker, *Woodrow Wilson and World Settlement*, Garden City, N. Y., 1922, III, 503-504.

10. Joseph P. Tumulty, *Woodrow Wilson as I Know Him*, Garden City, N. Y., and Toronto, Canada, 1921, 340.

11. Allan Nevins, *Henry White: Thirty Years of American Diplomacy*, New York and London, 1930, 360.

12. Charles Seymour, *The Intimate Papers of Colonel House*, Boston, 1928, IV, 362.

13. Lloyd George, I, 96-97.

14. Nevins, 475-476.

15. *Ibid.*, 409.

16. Lloyd George, I, 144, 150.

17. Nevins, 377-378.

18. *Ibid.*, 446.

19. Nicolson, 6.

313

1. Ray Stannard Baker, *Woodrow Wilson, Life and Letters*, New York, 1939, VIII, 580.

2. *Ibid.*, 554. Cf. Seymour, IV, 188.

3. Baker, VIII, 564-565.

4. Seymour, IV, 162.

5. *Ibid.*, 165.

6. *Ibid.*, 163-164.

7. *Ibid.*, 171.

8. *Ibid.*

9. *Ibid.*

10. *Ibid.*, 170.

11. *Ibid.*, 188. Lloyd George, I, 47, attempts to deny any discrepancy between his own and President Wilson's war aims. He explains that he merely wanted a perfectly reasonable clarification of some of the points. He cites only part of the record to prove his case and then accuses Colonel House of deliberate prevarication; "Even Colonel House, who knew better what actually happened than outside critics, sought to foster that false impression."

12. Lloyd George, I, 189.

13. David Hunter Miller, *My Diary at the Conference of Paris*, privately printed, 1928, II, 13-54, 81ff. Binkley, "New Light on the Paris Peace Conference," *Political Science Quarterly*, XLVI, 335-361, shows that there were actually two separate memoranda. Cf. Nicolson, 102-103.

14. Nicolson, 39.

15. Lloyd George, I, 189.

16. *Ibid.*, 252.

17. Seymour, IV, 118-124. For the background of the Rhineland question, see Mermeix (pseudonym for Gabriel Terrail), *Le Combat des trois*, Paris, 1922, 191-193. For text of the Franco-Russian agreement, see Cocks, *Secret Treaties*, London, 1918, 69-73.

18. Mermeix, 205-210.

19. *Journal of Modern History*, March, 1935, 93.

20. George Bernard Noble, *Policies and Opinions at Paris*, New York, 1935, 349.

21. Seymour, IV, 241.

22. Lloyd George, I, 78-80.

23. *Ibid.*, 54-66, 81-86.

24. Bernadotte E. Schmitt, *The Coming of the War*, New York, 1930, I, 329-341.

25. Lloyd George, I, 320-322.

26. Seymour, IV, 247, 249.

27. Lloyd George, I, 300.

28. *Ibid.*, 305.

29. *Ibid.*, 317. (Lloyd George's italics.)
30. *Ibid.*, 319. (Author's italics.)
31. *Ibid.*, 306-309. (Author's italics.)
32. Nicolson, 18.
33. *Ibid.*, 20.
34. Nevins, 358-359.
35. Seymour, IV, 280-283.
36. These and following italics are Bowman's own emphasis.
37. Nevins, 359.
38. Beer, *African Questions at the Peace Conference*, New York, 1923, 431-457.
39. Nicolson, 40-41.
40. Seymour, IV, 194-195.
41. *Ibid.*, 152-154.
42. *Ibid.*, 281.
43. Lloyd George, I, 71.
44. *Ibid.*, 71.
45. Miller, XIX, 191-192.
46. Seymour, IV, 251-253.
47. *Ibid.*, 254-255.
48. Lloyd George, I, 71.
49. *Ibid.*, 69, 413-417.
50. *Ibid.*, 68.
51. *Ibid.*, 69.
52. *Ibid.*, 112.
53. *Ibid.*, 113.
54. *Ibid.*, 114-115.
55. Beer, 27-45, 57-67.
56. Lloyd George, I, 71-77.
57. *Ibid.*, 118.
58. *Ibid.*
59. *Ibid.*
60. *Ibid.*
61. *Ibid.*
62. *Ibid.*
63. *Ibid.*, 118-119.
64. *Ibid.*, 119.
65. *Ibid.*, 343.
66. Miller, I, 123, 178.
67. *Ibid.*
68. Lloyd George, I, 120-121.
69. *Ibid.*, 122-123.
70. *Ibid.*, 122, 124.
71. Seymour, IV, 256.

72. *Ibid.*, 267-269.
73. *Ibid.*, 269. (Author's italics.)
74. *Ibid.*, 270-271.
75. *Ibid.*, 273-275.
76. *Ibid.*, 290-291.

CHAPTER III

1. Seymour, IV, 293.
2. Miller, XIV, 11.
3. *Woodrow Wilson and World Settlement*, I, 252-254.
4. Miller, XIV, 19-21.
5. *Ibid.*, 19-24.
6. The English edition, *The Truth about the Treaties*, London, 1938, I, 516.
7. Miller, XIX, 39.
8. Seymour, IV, 294-297. Cf. Miller, I, 94.
9. Seymour, IV, 296-297.
10. Miller, XIV, 36-52.
11. *Ibid.*, 52.
12. Seymour, IV, 297.
13. Lord Riddell, *Intimate Diary of the Peace Conference and After, 1919-1923*, New York, 1934, 16-18.
14. (Author's italics.) Text of the resolutions in Lloyd George, (American edition) I, 357-358; Seymour, IV, 319-320; Miller, XIV, 302-304.
15. There was later provision for a permanent commission to receive the reports.
16. Seymour, IV, 298.
17. Riddell, 17.
18. *Ibid.*, 18.
19. Lloyd George, I, 360.
20. Miller, XIV, 72-82. A copy of the same minutes are to be found also in Miller, *Drafting of the Covenant*, New York, 1928, II, 194-203.
21. Miller, *Diary*, XIV, 87-91. (Author's italics.)
22. *Ibid.*, 92-93. (Author's italics.)
23. Lloyd George, I, 359-360.
24. Miller, XIV, 95-98. Cf. Lloyd George, I, 359-362.
25. Miller, I, 97-99.
26. Beer, 431-457.
27. Seymour, IV, 299. (Author's italics.)
28. *Ibid.*
29. Nicolson, 68.
30. Beer, 269-278.

31. Miller, XIV, 99-103. Also, Baker, *Woodrow Wilson and World Settlement*, I, 427-428, and Lloyd George, I, 362-363.

32. Baker, I, 429, and Miller, *Drafting of the Covenant*, II, 272-275.

33. Baker, I, 430, and Miller, *Drafting of the Covenant*, I, 501-504.

34. Miller, *Diary*, XX, 349.

35. *Ibid.*, 513.

36. *Ibid.*, 420-421.

37. Baker, I, 430-431.

38. *Minutes of the Permanent Mandates Commission*, 1926 Sessions No. 8-10, especially No. 9, 132, 193-194.

CHAPTER IV

1. Miller, XIX, 39-40, 171-175. Cf. Baker, II, 228-231.

2. *Ibid.*

3. Robert Lansing, *The Peace Negotiations*, Boston, 1921, 253.

4. Lloyd George, I, 121.

5. Seymour, IV, 309.

6. *Ibid.*

7. *Ibid.*

8. *Ibid.*, 310-311.

9. *Ibid.*, 312.

10. *Ibid.*, 313. (Author's italics.)

11. Miller, I, 123.

12. *Ibid.*, 178.

13. Seymour, IV, 313-314.

14. *Ibid.*, 313.

15. Miller, *Drafting of the Covenant*, II, 323-325.

16. *Ibid.* Cf. Baker, II, 234-235.

17. Seymour, IV, 314-315.

18. *Ibid.*, 317-318.

19. Baker, II, 23-24, 236.

20. Miller, *Drafting of the Covenant*, I, 295, and Henry Borden (Ed.), *Robert Laird Borden: His Memoirs*, New York, 1938, II, 926-928.

21. Seymour, IV, 413-415.

22. *Ibid.*, 415.

23. Miller, *Drafting of the Covenant*, II, 258.

24. *Ibid.*, 387-392.

25. *Ibid.*, and Miller, *Diary*, I, 246.

26. *Ibid.* Cf. Seymour, IV, 428, and Miller, VIII, 268a, 277-281.

27. Miller, *Drafting of the Covenant*, II, 392.

28. Miller, *Diary*, I, 246, and VIII, 259.

29. Miller, *Drafting of the Covenant*, II, 702-704.

317

30. Miller, *Diary*, XIX, 195-197. (Author's italics.)
31. *Ibid.*, 176-177.
32. Lansing, 254.
33. Baker, II, 247-249.
34. Miller, XIX, 177-184.
35. *Ibid.*, 177-186.
36. *Ibid.*, 186-193.
37. *Ibid.*
38. *Ibid.*, 193.
39. Baker, II, 257-258.
40. Miller, XIX, 193-194.
41. *Ibid.*, 188.
42. *Ibid.*, 194-195.
43. Seymour, IV, 451.
44. Miller, XIX, 197.
45. Baker, II, 260-261, and Lansing, 254-255.
46. Baker, II, 261.
47. Miller, XIX, 195-197.
48. *Ibid.*, 198, and Baker, III, 312-314.
49. Seymour, IV, 451-452.
50. Miller, XIX, 199.
51. Seymour, IV, 454.
52. *Ibid.*, 455. (Author's italics.)
53. Miller, *Diary*, XIX, 199-201. Cf. Baker, II, 263-264.
54. Lansing, 255-261.
55. Baker, II, 266.
56. *Ibid.*, 262.
57. Lansing, 261.
58. Baker, III, 315-316. (Author's italics.)
59. Baker, II, 224.
60. Nevins, 475-476.
61. Ray Stannard Baker's unpublished journal for April 30 proves that Colonel House did not know the question had been settled that day. Baker himself announced the settlement to representatives of the press at noon of that day. The same evening Colonel House told the press that there had been no settlement.

CHAPTER V

1. Lloyd George, I, 141.
2. André Tardieu, *The Truth about the Treaty*, Indianapolis, 1921, 309.
3. Baker, I, 361.
4. Theodore Marburg, *Development of the League of Nations Idea*, two volumes, New York, 1932.

5. *House Collection.* House to Wilson, February 17, 1919.
6. Baker, III, 157-158. Also, Miller, *Drafting of the Covenant* (simply referred to as *Drafting* hereafter), II, 241-243. (Author's italics.)
7. Miller, *Drafting,* II, 241-243.
8. Noble, *Policies and Opinions at Paris, 1919,* 113.
9. Miller, *Drafting,* II, 264. (Author's italics.)
10. *Ibid.* Cf. Noble, 117.
11. Miller, *Drafting,* II, 264.
12. *Ibid.,* 291-292. (Author's italics.)
13. *Ibid.,* 293-294. (Author's italics.)
14. *Ibid.,* 295-297.
15. *Ibid.,* 292-293, 296.
16. *Ibid.,* 297. Cf. Miller, *Drafting,* I, 209.
17. Miller, *Drafting,* I, 216-217.
18. Miller, *Drafting,* II, 317-319.
19. *Ibid.,* 320-321.
20. Seymour, IV, 317.
21. *House Collection.*
22. *Ibid.*
23. Nevins, 385-394, *passim.* See also Denna Frank Fleming, *The United States and the League of Nations, 1918-1920,* New York and London, 1932, for a full account.
24. Miller, *Diary,* I, 154.
25. *House Collection,* communications between House and Wilson, March 3-4, 1919.
26. Seymour, IV, 411.
27. *Ibid.,* 411-412. (Author's italics.)
28. Nevins, 410, 415, 442-443.
29. Miller, *Drafting,* I, 300. (Author's italics.)
30. Miller, *Diary,* I, 190-191; VI, 476.
31. Miller, *Drafting,* II, 343.
32. Miller, *Drafting,* I, 321.
33. Miller, *Diary,* IX, 173.
34. Miller, *Drafting,* I, 324. (Miller's italics.) Cf. Miller, *Drafting,* II, 344-347.
35. *Ibid.,* 322-323.
36. Miller, *Drafting,* II, 347-350.
37. *Ibid.,* 357-359.
38. Miller, *Drafting,* I, 338.
39. Miller, *Diary,* I, 210-240.
40. Seymour, IV, 418.
41. *House Collection,* letter of April 8, 1919, endorsed in Colonel House's handwriting, "This is the letter mentioned in the diary, but which was not sent." House's motive for not sending the letter appears clearly in an extract

from his diary which President Seymour has sent me. Lloyd George had put the negotiations into Cecil's hands, and the latter was afraid that House's letter would provoke Lloyd George again to take hold. House had also made a tentative promise in the letter about modification of the uncompleted part of the American naval program, which he thought unwise.

42. Miller, *Drafting*, I, 425, and Seymour, IV, 422-423.

43. Miller, *Drafting*, I, 425-426.

44. Seymour, IV, 424.

45. *Ibid.*, 424-425.

46. Miller, *Drafting*, II, 369-374, and Miller, *Diary*, VIII, 282-291.

47. Miller, *Diary*, VIII, 291.

48. Miller, *Drafting*, I, 453-454. (Author's italics.)

49. *Ibid.*, 454, and Miller, *Diary*, I, 242-243.

50. Miller, *Drafting*, II, 381-392.

51. *Ibid.*, 706-719, and Seymour, IV, 430-431.

52. Nevins, 443.

53. *House Collection.*

CHAPTER VI

1. Miller, *Diary*, XIV, 3.

2. *Ibid.*, 4, and Tardieu, 127. (Author's italics.)

3. Baker, I, 362-363, and III, 191.

4. Seymour, IV, 324-326.

5. Miller, *Drafting*, II, 175-176, and *Diary*, XIV, 336-337. Also Seymour, IV, 326-328.

6. Tardieu, 130.

7. Seymour, IV, 328.

8. *Ibid.*, 327.

9. *Ibid.*, 328-329. (Author's italics.) Miller, *Drafting*, II, 176, and *Diary*, XIV, 337.

10. Seymour, IV, 329-330.

11. *Ibid.*, 332-333.

12. *House Collection,* House to Wilson, Feb. 19, 1919.

13. Seymour, IV, 335-336.

14. *Ibid.*, 334-335. (Author's italics.)

15. *Ibid.*, 340.

16. *Ibid.*, 341-342.

17. *Ibid.*, 348-350.

18. *Ibid.*, 340. See also the appendix to this chapter in Seymour, IV, 363-376.

19. *House Collection,* House to Wilson, Feb. 27, 1919.

20. *Ibid.*, Wilson to House, Mar. 3, 1919.

21. *Ibid.*, House to Wilson, Mar. 4, 1919.

22. *Ibid.*, Supreme Council Minutes, Mar. 17, 1919.

23. *Ibid.*, Minutes of the daily meetings of the American Commissioners, Mar. 18, 19.

24. Miller, *Diary*, XV, 135-136.

25. *Ibid.*, 136-143.

26. *Ibid.*, 177-178.

27. Noble, 178-179.

28. Miller, *Diary*, XV, 244-246.

29. *Ibid.*, 287-292. Cf. George Louis Beer, unpublished diary, March 26, 1919.

30. Miller, *loc. cit.*

31. *Ibid.*, 292-299.

32. *Ibid.*, 367.

33. *Ibid.*, 369-370.

34. *Ibid.*, 298.

35. *Ibid.*, 372-375, 395-398.

36. *Ibid.*, 396-398.

37. Tardieu, 135-137.

38. *Ibid.*, 138. (Author's italics.)

39. *Ibid.*, 138-139.

40. *Ibid.*, 140.

41. Winston S. Churchill, *The Aftermath,* New York, 1929, 228.

42. Baker, I, 375.

43. Nicolson, 327.

44. Miller, *Diary*, XVIII, 469.

45. Churchill, *loc. cit.*

CHAPTER VII

1. Mermeix, 191-193, and Cocks, *Secret Treaties,* 69-73.

2. Baker, III, 37-38.

3. *The Memoirs of Prince Max of Baden,* New York, 1928, II, 24, note 1.

4. Baker, III, 37-38.

5. *Ibid.*

6. *Ibid.* (Author's italics.)

7. House and Seymour, *What Really Happened at Paris,* New York, 1921, 75.

8. Seymour, IV, 153-154.

9. *Ibid.*, 200. Dmowski's memoirs indicate that Wilson himself was considering alternatives to the Polish Corridor as late as September 1918. Casimir Smogorzewski, *Poland's Access to the Sea,* London, 1934, 95-96.

10. René Martel, *The Eastern Frontiers of Germany,* London, 1930, 33-35.

11. Miller, *Diary*, XIV, 62-67.

12. *Ibid.*, IV, 224-226.

13. *Ibid.*, VI, 49-52.
14. *Ibid.*, IV, 224-226.
15. *Ibid.*
16. *Ibid.*, I, 370 ff., and Seymour, IV, 280-283.
17. Miller, *Diary*, I, 289, and Smogorzewski, 93-94. Also Lloyd George, I, 482, and II, 643.
18. Miller, *Diary*, XIX, 118.
19. Smogorzewski, 121.
20. Miller, *Diary*, XIX, 117-118.
21. Seymour, IV, 334-335.
22. *Ibid.*, 335-336.
23. Lloyd George, I, 188-189.
24. Miller, *Diary*, VI, 350-366.
25. *Ibid.*, XV, 422-431, and Lloyd George, II, 637-642.
26. *Ibid.*
27. Lloyd George, II, 642.
28. *House Collection*, Supreme Council Minutes, March 21, 1919.
29. Miller, *Diary*, VII, 75-78.
30. *Ibid.*, XV, 471-473.
31. *Ibid.*, I, 208-209.
32. Lloyd George, I, 266.
33. *Ibid.*, 266-273, Churchill, 198-201, and Baker, III, 449-457.
34. Riddell, 42.
35. Lloyd George, I, 273-276, Tardieu, 116-119, and Baker, III, 249-252.
36. Lloyd George, I, 276-277, and Baker, III, 51-52.
37. Riddell, 44.
38. Martel, 49-50.
39. Except for the Reparation question, which is the subject of a later chapter.
40. Miller, *Diary*, VIII, 335-340, I, 258, and XIX, 112, 120.
41. *Ibid.*, XIX, 112.
42. *Ibid.*, XIX, 121.
43. Baker, III, 483.
44. Martel, 55.
45. Miller, *Diary*, XIX, 95.
46. Baker, III, 498-504. The President's criticism of Lloyd George had chiefly to do with his attitude on the Reparation question discussed in a later chapter.
47. G. L. Beer, unpublished diary, June 3, 1919.
48. Baker, III, 484.
49. *Ibid.*, 482-483.
50. Miller, *Diary*, XIX, 95-97. Also Mermeix, 233-244, and Martel, 52-57.
51. Miller, *Diary*, XIX, 97-99, Mermeix, 244-246, Martel, 57-60.
52. Miller, *Diary*, XIX, 99-102, Mermeix, 246-255, Martel, 60-64.

53. Seymour, IV, 482.

54. Miller, *Diary*, XIX, 102-103, and Martel, 64-66.

55. Sarah Wambaugh, *Plebiscites Since the World War*, Washington, 1933, I, 206-271. It should be remarked that the Supreme Council made other modifications of the Polish Commission's report, returning to Germany a strip of Pomerania on the Baltic and the important rail center of Schneide-mühl. See Temperley, *History of the Paris Peace Conference*, London, 1924, VI, 250-252, and Miller, *Diary*, XIX, 89-92.

CHAPTER VIII

1. Seymour, IV, 118-124.

2. Mermeix, 205-210, and Lloyd George, I, 78-80.

3. Mermeix, *loc. cit.*

4. Tardieu, 134.

5. Mermeix, 210-219, and Baker, III, 227-237.

6. Noble, 249, and *Journal of Modern History*, March, 1935, 93.

7. Seymour, IV, 345-346.

8. *Ibid.*, 332-334.

9. *House Collection*, Wilson to House, February 20, 1919. This is a somewhat fuller version than that printed in Seymour, IV, 335-336. (Italics indicate omitted portions. The omissions do not alter the sense, but weaken the impression of Wilson's concern, and the force of his warnings.)

10. Seymour, IV, 334-335.

11. *Ibid.*, 347.

12. *Ibid.*, 349.

13. *Ibid.*, 383. President Seymour gives the date for this proposal of Colonel House as March 17, 1919.

14. *House Collection*, Balfour's "Brief Notes on the Present Conference Situation," February 25, 1919. (Author's italics.)

15. House diary, February 27, 1919. Not published in the *Intimate Papers*. President Seymour, while declining to permit me to see the diary, has courteously looked up special matters for me in the diary and has sent me the relevant excerpts.

16. Seymour, IV, 351. The text of the memorandum appears in Tardieu, 147-171.

17. One of the excerpts from the diary which President Seymour sent the author.

18. *House Collection*, House to Wilson, March 7, 1919. The italicized portion does not appear in the version printed in Seymour, IV, 358.

19. *House Collection*, Wilson to House, March 10, 1919. The italicized portion does not appear in Seymour, IV, 358. The only portion there quoted is in the footnote, No. 2.

20. Seymour, IV, 359.

21. Miller, *Diary*, VII, 57-59. Tardieu's version appears in Tardieu, 172-176.

22. Tardieu, 174-175.

23. Seymour, IV, 360.

24. Edith Bolling Wilson, *My Memoir*, Indianapolis, 1939, 245.

25. President Seymour's statement to me.

26. Beer, unpublished diary, March 12, 1919. (Author's italics.)

27. Edith Bolling Wilson, 245-246. The Lloyd George memoirs support the view that House had seriously compromised Wilson's position on the Rhineland, I, 262.

28. Mermeix, 198-199.

29. Tardieu, 177.

30. *Ibid.*, 178-182.

31. *House Collection*, minutes of the daily meetings of the American Commissioners, March 20 and 21, 1919. Cf. Nevins, 411.

32. Seymour, IV, 394.

33. *Ibid.*, 395, and *House Collection*, minutes of the American Commission meeting, March 27, 1919.

34. Lansing, 179-181.

35. Nevins, 411, and American Commission minutes, March 20, 1919.

36. Seymour, IV, 393.

37. Tardieu, 181-182.

38. Miller, *Diary*, VII, 29-40.

39. *Ibid.*, 55.

40. Tardieu, 134, 183.

41. Tardieu, 205-208. Clemenceau finally agreed, April 15, 1919, to the formula, "The present treaty will continue in force until on the application of one of the parties to it, the Council of the League, acting if need be by majority, agrees that the League itself affords sufficient protection."

42. Seymour, IV, 396, footnote No. 1, and House and Seymour, 464-465.

43. Miller, *Drafting*, I, 453-454.

44. Library of Congress, Washington, D. C., Division of Manuscripts, Lansing's unpublished diary, March 28, 1919.

45. Baker, II, 46-47, and Lloyd George, I, 277.

46. Seymour, IV, 406-407.

47. *Ibid.*, 407-408.

48. Lloyd George, I, 280.

49. Tardieu, 186.

50. Noble, 258.

51. Tardieu, 210-211.

52. *Ibid.*

53. Mermeix, 219-221.

54. Tardieu, 187, and Noble, 254-255.

55. Tardieu, 188-189.
56. Mermeix, 226-231.
57. Tardieu, 190-194, and Nicolson, 327.
58. Noble, 231, and Baker, III, 57.
59. Noble, 231-232. See also Lansing's unpublished diary for this period.
60. Lloyd George, I, 189.
61. Noble, 228-229.
62. Mermeix, 231-232.
63. *Ibid.,* 154-171.
64. *Ibid.,* 172-177, and Tardieu, 372-373.
65. Baker, I, 86-94, and Tardieu, 372.
66. Baker, III, 490.
67. Nicolson, 359.
68. Tardieu, 196-198.

CHAPTER IX

1. House and Seymour, 56.
2. Noble, 207.
3. Seymour, IV, 197.
4. Miller, *Diary,* IV, 212; V, 30-36; VI, 43-52.
5. Seymour, IV, 383 (undated.) President Seymour has since supplied the date, March 17, 1919.
6. Tardieu, 182.
7. *Ibid.,* 251-262.
8. *Ibid.,* 262.
9. E. G. Tardieu, 262-265.
10. Lloyd George, I, 141-142.
11. Tardieu, 265, and Lansing's unpublished diary, March 28, 1919.
12. Seymour, IV, 396 and footnote 1; House and Seymour, 464; and Tardieu, 265.
13. Tardieu, 265-266.
14. *Ibid.,* 266-268.
15. Lansing, diary, March 28, 1919.
16. Seymour, IV, 397.
17. *Ibid.,* 396.
18. Baker, II, 73-74.
19. *Ibid.,* 73.
20. Mermeix, 202.
21. *Ibid.,* and Tardieu, 269.
22. Miller, *Diary,* VII, 464-466.
23. Wickham Steed, "Is it Peace?" *The Fortnightly,* January, 1935, 6.
24. Seymour, IV, 397.
25. Mermeix, 202-203; Tardieu, 270; and Miller, *Diary,* VIII, 26-33.

26. Tardieu, 271, and Seymour, IV, 405.

27. Tardieu, 271-272, and Miller, *Diary*, VIII, 136; IX, 226-232.

28. Tardieu, 272-276, and Miller, *Diary*, VIII, 148-152.

29. Tardieu, 276-277, and Miller, *Diary*, IX, 230-232.

30. Sarah Wambaugh, *The Saar Plebiscite,* Cambridge, 1940.

31. Baker, III, 502.

CHAPTER X

1. Seymour, IV, 170-171, 187.

2. Lloyd George, I, 309.

3. *Ibid.,* 319.

4. Philip Mason Burnett, *Reparation at the Paris Peace Conference,* (The Paris Peace Conference: History and Documents), two volumes, Columbia University Press, New York, 1940, I, vi.

5. Seymour, IV, 125-126.

6. *Ibid.,* 176-177.

7. Baker, II, 370, and Miller, *Diary*, XIX, 265-266.

8. House and Seymour, 269-270. The Allied memoranda and a summary of the arguments are to be found in Miller, *Diary*, XIX, 267-269; a summary of the arguments in Tardieu, 286-292; and the full text of the arguments in Baruch, *The Making of the Reparation and Economic Sections of the Treaty,* New York and London, 1920, 289-337.

9. Tardieu, 291-292, and Burnett, I, 25-27.

10. *House Collection,* Minutes of the Meetings of the American Commissioners, February 11, 1919.

11. *Ibid.,* February 18, 1919.

12. Seymour, IV, 343, footnote.

13. *Ibid.,* 349.

14. Miller, *Diary*, XIX, 271.

15. *Ibid.,* VI, 316-317.

16. Seymour, IV, 343-344, 382, and Norman Davis's typed "Peace Conference Notes," July 5, 1919. Lamont was responsible for the nickname, "heavenly twins," Baker, III, 476.

17. Davis, "Peace Conference Notes."

18. *Ibid.*

19. *Ibid.*

20. *Ibid.,* and Burnett, I, 54-56.

21. Baker, III, 383-396.

22. Burnett, I, 59-60.

23. Seymour, IV, 399.

24. Davis, "Peace Conference Notes," Annex "B."

25. Tardieu, 296, and Baker, II, 378.

26. Burnett, I, 61.

27. *Ibid.*, 63.

28. *Ibid.*, 63-64, and House and Seymour, 271-272. Also Baruch, 28-31.

29. Burnett, I, 64-65; Baker, II, 383, and Baruch, 28-29.

30. Miller, *Diary*, I, 150. Dulles proposed to Miller the possibility of including pensions because the French supported it, March 4, 1919. Miller disapproved and Dulles suggested it only as a possible basis of compromise, disliking the idea himself.

31. Burnett, I, 61-62.

32. Tardieu, 292.

33. Burnett, I, 26-27, 66-68.

34. *Ibid.*, 69.

35. *Ibid.*, 142, and Seymour, IV, 408-409. Also, Miller, *Diary*, XIX, 288.

36. There has been much learned discussion as to whether Article 231 was intended to carry, or did legally carry, any meaning but that Germany began the war with a technical act of aggression. See Burnett, I, 142-157.

37. Baker, III, 480.

38. Baker, II, 378-379; III, 397-399.

39. Burnett, I, 72.

40. *The Parliamentary Debates: Official Report*, 5th series (House of Commons), CXIV, 1304-1350. Burnett, I, 866. Lloyd George, I, 372-375.

41. Burnett, Document 237, I, 832-833.

42. *Ibid.*, 833. Professor Slosson, in his summary of the official minutes has ascribed Colonel House's remark to Norman Davis, Miller, *Diary*, XIX, 300-301, (printed by Burnett as Document 238, I, 835-836). Baker, II, 380-381, gives exactly the version of the official minutes as they appear in Burnett, Document 237, I, 831-835, and those official minutes are consistent with Norman Davis' entire record. The full report of his remarks on that occasion makes it clear just why he regarded the French proposal as "a complete departure from the principles" of the American delegation. Moreover, Norman Davis told the author in a conversation on March 12, 1940, in Washington, that his remark was prompted by indignation at Colonel House's inability or unwillingness to see the difference. The author concludes that Professor Slosson has probably made an error in transcription.

43. Burnett, Document 239, I, 837-838.

44. Seymour, IV, 401.

45. *Ibid.*, 402.

46. Excerpt from the diary sent the author by President Seymour.

47. Seymour, IV, 405.

48. The French continued to make difficulties over "verbal niceties" and it was on the morning of April 7 that Wilson, in agreement with his advisers that the end of concessions had been reached, dispatched the order to the *George Washington* to come to Brest. Seymour, IV, 402-404.

49. "Behind the House-Wilson Break," chapter 12 of *The Inside Story*, by members of the Overseas Press Club of America, New York, 1940.

50. Seymour, IV, 402.
51. Lansing diary, May 19, 1919.
52. See above, chapter 8.
53. Lansing diary, April 4 and 5, 1919.
54. *Ibid.*, April 10, 1919.
55. Baker, III, 480.
56. *Ibid.*, 476-477.
57. *Ibid.*, 476, 480.
58. *Ibid.*, 503.
59. Nicolson, 209-210.
60. Baker, III, 470-481.
61. Burnett, I, 137.
62. The entire controversy is well analyzed by Burnett, I, 84-91.
63. There is evidence to suggest that the War Debts problem hampered the freedom of the American delegation in dealing with the Reparation question. Baruch, 54-55, says, ". . . American delegates came to the conclusion that they should not assume the responsibility of objecting to the effort by the Allies to collect from Germany what she owed them, provided they would agree to certain safeguards against the dangers of such a course." He suggests the fear (52), that the Allies might say, "If you ask us to lessen our claims upon Germany for indemnity, which she admits she owes, what will you do for the loan made to us for the prosecution of a war which was as much your war as our war, the amount of which clearly exceeds our ability to pay unless we are allowed to get the last possible dollar out of Germany?"

There is little evidence of *direct* influence of that consideration on the negotiations. For such as there is, see Baruch, 52-55; Lloyd George, I, 319; Riddell, 23; Nevins, 381-382, 384; Baker, II, 384; House and Seymour, 289; Burnett, I, 73.

CHAPTER XI

1. Pribram, *The Secret Treaties of Austria-Hungary*, Cambridge, 1921, II, 6.
2. Nicolson, 183-184.
3. René Albrecht-Carrié, *Italy at the Peace Conference*, (The Paris Peace Conference: History and Documents), Columbia University Press, New York, 1938, 63.
4. *Ibid.*, 97-98.
5. *Ibid.*, 100-101.
6. Baker, II, 135.
7. *House Collection*, Sonnino to House, March 11, 1919.
8. *House Collection*, Supreme Council Minutes, March 11, 1919.
9. Albrecht-Carrié, 96-103, and Baker, II, 135.
10. Baker, II, 133.

11. Albrecht-Carrié, 63, 65-66, 85, note 75.

12. *Ibid.*, 94-95.

13. Lansing diary, March 23, 1919.

14. Beer diary, March 16, 21. Miller, *Diary*, I, 157, 172; March 7, 16, 1919.

15. Miller, *Diary*, I, 202; March 25, 1919.

16. Beer diary, May 17, 1919.

17. *House Collection*, Charles Seymour memorandum of conversation with Colonel House, March 17, 1920.

18. Lansing diary, March 28 and May 19, 1919.

19. Beer diary, April 5, 1919.

20. *Ibid.*, March 15, 1919.

21. Statement made by one of the persons in question in a conversation, February 14, 1940.

22. *Ibid.*

23. Albrecht-Carrié, 120, note 18.

24. *Ibid.*, 120.

25. *Ibid.*, 121-123.

26. *Ibid.*, 126-128.

27. Baker, II, 146.

28. Seymour, IV, 442.

29. Miller, *Diary*, I, 255-257; April 16, 17, 1919.

30. Lansing diary, April 17, 1919, and Albrecht-Carrié, 128.

31. Miller, *Diary*, I, 256-257, 260; April 16, 17, 19, 1919.

32. Statement by Professor Douglas Johnson in conversation, February 14, 1940.

33. *House Collection*, Miller to House, April 19, 1919, and Mezes to Johnson, April 21, 1919.

34. Lansing diary, April 17, 1919.

35. *Ibid.*, April 18, 1919.

36. Text of letters in Albrecht-Carrié, 129-130, and Baker, II, 153-154. The circumstances surrounding the dispatch of the letter to Wilson and his reply were described to me by one of the six men concerned in a conversation of June 13, 1940.

37. Lansing diary, April 18, 1919. (Lansing's italics.)

38. *House Collection*, minutes of the daily meetings of the American Commissioners, April 18, 1919.

39. Conversation with one of the six, June 13, 1940.

40. *Ibid.*

41. Seymour, IV, 444.

42. Lansing diary, March 18, 22, 23, 28, April 3, 4, 5, 1919. It is true that Lansing records, on March 22, 1919, Colonel House's complaint that he had not been able to see President Wilson alone for a week, in other words, since a day or so after Wilson's return from the United States. If that were true, it would indicate even more substance to the view that Wilson felt that Colonel

House had compromised the American position during his absence. However that may be, during the last week in March and the first two weeks of April the President saw Colonel House constantly and alone. This was the period of complaint by the other Commissioners.

Ray Stannard Baker's unpublished journal supports the view that the Fiume question merely widened an existing breach. His entry for April 19, 1919, reads:

"The rift between the President and Colonel House seems to be widening. The Colonel compromises everything away—and he has gone so far with the Italians that they are now heralding him as the Great Man of the Conference and comparing him unfavorably *(sic)* with the President. It makes it difficult now for the President. The Colonel is still declaring that if he had the peace to make it would all be done in a day or so—and it would—by giving away everything we came to fight for."

On the other hand, Colonel House and his partisans maintain that no important issue of policy ever separated the two men. They attribute the personal rift entirely to the jealousy of Mrs. Wilson and her efforts to discredit Colonel House in the President's eyes. The two published accounts to this effect, George Sylvester Viereck's "Behind the House-Wilson Break" in *The Inside Story* (New York, 1940), and Arthur D. Howden Smith's *Mr. House of Texas* (New York and London), 1940, clearly derive from Colonel House's own statements, as do the many hints to the same effect which the author has heard directly from friends of Colonel House. There is clearly some substance to the story, but it is not more than half the truth. The present chapter of this book reveals the very deep cleavage of philosophy and method which separated the two men and ultimately ended their friendship.

43. Seymour, IV, 445-446, and Lansing diary, April 19, 1919.

44. Seymour, IV, 445-446, and Albrecht-Carrié, 135.

45. Lansing diary, April 21, 1919.

46. Seymour, IV, 446.

47. Excerpt from House diary, April 23, 1919, sent me by President Seymour.

48. *Ibid.*, April 24, 1919.

49. Lansing diary, April 25, 1919.

50. Excerpt from House diary, April 24, 1919, sent me by President Seymour.

51. Seymour, IV, 451, and additional excerpt from House diary, April 26, 1919, sent me by President Seymour.

52. Seymour, IV, 451.

53. Seymour, IV, 454, and additional excerpt from House diary, April 29, 1919, sent me by President Seymour.

54. *Ibid.*, May 3, 1919.

55. *Ibid.*, May 5, 1919.

56. Beer diary, May 9, 1919.

57. Lansing diary, May 5, 1919.

58. *Ibid.*, May 19, 1919.

59. Letter from President Seymour, June 26, 1940.

60. Beer diary, April 29, 1919.

61. *Ibid.*, May 9, 1919.

62. Conversations with two different members of the six experts, February 14, 1940, and June 13, 1940. I had heard this account twice before discovering it in the Beer diary.

63. *House Collection*, minutes of the daily meetings of the American Commissioners, May 7, 1919; and statement by Dr. Bowman, July 13, 1940.

64. Lansing diary, May 9, 1919.

65. Excerpt from House diary, May 13, 1919, sent me by President Seymour.

66. *Ibid.*, May 12, 1919.

67. Miller, *Diary*, I, 301; May 12, 1919.

68. *Ibid.*, 303-304; May 13, 1919.

69. *Ibid.*, 309-311; May 14, 1919. (Miller's italics.)

70. Excerpt from House diary, May 13, 1919, sent me by President Seymour.

71. *Ibid.*, May 16, 1919. Also Beer diary, May 16, 1919, and Miller, *Diary*, I, 314 of same date.

72. Beer diary, May 16, 1919, and Miller, *Diary*, I, 315 of same date.

73. Excerpt from House diary, May 16, 1919, sent me by President Seymour.

74. Beer diary, May 17, 1919, and Miller, *Diary*, I, 316 of same date.

75. *House Collection*, Charles Seymour memorandum of conversation with Colonel House, March 17, 1920.

76. Beer diary, May 19, 1919.

77. *Ibid.*, May 17, 1919.

78. Lloyd George, I, 159.

79. Excerpts from House diary of those dates, sent me by President Seymour.

80. Lansing diary, June 10, 1919.

81. *Ibid.*, June 5 and 21, 1919.

82. Seymour, IV, 487.

83. Nevins, 476.

84. *Ibid.*, 475. This same passage has been quoted in chapter I of the present book to give a forecast of Colonel House's rôle. It is repeated here in its proper context.

BIBLIOGRAPHY

Note: The bibliography lists only materials consulted in the preparation of this book. For more general guides to a somewhat wider range of Peace Conference literature, refer to "Bibliographical Aids" below.

BIBLIOGRAPHICAL AIDS

Binkley, Robert C., "Ten Years of Peace Conference History," *The Journal of Modern History*, Dec., 1929, I, 607-629.

Birdsall, Paul, "The Second Decade of Peace Conference History," *The Journal of Modern History*, Sept., 1939, XI, 362-378.

UNPUBLISHED RECORDS

Edward M. House Collection, Sterling Memorial Library, New Haven, Conn. Private papers, diary, and sets of official minutes.

Division of Manuscripts, Library of Congress, Washington, D. C. Papers of Tasker Bliss, Robert Lansing, Henry White, and Woodrow Wilson. The Wilson papers have just been opened, too late for use in the preparation of this book. The Lansing papers, especially the appointments books—which are practically a diary —are the most important item.

(Department of State, Washington, D. C. The full set of official Peace Conference records, not open to the private investigator, is being prepared for publication by the Division of Research and Publication.)

PRIVATE COLLECTIONS

George Louis Beer typescript diary in the possession of Professor James T. Shotwell of Columbia University.

Ray Stannard Baker journal in Mr. Baker's possession at Amherst, Mass.

Norman Davis' typescript "Peace Conference Notes," in Mr. Davis' possession at Washington, D. C.

PUBLISHED WORKS

Note: Most of the works listed below contain important source materials; letters and excerpts from diaries and official minutes.

Albrecht-Carrié, René. *Italy at the Peace Conference* (in the series, *The Paris Peace Conference: History and Documents,* published for Carnegie Endowment for International Peace). New York, Columbia University Press, 1938.

Baker, Ray Stannard. *Woodrow Wilson and World Settlement.* (Three volumes.) Garden City, N. Y., Doubleday, Page and Company, 1922.

Baruch, Bernard M. *The Making of the Reparation and Economic Sections of the Treaty.* New York and London, Harper and Brothers, 1920.

Beer, George Louis. *African Questions at the Peace Conference.* New York, The Macmillan Company, 1923.

Burnett, Philip Mason. *Reparation at the Paris Peace Conference* (in the series, *The Paris Peace Conference: History and Documents,* published for Carnegie Endowment for International Peace). New York, Columbia University Press, 1940.

Carnegie Endowment for International Peace. *Official German Documents Relating to the World War.* (Two volumes.) New York, Oxford University Press, 1923.

Churchill, Winston S. *The Aftermath.* New York, Charles Scribner's Sons, 1929.

Cocks, F. Seymour (Ed.). *The Secret Treaties.* (Second edition.) London, Union of Democratic Control, 1918.

Fleming, Denna Frank. *The United States and the League of Nations, 1918-1920.* New York and London, G. P. Putnam's Sons, 1932.

House and Seymour (Ed.). *What Really Happened at Paris.* New York, Charles Scribner's Sons, 1921.

Keynes, John Maynard. *The Economic Consequences of the Peace.* New York, Harcourt, Brace and Howe, 1920.

334

Lansing, Robert. *The Peace Negotiations: A Personal Narrative.* Boston and New York, Houghton Mifflin Company, 1921.

League of Nations. *Minutes of the Permanent Mandates Commission,* Sessions 8-10, 1926. Geneva, 1926.

Lloyd George, David. *Memoirs of the Peace Conference.* (Two volumes.) (American Edition); New Haven, Yale University Press, 1939. (English Edition); *The Truth about the Peace Treaties.* (Two volumes.) London, Victor Gollancz, Ltd., 1938.

Marburg, Theodore. John N. Latané, (Ed.). *Development of the League of Nations Idea.* (Two volumes.) New York, The Macmillan Company, 1932.

Martel, René. *The Eastern Frontiers of Germany.* London, Williams and Norgate, Ltd., 1930.

Mermeix (pseudonym of Gabriel Terrail). *Le combat des trois.* Paris, Librairie Ollendorff, 1922.

Miller, David Hunter. *My Diary at the Conference of Paris.* (Twenty volumes.) Privately printed. 1928.

Miller, David Hunter. *The Drafting of the Covenant.* (Two volumes.) New York and London, G. P. Putnam's Sons, 1928.

Nevins, Allan. *Henry White: Thirty Years of American Diplomacy.* New York and London, Harper and Brothers, 1930.

Nicolson, Harold. *Peacemaking 1919.* Boston and New York, Houghton Mifflin Company, 1933.

Noble, George Bernard. *Policies and Opinions at Paris, 1919.* New York, The Macmillan Company, 1935.

The Parliamentary Debates: Official Report, 5th Series (House of Commons), CXIV.

Pribram, Alfred Franzis. *The Secret Treaties of Austria-Hungary.* (Two volumes.) Cambridge, Harvard University Press, 1920.

Prince Max of Baden. *Memoirs of Prince Max of Baden.* (Two volumes.) New York, Charles Scribner's Sons, 1928.

Riddell, George Allardice. *Lord Riddell's Intimate Diary of the Peace Conference and After, 1918-1923.* New York, Reynal and Hitchcock, Inc., 1934.

Seton-Watson, Robert William. *Britain and the Dictators.* New York, The Macmillan Company, 1938.

Seymour, Charles (Ed.). *The Intimate Papers of Colonel House.* (Volume four, "The Ending of the War.") Boston and New York, Houghton Mifflin Company, 1928.

Shotwell, James T. *At the Paris Peace Conference.* New York, The Macmillan Company, 1937.

Smith, Arthur D. Howden. *Mr. House of Texas.* New York and London, Funk and Wagnalls Company, 1940.

Smogorzewski, Casimir. *Poland's Access to the Sea.* London, G. Allen and Unwin, Ltd., 1934.

Tardieu, André. *The Truth about the Treaty.* Indianapolis, The Bobbs-Merrill Company, 1921.

Temperley, H. W. V. (Ed.). *A History of the Peace Conference of Paris.* (Six volumes.) London, Institute of International Affairs, 1920-1924.

Tumulty, Joseph P. *Woodrow Wilson as I Know Him.* Garden City, N. Y., and Toronto, Canada, Doubleday, Page and Company, 1921.

Viereck, George Sylvester. *Behind the House-Wilson Break,* chapter twelve of *The Inside Story,* by members of the Overseas Press Club of America. New York, Prentice-Hall, Inc., 1940.

Wambaugh, Sarah. *Plebiscites Since the World War.* (Two volumes.) Washington, Carnegie Endowment for International Peace, 1933.

Wambaugh, Sarah. *The Saar Plebiscite.* Cambridge, Harvard University Press, 1940.

Wheeler-Bennett, John W. *The Forgotten Peace: Brest-Litovsk.* London and New York, W. Morrow and Company, 1939.

Wilson, Edith Bolling. *My Memoir.* Indianapolis, The Bobbs-Merrill Company, 1939.

INDEX

INDEX

Adriatic question, 107, 267-268, 281. *See also* Dalmatia; Fiume; Yugo-Slavia.

Akers-Douglas, Aretas, 179.

Allenstein, 181, 188, 192.

Allied and Associated Powers, 6, 10, 22, 32, 102, 109, 121, 290; and "War Guilt" Clause, 34, 254.

Allied High Command, 166, 215.

Allied Premiers, 60, 259.

Albania, 265.

Alsace-Lorraine, 27, 29-31, 195-197, 225.

American Commissioners, 12, 283. *See also* American Peace Delegation.

American Exclusion Acts, 90.

American Experts. *See* American Peace Delegation.

American Inquiry. *See* American Peace Delegation.

American Intelligence, 41. *See also* American Peace Delegation.

American Intelligence for Territorial, Political, and Economic Questions. Report on German boundaries, 177. *See also* American Peace Delegation.

American Peace Delegation.
American amendments, 138-139.
Anglo-American Treaty of Guarantee, 136.
Armistice renewal, 150.
British collaboration, 117, 120, 252.
conscription, 159.

disarmament of Germany, 167.
French program, 197-198.
German conscript army, 163.
guarantees, 121.
and House, 13-14, 282.
internal conflicts, 12, 20, 113, 142-143, 185, 273-276, 279-282, 290, 292.
Italian claims, 7, 269, 271, 273-276, 279-280, 282.
Japanese claims, 74, 96-99.
naval question, 142-143, 185.
pensions, 251-252.
Polish question, 174, 178, 180, 190.
Reparation, 243-245, 249-250, 255, 258, 299.
Treaty, 158, 286, 291.
"War Guilt" Clause, 253.
and Wilson, 9, 41, 44, 189, 209, 222, 231.

Anglo-American Treaty of Guarantee, 136, 168, 205, 207-209, 214, 217, 226, 295-297; Anglo-American draft of, 211; violation of Wilson's principles, 210.

Appeasement, 302.

Armistice, 22, 24, 30, 44, 173, 218-219, 240; renewal of, 148-150; military terms of, 195.

Armistice Commission, 215.

Armistice Convention, 240-241.

Associated Chambers of Commerce, 37-38.

Aubert, Louis, 124.

Auchincloss, Gordon, 133, 271, 274-275.
Australia, 36, 45-46, 49, 61, 71, 74-75; and racial equality, 90. *See also* British Dominions.
Austria, 26, 81, 201.
Austria-Hungary, 7, 8, 46, 266-267.

Baden, 219.
Baden, Prince Max of, 2, 174.
Baker, Ray Stannard, 60, 114; on French diplomacy, 118; on House, 155-156, 213.
Balance of power, 46, 116, 291.
Balfour, Lord. Attitude toward the League of Nations, 48, 54; Australia, 49; Franco-Russian agreements, 30; German conscript army, 163; German disarmament, 159; and House, 155; on Hughes, 52, 93; Japanese claims, 109-111, 113; and Lloyd George, 142; London Conference, 33; Polish boundaries, 117; Rhineland, 196, 199-204, 208.
Baruch, Bernard, 262.
Barzilai, S., 267.
Bavaria, 218-220.
Beer, George Louis, 42, 48, 77, 271, 285; on House and Wilson, 206, 273, 279, 281-282; on mandates principle, 75.
Bela Kun (Hungary), 185.
Belgium, 3, 30-31, 33, 42, 164, 195, 202-203, 242, 299, 305; colonial armies, 78.
Benson, Admiral, 159.
Bismarck, Prince Otto von, 3, 26-27, 196, 265-266.
Bliss, General Tasker, 113-115, 131, 150, 163-164, 243; Anglo-American Treaty of Guarantee, 209; and House, 260; Italian claims, 275-276, 278-280, 282, 286.
Bohemia, 163, 186.
Bolshevism, 28-29, 184-186.
Borah, Senator William E., 133.
Borden, Premier, 46-47, 53, 63, 68.

Botha, General Louis, 61-62, 68, 72-73.
Bouillon, Franklin, 225.
Bourgeois, Léon, 19, 80, 117-119; Covenant and French amendments, 122, 124, 125-132, 137-139, 145-146, 149, 166-167, 196, 199, 205, 210, 212.
Bowman, Isaiah, 41, 179, 184, 270, 275, 281-282.
Brandegee, Senator, 133.
Brenner Pass, 267, 269.
British Dominions. Annexation aims, 18, 40, 45, 51, 71, 75, 84; and mandatory principle, 59-61, 63-65, 70, 268; and racial equality, 90, 92, 97. *See also* Great Britain.
British Empire, 47, 52. *See also* British Dominions.
British Empire Peace Delegation, 52-53, 60, 68, 74, 76, 190; and racial equality, 94.
British Peace Delegation. American collaboration, 117, 120, 252.
conscription, 159.
diplomatic strategy of, 18.
French program, 197-198.
German conscript army, 163.
German disarmament, 169.
guarantees, 121.
and House, 77.
Italian claims, 7, 266, 274.
Japanese claims, 99.
Polish question, 173, 180, 189.
and Wilson, 65-66, 261-262.
Bromberg, 180.
Bugeaud, Marshall, 160.
Bullitt, William, 293.

Cambon, Jules, 181, 219-220; Grey-Cambon correspondence, 63.
Cambresis, Cateau, 26.
Cameroons, 63-65, 80.
Canada, 46; and U. S., 53. *See also* British Dominions.
Caporetto, 266.
Cavallero, General, 164.

340

Cecil, Lord Robert, 53, 62-63, 76, 80, 94, 97, 156; and American amendments, 134, 142-144; and Bourgeois, 128-130; on Clemenceau, 132, 137; on Hughes, 52, 93; on racial equality, 98.
Cellere, Count Macchi di, 271, 285.
China, 19, 41; foreign concessions in, 109, 111; German rights in, 84-85, 87-89; Japanese claims, 102-115, 268. See also Shantung; Twenty-One Demands.
Chinda, Viscount, 83, 90; and racial equality, 91-99 passim, 110; and Shantung, 102-113 passim.
Chinese Peace Delegation, 87, 89, 106.
Churchill, Winston, 171, 261.
Clausewitz, Karl von, 3, 116, 304.
Clemenceau, Georges, 27-28, 44, 47, 52-53, 95, 153, 182, 286, 297.
    Anglo-American Treaty of Guarantee, 136, 207-208, 210-212.
    censorship, 32, 199, 214-215.
    colonial armies, 78-80.
    diplomatic strategy, 19, 32-33, 60, 116, 118-119, 124, 146.
    disarmament, 169-170.
    federalization of Germany, 29, 180, 219-220.
    final peace terms, 151, 179.
    and Fourteen Points, 24-25.
    French public opinion, 146.
    French security, 117, 124, 126, 132, 137, 207, 214, 217.
    and Foch, 170, 216-218.
    German demobilization, 149.
    and House, 20, 54-56, 160, 213.
    and Hughes, 51.
    Italian claims, 276, 278-279, 286.
    Japanese claims, 106-107.
    League of Nations, 45, 54, 56, 118, 163, 210.
    and Lloyd George, 64, 141, 187, 217.
    military terms, 159-162, 164, 166.
    Poland, 187-188, 190, 192-193.
    Reparation, 240, 244-249, 253, 257.
    Rhenish Republics, 154, 201, 204.
    Rhineland, 30, 32, 46, 160, 195-199, 202-204, 207, 222.
    Saar, 225, 227-229, 231-232, 234.
    Separatist movement, 221, 299.
    "War Guilt" Clause, 254.
    and Wilson, 5, 13, 24-26, 29, 45, 76, 117, 140, 167, 183, 209, 212, 228-229, 233.
Clive, Consul, 300.
Cobb, Frank, 43-44, 175-176, 269.
"Commission of Verification" (credentials), 219-220.
Conscription, 123, 126, 158, 196-197; German, 120, 160-162.
Control Commissions, 165.
Cornwall, Lt. Col., 179.
Council of Four. Supplants Council of Ten, 182; Reparation, 262; Saar, 228; "War Guilt" Clause, 254; Wilson's absence, 256, 260. See also Supreme Council.
Council of Ten, 57, 59-60, 69, 87, 154; supplanted by Council of Four, 182, 209; mandates principle, 73. See also Supreme Council.
Covenant. See League of Nations, Covenant.
Croatia, 267.
Crowe, Sir Eyre, 184, 291.
Cunliffe, Lord, 37-38, 246-247, 255, 261.
Curzon, Lord, 53; Customs Union, 7, 187, 198-199, 234; for Europe, 306.
Czechoslovakia, 8, 59, 163.

Dalmatia, 267, 269, 271, 274, 277.
Danubian Confederation, 7.
Danzig, 8, 176-181, 183, 187-188, 201, 206, 226, 228.
Davis, Norman, 245-248 passim, 254, 257-259 passim, 261-263 passim; on House, 280.
Day, Clive, 270, 274-275, 281.
Dell, Robert, 303-304, 306-307.
Desgouttes, General, 162, 164.
Disarmament (general), 117, 128, 140, 148, 169-170, 185. See also Naval question, Anglo-American.
Disarmament Conference (Geneva), 171.

Dmowski, Roman, 176, 178, 189.
Dominions. *See* British Dominions.
Doumer, Paul, 215.
Doumergue, Gaston, 29.
Dulles, John Foster, 240-242, 254.

East Prussia, 175-177, 180-182, 188, 219. *See also* Danzig.
England. *See* Great Britain.

Federation (Europe), 306-307, 309, 311.
Federation of British Industries, 37-38.
Fisher, Lord, 261.
Fiume, 13, 20-21, 260, 268-269, 273-277, 280-283, 286-287, 292; suburb Susâk, 267, 293.
Foch, Marshal, 26-29 *passim*, 118, 166, 170; appeal to French Cabinet, 216-217; attack on peace terms, 215-216; on German demobilization, 149; on Poland, 180; on Preliminary Treaty, 150-151, 153-154, 158; Rhineland proposals, 30-33, 196, 198, 200, 214, 216; Rhineland intrigues, 221.
Foster, Sir G. E., 37.
Fourteen Points, 10, 18, 28, 38, 118, 174, 181, 189, 233, 269-270, 272, 292-293, 296; Cobb-Lippmann commentary on, 43-44, 175-176, 225, 269; and Foch memorandum, 34; legal basis of peace, 25, 290-291; opposition to, 24; on Reparation, 239, 243. *See also* Pre-Armistice Agreement; Self-Determination.
France, 4-5, 12-13, 25, 33, 42, 63, 163, 186.
  colonial armies, 77-82.
  colonies, 3.
  disarmament (general), 128.
  defeat 1940, 268, 303-305, 310.
  Franco-Italian agreements (Treaty of London), 266.
  Franco-Japanese agreements, 106-107.

Franco-Russian agreements, 29-31, 173-174.
  Lloyd George's appeal to, 184.
  national traditions, 26-29, 116-117, 125-128, 296-297, 303-305.
  naval question, 141-143.
  public opinion, 130, 161, 245-246.
  Treaty enforcement, 298-300.
  war aims (World War I), 19-20; (World War II), 224-225.
  See also Alsace-Lorraine; Germany, disarmament of; Germany, dismemberment of; Poland; Reparation; Rhenish Republics; Rhineland; Saar; Security, French.
Francis I, 172.
Frazier, Arthur H., 285.
"Freedom of the Seas," 24.
French, General, 200.
French Peace Delegation, 77; Armistice renewal, 149; coordination, 19, 118, 208, 234; diplomatic strategy, 18-20, 54, 138, 145, 165, 212, 233; federalization of Germany, 218-219; Reparation, 240, 244, 250, 252; Rhineland policy, 195-196; Saar, 226. *See also* France.
Fromageot, Henri, 80, 157.

Geddes, Sir Eric, 39.
The George Washington, 40; Wilson's return trip to France (March 1919), 204, 206; Wilson's order to return to France (April 7, 1919), 141, 184, 212, 233.
German Colonies, 18, 40-41, 45-46, 48-49, 51; *Chap. III passim*.
German East Africa, 44, 49.
German Peace Delegation, credentials, 219-221; Danzig protest, 188.
German Southwest Africa, 46-49, 67, 75.
Germany, 8, 10-11, 19-20, 22.
  colonial aims, 49.
  colonial policy, 48, 60, 78.
  concessions in China, 84-89, 102, 105, 107-110, 112.

conscript system, 120, 148, 159-161.
disarmament of, 20, 117; *Chap. VI;*
196-197, 296.
dismemberment of, 116; *Chaps.
VII-IX passim;* 198, 203, 207,
240, 268-269, 299, 303, 305-306.
federalization of, 29, 180, 204, 218-
219, 306.
financial capacity, 36-38, 40-41, 189,
245-249, 251-258.
and France, 26-29, 172-173, 298-299.
inflation, 300-301.
Japanese alliance, 308.
and League of Nations, 170, 203,
260.
national traditions, 303-304.
military occupation. *See* Rhineland; Saar.
peace terms of 1916, 2-4.
Polish boundaries, *Chap. VII.*
post-war Germany, 298-302. *See
also* Hitler.
Pre-Armistice Agreement, 25.
Reparation, *Chap. X.*
Rhineland, *Chap. VIII.*
Saar, *Chap. IX.*
Self-Determination, 8, 174. *See also*
Rhineland; Saar; Poland.
special boundary commission, 181,
204-206.
"War Guilt," 242, 253-255.
Gibbs, Herbert, 37-38.
Grayson, Admiral Cary, 287.
Great Britain, 4-5, 12, 25, 33, 42, 63,
106, 129, 203, 205.
Anglo-Japanese agreements, 45, 49-
51, 83-84, 86, 102, 104, 107.
Anglo-Italian agreements (Treaty
of London), 266.
colonial policy, 61, 75.
and conscription, 123, 148-149, 305.
and France (post-war), 303-305, 310.
national traditions, 119-122, 124-
125, 127-128, 131, 140, 146, 305.
naval question, 141-144.
public opinion, 51, 202, 245-247,
303.
and United States (post-war), 308-
311.

World War II, 306-307. *See also*
British Peace Delegation; Im-
perial War Cabinet; Mandates;
Reparation.
Grey, Sir Edward, 85.
Grey-Cambon correspondence, 63.
Guarantees, 17, 120-121, 128, 135, 139,
295. *See also* Anglo-American
Treaty of Guarantee; League of
Nations; Security.

Haig, Marshal, 30, 195.
Haskins, Charles H., 179, 231-232,
236-237.
Headlam-Morley, James W., 179, 206,
232.
Herriot, Edouard, 300.
Hewins, W. A. S., 37.
Hitler, Adolf, 1-2, 8, 197, 255, 265,
289, 297, 302-305; and Ludendorff, 3-4, 308.
Holt, Hamilton, 309.
Hornbeck, Stanley K., 281.
House, Colonel Edward M., 11, 32-33,
44, 46, 62, 80, 95, 131, 150, 163.
Anglo-American Treaty of Guarantee, 210-211.
and Clemenceau, 20, 54-56, 160,
213.
in Council of Four, 256-257, 260.
disposition to compromise, 14, 20,
63, 76, 115, 133-134, 152-153, 207,
212-213, 259, 272, 274, 280-281,
287.
and final Treaty, 155-156.
Italian claims, 264, 267, 271-286,
288.
Japanese claims, 91-94, 97, 109, 292.
and League of Nations, 12, 16, 156,
199, 202, 272, 288, 292.
and Lloyd George, 142, 213.
Monroe Doctrine amendment, 139,
143-146.
as negotiator, 12-13, 54-56, 68.
Polish settlement, 180, 190, 193.
Pre-Armistice Agreement, 22-26,
241.
Reparation, 35, 40, 244, 246-247,
257-258.

343

Rhineland, 160, 196, 199-209, 293.
Saar, 225, 232-234.
Self-Determination. *See* Rhineland *above.*
"War Guilt" Clause, 254.
and Wilson, 55, 65, 113, 147, 154, 178-179, 206, 231, 258-260, 264, 273, 276-280, 283-287, 294.
See also American Peace Delegation, internal conflicts; Mandates.
Hughes, Premier William H., 36, 46, 61-63, 68-69, 76, 100; opposition to Wilson, 51-53, 65, 70-72; and racial equality, 90, 93, 96-97; Reparation (war costs), 36-37, 241-242.
Hungary, 185.

Imperial War Cabinet, 36, 38, 45-46, 51, 53.
Indemnities, 11-12, 35, 38, 40, 50, 244; German terms of 1916, 3. *See also* Reparation, War Costs.
Inquiry. *See* American Peace Delegation; American Intelligence for Territorial, Political, and Economic Questions.
"Inspection," 122, 127, 129, 137, 166-168, 205, 207, 209, 211-212. *See also* League of Nations, French amendments.
Inter-Allied Commission of Experts (Reparation), 35, 40.
Inter-Allied Conference (December 1918), 38. *See also* London Conference.
International army, 122-123, 127. *See also* League of Nations, French amendments.
Intervention, American (World War I), 1, 307; (World War II), 308, 310.
"Irreconcilables," 12, 17, 102, 133, 295.
Ishii, Viscount, 91.
Isolationism, American, 1, 12, 17, 307-308.
Italian Peace Delegation, 20, 164;

break with Wilson, 277, 279, 281-283; diplomatic strategy, 264, 266-267, 271.
Italy, 12, 25; national claims, 50, 107, 266-272, 274-287 *passim;* national traditions, 264-265, 273, 303; Sino-Japanese agreements, 266, 269. *See also* Adriatic question; Dalmatia; Fiume; Yugoslavia.

Japan, 12, 42, 74-75.
Anglo-Japanese agreements, 45, 50, 85, 102, 104.
German alliance, 308.
Imperialist aims, 19, 45, 50, 63, 83-88, 102-115, 268.
racial equality, 19, 90-99, 110.
Sino-Japanese agreements, 88-89, 102, 104-105, 107, 109, 112-113. *See also* German Colonies; Japanese Peace Delegation; Mandates; Shantung; Twenty-One Demands.
Japanese Peace Delegation.
diplomatic strategy, 18; *Chap. IV passim;* 118, 268, 293.
Johnson, Douglas, 179, 270, 274-275, 281, 285.
Johnson, Senator Hiram, 114.
Jusserand, Ambassador, 29.

Kerr, Philip (late Lord Lothian), 204-205, 285.
Keynes, John Maynard, 7, 170, 246-247, 255; *Economic Consequences of the Peace,* 262, 298; on Wilson, 5-6.
Kiao-Chow, 84-87, 105, 108-109.
Klotz, Louis, 117-118, 240-242, 249, 256-258.
Koo, Wellington, 87-89, 106-108.
Korfanty, 194.

Lamont, Thomas W., 247, 259-262.
Lansing, Robert, 40, 89, 102-103, 109, 113, 115, 156, 163, 165, 218, 220, 231, 243, 271, 275-276, 278, 282, 286-287; on Anglo-American Treaty of Guarantee, 209-210; on

House and "House Group," 260, 271, 273, 294; opposition to League of Nations, 12; on Wilson, 294.

Larnaude, Ferdinand, 19, 99, 119, 137; on Monroe Doctrine amendment, 144-146, 212.

Law, Bonar, 37-38, 218, 239, 257.

League of Nations, 7, 9-13, 15-17, 24, 52-57, 61, 63, 86, 108-109, 112, 167, 177, 211, 292, 306, 310.
American opposition, 12, 17, 102, 132-134, 207, 295, 297.
Commissioner for Free City of Danzig, 187.
French views on, 45-46, 118-119, 121-122, 124, 163, 244, 272, 295.
and Germany, 170, 203, 260.
governing Commission for Saar, 235-237.
guarantees and sanctions, 120-122, 135, 139.
and Colonel House, 12, 156, 199, 202, 272, 292.
and Italy, 272.
and Mandates, 42, 48-49, 58-59, 61-77 passim.
as part of Peace Treaties, 28, 41, 57.
proposed administration of Fiume, 274.
and Wilson, 16-17, 54, 58-59, 64, 118.

League of Nations. Council, 167, 235-236.

League of Nations. Covenant, 13, 141, 311.
adoption, 95, 100, 110, 127, 131, 279.
Amendments, American, 96, 134-135, 138-140.
Amendments, French, 125-130, 137-138, 145-146, 166-167, 196, 205, 210.
Amendments, Japanese, 92-101.
Anglo - American (Hurst - Miller) draft, 124-125, 158.
and disarmament, 169.
French (Bourgeois) draft, 122-124.

Mandates Article, 58, 66, 74, 79-80.
opportunity for diplomatic bargaining, 16-19, 158, 292.
racial equality, 19, 90-92, 94, 97, 100. See also Japanese Amendments above.
Smuts resolutions. See Mandates Article above.

League of Nations Commission, 57, 83, 91, 93, 96, 102, 122, 124, 184, 294; Anglo-American cooperation, 141; diplomatic strategy, 16-19, 158, 292; final draft of Covenant, 130-131; final meeting, 97, 146; reconvened, 136.

League of Nations societies, 309; British, 120, 309; French, 120.

League to Enforce Peace, 120, 309.

Liggett, General, 221.

Lippmann, Walter, 43-44, 175-176, 269.

Lloyd George, David.
Anglo-American Treaty of Guarantee, 205, 207-208, 211, 226.
Apologia, 6.
appeal to France, 184, 186-187.
on Bolshevism, 184-185.
and Bourgeois, 147.
and Clemenceau, 33, 64, 141, 187, 217.
on colonial armies, 79.
diplomatic strategy, 59, 141-142, 259, 261.
on disarmament (general), 148.
Dominion claims, 49, 61, 66, 68, 76, 83.
election commitments, 36-37, 39, 246, 249-250, 253, 257, 262.
and Foch, 34, 215-216.
and Fourteen Points, 23-24, 44.
and German conscript system, 159-163.
and House, 142, 213.
and Hughes, 51-52, 68-69.
Italian claims, 276, 278-279, 285.
Japanese claims, 86, 103-104, 106-107, 109-110, 113.
League of Nations, 48, 54.
Mandates, 44-46, 61, 64, 66, 73, 79.

345

Monroe Doctrine amendment. *See* naval question, Anglo-American *below.*

naval question, Anglo-American, 141-144, 185.

Polish question, 179-183, 187-189, 191-194, 209, 293.

as politician, 51, 185, 189.

Pre-Armistice Agreement. *See* Reparation *below.*

and publicity, 182.

Reparation, 35-39, 41, 50, 185, 239, 241, 244-253 *passim,* 255, 257-258, 260-261, 299.

Rhineland, 30, 32, 196-199, 203-205, 207, 209, 222.

Saar, 228-229, 234-235, 237.

Treaty revision, 189-190, 260, 286.

"War Guilt" Clause, 253-254.

and Wilson, 5, 11, 15, 23-24, 26, 34, 47, 52, 70, 76, 214, 260-263.

Locarno, 197, 236, 302.

Lodge, Senator, Henry Cabot (senior). Opposition to Wilson, 10-11, 14-15, 17, 133.

London Conference, 33-36. *See also* Inter-Allied Conference (December 1918).

Long, Walter, 37.

Lord, Robert H., 178-179, 190-191.

Loucheur, Louis, 118, 149, 208, 227-229, 234, 246-247, 256-257, 261.

Louis XIV, 27, 116, 227.

Lowell, A. Lawrence, 309.

Ludendorff, General Eric von, 2-4, 174, 304.

Lunt, W. E., 270, 274-275, 281.

Luxembourg, 30-31, 33, 195, 224.

McCormick, Vance, 243.

MacDonald, Premier Ramsay, 300.

Makino, Baron, 61, 65, 83, 86, 88, 126; and racial equality, 90-101, 146; and Shantung, 102-110 *passim.*

Mandates, 48, 89; distribution, 48, 64-65, 67, 70-74, 76; and military service, 78-80.

Mandates Principle, 7, 18, 42, 49; *Chap. III;* Cobb-Lippmann commentary on, 43-44; and Japanese claims, 84, 86; Smuts memoranda, 46-47, 66-67, 78. *See also* League of Nations; League of Nations. Covenant.

Mangin, General, 211-222, 230.

Marburg, Theodore, 120.

Marienwerder, 180-181, 183, 188. *See also* Danzig; Poland.

Massey, Premier, 61, 68, 71-73, 76.

Mein Kampf, 3.

Mesopotamia, 66. *See also* Mandates Principle.

Metternich, Prince, 227.

Mezes, Sidney, 179, 183-184; and Italian claims, 271-276, 279, 281-282, 292; special commission on German boundaries, 204-205.

Military Commission, 155.

Military High Command. *See* Allied High Command.

Miller, David Hunter, 62, 74, 80, 97-98, 134, 137, 262; and American Amendments, 135-136, 139, 141-142, 145; on Anglo-American Treaty of Guarantee, 136; Italian claims, 271-272, 274-276, 284-285; Polish question, 183-184; Saar question, 142, 234.

Milner, Lord, 47.

Moltke, Helmuth Karl von, 196.

Monroe Doctrine, 17, 133-134; amendment, 139, 141, 143-145, 167-168, 185, 212-213; Japanese Monroe Doctrine for Asia, 85, 88.

Montagu, Edwin S., 246-247, 255-256.

Montenegro, 265.

Munich Settlement, 8, 298, 308.

Mussolini, Benito, 265.

Napoleon I, 27, 116, 160.

National sovereignty, 121, 306, 309-310. *See also* League of Nations. Covenant. Amendments, American, French, and Japanese.

Nationalism, 5, 9-10, 11-12, 18.

Naval Commission, 159.

Naval question, Anglo-American, 141-144.

Nazism, 3, 5, 302.

New Guinea, 45-46, 52, 68, 71-72, 75.

New Zealand, 45-46, 61, 71, 74-75. *See also* British Dominions.

Nicolson, Harold, 16, 29, 39-40, 222, 266, 292; on boundary decisions, 7; on diplomacy, 77, 81; on House, 76; on Wilson, 5, 262, 291.

Noble, George B., 124.

Nudant, General, 215-216.

"Open Door," 42, 61, 66-67, 74-75. *See also* Mandates Principle.

Orlando, Premier, 33, 44, 61, 107-108, 182, 267-268, 274, 277, 284-285; departure from Paris, 278; and League of Nations, 272; return to Paris, 283. *See also* Italy, national claims.

Pacific Islands, 45-47, 49, 53, 62, 67-68, 75, 83. *See also* German Colonies; Mandates Principle.

Paderewski, Premier, 192-194.

Page, Thomas Nelson, 283-284.

Pensions, 250-253, 258. *See also* Reparation.

Permanent Mandates Commission, 81.

Pershing, General, 221.

Piacentini, Renato, 271.

Pichon, L., 27, 78, 173, 176, 208, 215, 218-219.

Plebiscites. Allenstein, 181, 188, 192; Marienwerder, 188; Saar, 233-236; Upper Silesia, 189-194, 260.

Poincaré, President, 29, 95, 216-217, 222, 299-300.

Poland, 8, 20, 28, 59, 81, 142, 163; *Chap. VII;* 206, 209, 228.

Polish Corridor, 8, 175-177, 180.

Polish Commission, 180-182, 184, 188-189, 193, 228.

Posen, 177, 180. *See also* Polish Corridor.

Pre-Armistice Agreement, 53, 292; acceptance, 25; and final peace terms, 241-242; and Mandates Principle, 42-44, 74; pensions, 250-252, 258; and Reparation, 35, 54, 238, 240, 243, 250, 254, 258, 263; violations, 6, 35-36, 38, 40, 244-245. *See also* Fourteen Points; Self-Determination.

Prussia, 26, 219-220, 227, 229-230.

Racial equality. *See* Japan; League of Nations. Covenant, racial equality.

Rault, M., 236.

Reading, Lord, 47.

Reparation, 20, 34-35, 81, 117, 183, 227; *Chap. X;* Lloyd George and, 36-39, 50, 299; post-war, 301, 306; violation of Pre-Armistice Agreement, 6.

Reparation Commission, 248-250, 252-253, 255-258, 262-263, 299.

Rhenish Republics, 33, 154, 179, 198-201, 203-205, 208, 219, 221, 226. *See also* Rhineland; Separatism.

Rhineland, 20, 26-27, 40, 46, 51, 54, 81, 146, 154, 158, 160, 167-168, 183-184; *Chap. VIII;* 225-227, 229-230, 249, 259, 293, 304; Foch memorandum, 30-34; French intrigues, 221, 299-300; military occupation, 29-30, 32, 149, 195-196, 199, 205, 207-209, 211, 213-214, 217, 221-223, 252, 260, 274, 295, 299, 301. *See also* French Peace Delegation, diplomatic strategy; Saar; Rhenish Republics.

Ribot, A. F. J., 56.

Richelieu, Cardinal, 26-27.

Riddell, Lord, 70, 185-186.

Rogers, John Jacob, 14.

Roosevelt, Franklin D., 308.

Roosevelt, Theodore, 10-11, 15, 90.

Root, Elihu, 135.

Ruhr valley, 149, 222; French occupation, 299, 301-302.

Rumania, 2.

Russia, 2, 28, 46, 186, 303-304; Franco-Russian agreements, 29-31, 173-174.

Saar, 20, 27, 29, 81, 142, 183-184, 209, 212-213; *Chap. IX;* 249, 293; military occupation, 227, 230, 233-237; Saar Commission, 233, 235-237.
Saarlouis, 227.
Sadowa, 26.
Samoa, 45-46, 71.
Sanctions, 121-122. *See* League of Nations, guarantees and sanctions.
Schleswig, 192.
Secret Treaties. *See* France, Franco-Russian agreements; Great Britain, Anglo-Italian agreements; Anglo-Japanese agreements; Grey-Cambon correspondence.
Security, 296; American, 308; Australian, 46, 49, 52; British Empire, 46, 53, 61; French, 19, 54 77, 81, 116, 124, 126, 128, 130, 132, 137, 139-140, 170, 197-198, 200, 205 207, 212, 214-215, 217, 295, 297, 299; Great Britain, 305; Italian, 267, 272; Japanese, 62; Polish, 182.
Self-Determination, 6, 34, 192; and Foch memorandum, 32; and France, 27, 81, 116; and Poland, 174-176; and Rhineland, 199, 201-202; and Russia, 172; and Saar, 227-231; and strategic boundaries, 7-8. *See also* Fourteen Points; Pre-Armistice Agreement.
Senate (U. S.). Opposition to Wilson, 10-11, 14, 132, 214; and Versailles settlement, 96, 133-134, 136, 143, 156-158, 236, 295.
Separatism (Rhineland), 221-223, 299-300. *See also* Rhenish Republics.
Serbia, 267. *See also* Yugoslavia.
Seton-Watson, R. W., 8.
Seymour, Charles, 179, 270, 274-275, 281.
Sforza, Count, 265.

Shantung, 19-20, 62, 84-87, 89-90, 101-115, 278, 294. *See also* Japan.
Shotwell, James T., 206, 271, 276, 281.
Simon, M., 63.
Simonds, Frank, 206.
Sino-Japanese agreements (1915 and 1918), 88-89, 102, 104-105, 107, 109, 112-113. *See also* Twenty-One Demands.
Smuts, Premier Jan, 76, 97; Mandates Principle, 46-47, 58, 56-68, 71, 73, 77-78; and pensions, 251.
Society of Nations, 122. *See also* League of Nations.
Sonnino, Baron, 24-25, 108, 267, 283; on Wilson, 272. *See also* Italy, national claims.
Spartacists, 185. *See also* Bolshevism.
Stalin, Josef, 303.
Steed, Henry Wickham, 233.
Strauss, Oscar, 145.
Streit, Clarence, 309-311.
Stresemann, Gustav, 300, 302.
Succession States, 7.
Sumner, Lord, 246-247, 251, 255, 261.
Supreme Council, 30, 103, 106-107, 109-110, 220; and German conscript system, 160-161; and military service in Mandates, 80; Polish question, 176, 178, 181, 183, 188, 193; Reparation, 244, 247-248; Saar question, 234-235; and Treaty of peace, 150, 155, 157; Wilson's absence, 153, 165, 233. *See also* Council of Four; Council of Ten.
Supreme Economic Council, 218.
Susâk. *See* Fiume.
Switzerland, 42.
Syria, 66, 187. *See also* Mandates Principle.

Taft, William Howard, 309.
Tardieu, André 118, 167-168, 181; reply to Lloyd George, 186; Rhineland, 196, 198, 201-205, 208-209, 211; Saar, 227-229, 232-235.
Thiers, Louis, 26.

Thirty Years' War, 27.
Togoland, 63-65, 75, 80.
Treaty of Brest-Litovsk, 2.
Treaty of Bucharest, 2.
Treaty of Frankfort, 220.
Treaty of London, 266-269, 279. *See also* France; Great Britain; Italy.
Treaty of Prague, 27.
Treaty of Versailles, 6, 74, 185, 194, 214, 236, 263, 296-297, 302-303; alleged iniquities, 1, 4; compromise character, 295; negative accomplishments, 9, 294; post-war disillusionment about, 289-290, 298; Wilsonian Features, 7, 295; "War Guilt" Clause, 242, 254-255. *See also* Senate (U. S.).
Treaty of Westphalia, 27.
Trentino, 267, 269. *See also* Treaty of London.
Trieste, 267. *See also* Treaty of London.
Trumbitch, Ante, 285.
Tsinan, 86, 110.
Tsingtao-Tsinan Railway, 85, 88, 105, 108, 110. *See also* China; Japan.
Turkey, 46, 66.
Twenty-One Demands, 85-86, 88, 104, 113. *See also* Sino-Japanese agreements.

Union of South Africa, 45-46, 49, 61, 75. *See also* British Dominions.
United States, 5, 11, 24, 38, 44, 46, 55, 89, 106, 129, 203, 205, 220.
and Canada, 53.
immigration policies, 90, 92, 96-97.
isolationism, 1, 12, 17, 307-308.
and League of Nations, 129, 132-135, 157, 207, 295.
national traditions, 119-122, 124-125, 128, 131-132, 140, 146, 307-308.
naval question, Anglo-American, 141-143.
public opinion, 202.
recent trends of policy, 307-311.

and Versailles settlement. *See* Senate (U. S.).
See also American Peace Delegation; League of Nations. Covenant, Amendments, American.
Upper Silesia, 176, 189-194, 260. *See also* Poland.

Vichy, 303. *See also* France, defeat, 1940.
Viereck, George Sylvester, 259.
Vistula River, 175-177, 180-181. *See also* Poland.

War Costs, 35-36, 38-39, 241-243, 258. *See also* Reparation.
"War Guilt," 4, 34, 242, 253-255.
Warrin, Frank L., 274.
Warsaw, 180.
Weimar Republic, 220, 302. *See also* Germany, post-war Germany.
West Prussia, 177, 180. *See also* Polish Corridor.
Weygand, General, 164, 216.
White, Henry M., 40, 113, 135, 220, 243; Anglo-American Treaty of Guarantee, 209; on House, 13, 16, 115, 260, 288; and Italian claims, 275-276, 278 282, 284, 286; on Wilson, 13-15, 287.
William II, Kaiser, 4, 34.
Wilson, Edith Bolling (Mrs. Woodrow), 206, 278.
Wilson, Sir Henry, 33.
Wilson, Woodrow.
absence from Paris, 95-96, 131, 152-153, 179, 199, 201.
and American Peace Delegation, 9, 41, 44, 189, 209, 231.
American Amendments (League Covenant), 96, 134, 139-141, 144-145.
Anglo-American Treaty of Guarantee, 208-211, 226.
appeal to Italian people, 283.
and Clemenceau, 5, 13, 45, 117, 140, 151-152, 167, 209, 212, 217, 221, 229.

criticism for personal attendance at Conference, 294.

Disarmament, 164-165, 169, 200.

English visit, 47, 51-53.

on Foch, 201, 215-216.

French Amendments (League Covenant), 126-128, 131.

French press attacks on, 213-214.

and Colonel House, 20, 55, 115, 152-154, 207, 231, 258-260, 264, 273, 276-280, 283-287, 294.

and Hughes, 51-53, 65, 70-72.

illness, 184, 212-213, 233, 256, 258, 295.

Italian claims, 107-108, 266-270, 273-286, 293-294.

Japanese claims, 86-87, 89, 91-92, 95, 97-99, 103-114, 278-279, 293.

and League of Nations, 16-17, 52, 54, 58-59, 64, 118, 294.

and Lloyd George (and British Peace Delegation), 5, 11, 15, 34, 47, 76, 189-190, 214, 261-263.

Mandates Principle, 41-44, 49-53; *Chap. III passim.*

negative accomplishments, 2, 294.

as negotiator, 9, 12, 14, 76-77.

neutrality efforts, 1.

on occupation of Germany, 150.

opposition to (United States), 10-11, 23, 132-134, 214. *See also* Senate (U. S.).

peace program, 6, 19, 22-26, 29, 40, 60, 289. *See also* Fourteen Points.

Polish question, 174-175, 177-178, 181-183, 188-194, 293.

preliminary peace, 151-158 *passim.*

racial equality, 91-92, 95, 97, 99.

Reparation, 38, 40-41, 239, 241, 243-244, 247-248, 251, 259 293-294.

reputation, 5, 13-15, 293.

return to Paris, 96, 133-134, 156-157, 204, 206, 226, 243-244, 246.

Rhineland, 197-209 *passim,* 222.

Saar, 228-229 231-237, 293.

See also American Peace Delegation.

Wilsonian Principles, 10-11, 18; *Chap. II passim;* 268. *See also* Fourteen Points; Pre-Armistice Agreement; Wilson, Woodrow, peace program.

Wiseman, Sir William, 62-63, 76, 278, 286.

World War I, 4, 266, 307.

World War II, 305, 308.

Württemburg, 219.

Yugoslavia, 51, 267-268, 271, 273-274, 276, 284-285. *See also* Adriatic questions; Dalmatia; Fiume.

Young, Allyn A. 270, 274-275, 281.

Zimmermann, colonial program, 49, *See also* Germany, colonial aims, colonial policy.